THE DRAGON'S BREATH

THE DRAGON'S BREATH

HURRICANE AT SEA

Cdr. Robert A. Dawes, Jr., USN (Ret.)

Naval Institute Press ▪ *Annapolis, Maryland*

Library of Congress Cataloging-in-Publication Data

Dawes, Robert A., Jr.
 The dragon's breath : hurricane at sea / Robert A. Dawes, Jr.
  p. cm.
 Includes bibliographical references (p.) and index.
 ISBN 1-55750-153-X (alk. paper)
 1. Warrington (Destroyer) I. Title.
VA65.W297D39 1996
359.3′254′097309044—dc20   95-12441

Printed in the United States of America on acid-free paper ∞
03 02 01 00 99 98 97 96 9 8 7 6 5 4 3 2

First printing

When the Dragon breathes, the shouts of men are drowned out.
— CHINESE PROVERB

CONTENTS

ILLUSTRATIONS

PHOTOGRAPHS

FIGURE

MAPS

CHARTS

FOREWORD

On 13 September 1944, the USS *Warrington,* DD 383, capsized and sank in a hurricane some three hundred miles off the coast of northern Florida. Three-fourths of her officers and crew, including one of my dearest friends, were lost after herculean efforts to save the ship, most of them because of an inexcusable delay in rescue operations. After a lengthy inquiry, three officers faced courts-martial. The records tell a gripping story of a tired crew and overworked ship under a new captain barely acquainted with his vessel, officers, and men, ordered to sail despite a lack of urgency into the teeth of an already identified hurricane. She was escorting and was subject to the orders of a new and much larger ship also commanded by a new captain. A lack of cooperation between the two captains played a major role in the catastrophe. Using his best judgment, the *Warrington*'s captain made mistakes that are far more obvious to the historian who knows the results than they were to the captain struggling to save his ship. But for a careless error at the Brooklyn Navy Yard, the *Warrington* would have been on another assignment nowhere near the hurricane on 13 September.

The story of the *Warrington,* however, does not begin with the hurricane. She had served the navy well for a number of years and her achievements are also worth remembering. Cdr. Robert A. Dawes was her captain until fourteen days before she sank. For a year he had commanded her through various adventures and long exhausting cruises in the Pacific. Until the day of his relief he was pleading for much-needed repairs and alterations. Those who died were his friends in a special way that only shipmates under adverse circumstances can fully understand. The survivors are still devoted to him, and to a man they are convinced that if he had been in command, the ship would have lived. For many years, he and Sarah Moore Traylor, whose brother was lost, have been gathering information from the records and through voluminous correspondence with survivors and with earlier members of the *Warrington*'s crew. Then, in 1991, some 1,300 pages of the official inquiry became available.

From all of this information, Commander Dawes has written the biography of a ship that is well worth remembering because of the brave men who died and because of the many lessons that can still be learned from her tragedy. Oliver Wendell Holmes once wrote that a ship is the most lifelike of all inanimate objects. All sailors and all readers of this book will understand his meaning.

—Elbert B. Smith
Communications Officer on
USS *Oswald*, DE 767

ACKNOWLEDGMENTS

This book could not have been written without the help of many people. It began as a joint enterprise conducted by Sarah Moore Traylor and myself. Mrs. Traylor, in addition to being a writer, is the sister of the late Lt. (jg) Robert B. Moore, U.S. Naval Reserve, one of the officers who lost his life when the *Warrington* went down. Unfortunately, as the work progressed, Mrs. Traylor found that the technical language as well as the type of book itself were outside her area of expertise, whereupon she withdrew and left the job to me. I thank her for her efforts, however, and her advice on such foreign (to me) subjects as dealing with publishers. Her continued interest and encouragement are also appreciated.

Many of the names of my other helpers appear in the following text. The help of the former ship's company of the *Warrington,* both survivors and those who served earlier, has been above and beyond the call of duty. I am deeply grateful to them all for their patience and willingness to supply personal recollections whenever I asked. In my estimation, many of these men are heroes; they are a fine group of men.

Others, whose names do not appear, include Professor Elbert B. Smith, formerly of the History Department of the University of Maryland, a close friend of Mrs. Traylor's family, and a veteran of the same confrontation with the Dragon; his help and advice have been invaluable. My cousin, Rear Adm. Julian T. Burke, Jr., U.S. Navy, Retired, who helped mightily in prying part of the record of the Court of Inquiry out of the very reluctant office of the Judge Advocate General of the Navy. My friend and classmate, Rear Adm. Charles A. Curtze, formerly of the Naval Construction Corps, provided expertise on the subjects of ship design and seaworthiness. Another classmate and friend, Rear Adm. Norman J. Drustrup, Civil Engineer Corps, Retired, and Capt. Eugene C. Rook, U.S. Navy, Retired, gave this book a preliminary review and offered helpful suggestions and ideas. My former gunnery officer, then-Lt. (jg) Philip G. Koelsch, U.S. Navy, not only corrected some of my historical errors, but also provided insight into the proper actions to take when a hurricane appears on the horizon. Phil, who ultimately became a rear admiral, U.S. Naval Reserve, and who had had experience with hurricanes in the Gulf of Mexico, was fighting his final, fatal, battle with illness while generously giving me his time and encouragement. My undying gratitude goes to all of these gentlemen.

Among the former crew members, I am particularly grateful to David H. Miller, whose anecdotes occupy a considerable part of the story of the early days of the *Warrington*. Dave is now a successful and very busy attorney, in spite of which, he has given me many hours of his time in helping to make this story a success. His excellent analysis of the causes of the ship's sinking is contained in appendix B.

My thanks would not be complete without acknowledgment of the help of two other gentlemen who were not members of the ship's company. Richard J. Reynolds is the nephew of the late shipfitter first class Howard T. Reynolds—one of Mother Carey's chickens—and has taken a deep interest in the preparation of this book from its inception. In addition to many helpful ideas, he has prepared the study of weather phenomena presented in appendix A. His friend, David Nieri, a Naval Reserve officer himself, provided the pencil sketch on page 223. They both have my deep appreciation.

This was truly an all-hands operation.

INTRODUCTION

Old sailors tell us that there is a huge ship lying on the bottom of the ocean at the equator. Her name is *Fiddler's Green,* and she is the last home of the souls of drowned sailors. A woman named Mother Carey is in charge of *Fiddler's Green,* and she sees to it that her guests, who as sailors have led a rough and uncomfortable life (as everyone knows), lead a life of ease and plenty, being waited upon by nonsailors such as passengers and aviators.

Far down in the bilges of *Fiddler's Green* are the domains of Davey Jones; this is where souls go who have not brought honor to the profession of sailors in their lifetimes. They spend eternity chipping paint with rubber chipping hammers, under the watchful eye of marines.

Fiddler's Green was established long ago, before the age of steam, when sailors were truly sailors. Therefore, when steamships became the latest fad, engineers were not regarded as sailors at all, somewhat like aviators today. They were assigned their own home, at the North Pole, where they spend eternity stoking the fires under the Northern Lights. Nevertheless, they have come to be accepted as being sailors, although in a somewhat qualified sense.

From time to time, Mother Carey permits some of her guests to visit their old haunts in the upper world. When this occurs, they are given the form of seabirds known to sailors as storm petrels, or Mother Carey's chickens. For this reason, no real sailor will ever harm a storm petrel.

During the three days from 13 through 15 September 1944, Mother Carey received more than 300 new guests, 247 of whom had been serving aboard the U.S. destroyer *Warrington* (DD 383); the remainder were coast guardsmen from the cutters *Jackson* and *Bedloe* and the lightship no. 73, *Vineyard Sound.*

This is primarily the story of the *Warrington,* and how she came to feel the breath of the Dragon, but the coast guardsmen must not be forgotten; all these men lost their lives in the service of their country. This is an attempt to speak for those who can no longer speak for themselves, and who have never received the recognition that was their due.

What happened to the *Warrington* brought to light a number of lessons that seagoing readers will probably spot for themselves, but since this book was not originally intended to be a textbook, I feel that there is only one lesson that should be emphasized here.

All of the ships lost had one thing in common: they were serving under someone else's orders, therefore, the captains were somewhat restricted in their freedom to act. Later in this book, I have quoted an alleged statement by Adm. Ernest J. King, commander in chief, U.S. Fleet, at the time of this incident. He is said to have remarked that "no modern man of war should ever be lost to weather." Whether or not he really said this we do not know, but such a remark overlooks one important factor—that modern men of war frequently find themselves under the orders of someone other than their own captain. When this occurs, the captains will almost always do their very best to carry out their orders, whatever they may be; consequently, they tend to be slow to take action on their own initiative, fearing criticism from above that could well affect their careers. Admiral Nimitz recognized this tendency when three destroyers were lost in a typhoon in the Pacific only three months after the *Warrington* went down. He gave the rough side of his tongue to the task force commander who put the ships in jeopardy. To use a legal phrase, the burden of proof should be on the person issuing the orders, not on the poor soul who is stuck with them.

This is not to say that the "poor soul" should be exempt from criticism; but what it does say is that he should not suffer alone. Captain Quarles suffered alone.

Unfortunately, his ship's company also suffered to some extent as a result of heckling and harassment by members of the Court of Inquiry and later, by some of the members of the courts-martial. These men had no responsibility for what happened; they were victims of a series of mistakes made by their superiors. It is incumbent upon seniors in the chain of command to know what they are doing, and to understand the risks they impose on others; to escape responsibility by laying all responsibility upon the shoulders of men under orders is not proper.

In response to a question by the Court of Inquiry, Captain Quarles named eleven men who, he thought, deserved recognition for their heroic conduct. He emphasized that these were men whose activities he had witnessed himself, and that there were many others who deserved recognition. The court ignored his recommendations completely. Therefore, in an effort to rectify this rank injustice, I, with the help of Lt. Patrick B. Davis, have brought the conduct of Lt. (jg) Robert M. Kennedy and the two radiomen, Paul Klingen and Linder G. Pirtle, to the attention of the Chief of Naval Operations, without success. Their actions are described hereafter.

The loss of a ship in a hurricane is not unusual; it has happened hundreds of times over the centuries, and it almost always results in either total or near-total loss of the ship's company. In this respect, the loss of the *Warrington* is unusual because a comparatively large number of men were rescued, thereby permitting us to piece together a fairly coherent story of what happened. They all deserve our thanks and our respect.

The opinions expressed in this book, except in appendixes A, B, and C, are entirely my own, and do not necessarily reflect the opinions of anyone else in the naval service.

THE DRAGON'S BREATH

PART ONE
NIGHT OF DISASTER

chapter one

SOUTH PACIFIC DAYS

In the summer of 1943, I
was serving as executive officer and navigator of the USS *Converse* (DD
509). She was a 2,100-ton destroyer of the *Fletcher* class, which we had put
in commission in Bath, Maine, the preceding winter. Early in the summer,
we arrived in the South Pacific, escorting, with two other destroyers, the
British aircraft carrier HMS *Victorious*. Few people knew, at that time, that
we had only one operational carrier left in the Pacific, and the Royal Navy
had lent us this one for the time being. Her British fliers used American
planes with American markings to deceive the Japanese. *Victorious*—the
conqueror of the mighty *Bismarck*—was a fine ship to operate with, and we
parted from her with real regret after reporting to the South Pacific Force.

We were assigned as parts of destroyer screens for convoys running
from the island of Espíritu Santo to Guadalcanal. The fighting on Guadalcanal had ended, to all practical purposes, by this time. The army had
replaced the marines, and, while there were a few Japanese soldiers still on
the island, they were no real threat to anyone. The army had started
withdrawing some of its men, but marines were still fighting on nearby
islands, such as New Georgia. Guadalcanal was still being subjected to an
occasional air attack, but that was about all. In fact, in June the *Converse* was
present when the last large attack took place—a major defeat for the
Japanese.

On arrival at Guadalcanal, the destroyers would form a screen around
the transports and cargo vessels, as they loaded or unloaded their cargoes.
On one occasion, the *Converse* went alongside one of the transports for

3

some reason or other; while there, the soldiers tried to sell tobacco bags full of Japanese teeth to our men.

This routine went on until, near the end of August, I received a dispatch, directing me to report aboard the USS *Warrington* as relief for the commanding officer, Cdr. Harold R. Demarest. At about the same time, the *Converse* received orders to join a convoy, so there followed a scene of confusion, as I started packing my gear while turning over my duties to Lt. Ellis McDowell, the chief engineer, the radiomen started trying to find out where the *Warrington* might be, and a start was made at finding me some air transportation to that unknown point. Within the hour, I was off the ship, trying to find a jeep to take me to the airfield on Espíritu Santo, having said my farewells to Capt. D. C. E. Hamberger, a fine skipper. Although I was naturally thrilled at the idea of having my own command, I also regretted leaving the *Converse*. She later became a member of the famous "Little Beaver Squadron."

After a cold and uncomfortable airplane ride, I arrived on Guadalcanal the next morning, to be greeted (much to my surprise) by a friend I had known when we were putting the *Converse* through her final building phases at Bath. He was the supply officer for the naval installation on Guadalcanal, and he appointed himself my guide and mentor during my stay on the island.

His name was Jim Witherill, and he went far out of his way to show me the sights, such as Bloody Ridge; he also "liberated" for me a sun helmet (which proved invaluable in heavy rains, too), a poncho, and two pairs of "boondocker" shoes, which I was still wearing twenty years later. He made a special point of showing me the *pièce de résistance* of island sights—the commodore's latrine.

The island commander's actual rank was commodore (the equivalent of a brigadier general). At that time, all food, liquor, and so on was being supplied by the army, and the army was sort of particular as to who got its goodies; as far as it was concerned, the navy was a poor relation, so the only naval person who could get beer was the commodore. He had a habit of sitting outside his hut every evening in his undershirt, drinking beer in full view of his deprived men. This did not improve his popularity.

As one would expect, everything on Guadalcanal was fairly primitive, and this included the toilet arrangements. There were several latrines for the enlisted men and one for the officers, but this was not good enough for the commodore, who had to have his own. The CBs were very busy at that time, so they did not appreciate having to build an extra "john"; having no choice in the matter, however, they made the best of it, by building a latrine that resembled a gingerbread house in a fairy tale—pagoda-type roof and all. The "throne" was solid mahogany, with armrests, and a mahogany magazine rack hung on the wall. It was painted tastefully so as to harmonize with the surroundings.

As I mentioned earlier, there was little Japanese activity. There was, however, a lone Japanese plane that flew over at night, once or twice a week. It might drop a bomb or two, but was never known to hit anything. Nevertheless, it was quite a nuisance, keeping people awake, or disrupting loading and unloading operations. It was known to all hands as "Washing Machine Charlie" because of the sound of its engine. It came over once during my stay, and I found out why it was so cordially disliked when I had to dive into a dugout in the middle of the night and sit fighting hordes of mosquitoes until the "All Clear" sounded about an hour later.

After about a week, I was finally notified that the USS *Warrington* had appeared off the island. I rounded up my gear, found a boat, and headed for the ship.

Captain Demarest greeted me warmly, and we proceeded through the routine of a relief of command. I hoped to complete the routine within about twenty-four hours, but it was not to be. The night I came aboard (30 August 1943), the *Warrington* ran into a very heavy electrical storm while patrolling her station in the screen. The radar antennas glowed like neon signs. In the midst of this, the radarmen reported an unidentified ship, making about twenty knots. So Captain Demarest headed for the contact— and bumped a propeller on a shoal; the twenty-knot contact was a small island.

The next morning, having reported this incident to the commander, South Pacific (ComSoPac), Demarest ran the ship over near the shoreline, so that her bow just touched the sand, while divers went down to inspect the damage. The damage was not great, so the ship was ordered to sail to Noumea for repairs. In the meantime, I had to wait until ComSoPac decided what action to take, if any (he eventually took no action), before I could finish relieving Demarest. Consequently, I did not take command until about the end of the first week in September, but I did get an opportunity to see how the ship handled.

My first assignment was as the screen commander for a convoy headed for Guadalcanal. The convoy commander was a merchant marine captain (a Naval Reservist), and the screen consisted of three or four DEs. There were four ships in the convoy.

Before getting under way, I held a conference with the convoy commander, discussing courses, speeds, and formations, but one thing was not mentioned—communications at night. I had a lot to learn, and so did my merchant marine friend.

In due time, we departed from Noumea and headed north. At about midnight, we encountered another convoy, headed south; we were headed directly for each other.

Frantically, I tried to warn the convoy commander and my screen ships, but I might as well have been on another planet. Nobody would answer any TBS (voice radio) signal, and since all ships were darkened, we couldn't show a light. In frustration, I finally just paid attention to the *Warrington,* and hoped for the best with the other ships. Miraculously, our convoy combed its way through the other without incident, although, as far as I could tell, nobody changed course as much as a degree. At Guadalcanal, the *Warrington* was detached from this convoy, to my relief, and was assigned to another, headed back to Noumea. I was not screen commander this time.

One or two nights after our departure, the sonarmen picked up an echo. It could have been anything—a school of fish, a whale. But since it had that metallic submarine ring, I proceeded to attack after notifying the screen commander. I deliberately refrained from sounding General Quarters until after the first depth charges had been dropped, since I wanted to find out how the men on watch would handle such an emergency; I also wanted to find out how fast my new crew could man their battle stations. I was delighted with the answers to both questions. Depth charges dropped right on command, and it took the crew only two minutes to climb out of their bunks and man their stations. I was proud of them, and never again did I doubt their ability to carry out their jobs.

We broke off from this convoy and sailed into the harbor of Espíritu Santo, where we were informed that, from then on, we and the USS *Balch* (DD 362) would be operating directly under the orders of ComSoPac as high-speed escorts not attached to any division or squadron. It turned out the high speed in this case meant the ships being escorted could make at least fifteen knots. This differentiated them from many cargo vessels and all LSTs, the majority of which could not steam at more than eight knots.

The orders also meant that we would spend most of our time running back and forth between Espíritu Santo and Guadalcanal, not much more than overnight runs. From September through October, we had little time to sit around; the usual routine was to enter Espíritu Santo, fuel, take on provisions and mail, and wait for the next set of orders. These were generally quick to arrive, and had us back on the high seas within twenty-four hours. On reaching Guadalcanal, the ship would patrol a sector of "Ironbottom Sound," just as the *Converse* had earlier, until time to return to

Espíritu Santo. This became boring, in time, especially since there was no leave or liberty for anyone at either end of the run. About the only relief was provided by our old friend, Washing Machine Charlie; on his arrival, Guadalcanal would announce "Condition Red" over the radio, and all hands would go to General Quarters, thus losing a substantial part of a night's sleep. We could, however, watch the fireworks, as the AA batteries on Guadalcanal peppered the sky in an effort to discourage Charlie. This worked to no avail until one night when two of our night fighters, visible to us only as streams of tracer bullets, ended Charlie's career. The Japanese never found a substitute for Charlie.

Our first big break in the routine came in early November. The marines had landed at Cape Torokina, on the island of Bougainville. Bougainville is at the northwest end of the Solomon Islands, and is the closest of those islands to the great Japanese naval base of Rabaul, at the northern end of New Britain; from Bougainville, Allied aircraft would be within easy striking range of that base. Cape Torokina formed an arm, partially surrounding Empress Augusta Bay.

On the initial invasion, one of the screening destroyers, the USS *Fullam,* bumped a propeller on an uncharted coral head, and had to be sent elsewhere for repairs. The *Warrington* was designated as her substitute for the first follow-up shipment of men and supplies, known as the "second echelon"; accordingly, I reported to a destroyer division commander for temporary duty. He assigned us our place in the destroyer screen supporting the transports and cargo ships.

We reached Empress Augusta Bay on the morning of 8 November 1943, and the convoy immediately started unloading, while the screening ships formed an arc around the bay. At about 10:00 A.M., we received a warning that a large force of enemy planes appeared to be headed our way. The ships ceased unloading and started out to sea, while the destroyers formed around them in a circular screen. The *Warrington*'s station was about at the middle of the port (left) side of the screen.

Most of the incoming aircraft seemed bent on making torpedo attacks; they came in fairly low. And most of them came in from the starboard side of the formation, so the destroyers on that side had their hands full, but proved to be well up to the job requirements.

On our side of the formation, only two planes approached. The first tried to break into the screen between us and the ship astern of us; our after 40 mm gun, commanded by Gunner's Mate 2d Class Robert "Whiz" Allen, shot pieces off the plane's tail, and it was seen to crash shortly thereafter. The second plane was fired on by the *Warrington* and the ship astern; it, too, was seen to crash, but we could not take full credit for it.

While this was going on, our gunnery officer, Lt. (jg) Philip C. Koelsch, champing at the bit, opened fire across the formation at the low-flying planes with his five-inch main battery, using so-called VT shells. These shells are influenced by magnetism, and explode if anything metallic passes close by them. They were Phil's only hope of hitting anything, but it gave me gray hairs, thinking one of them might be set off by passing over one of our own ships at too low an altitude. As it turned out, nothing happened— including hitting anything.

The Japanese survivors pulled out in a few minutes, and everyone went back to the unloading operation, finishing it off a little after dark. We all then formed up again and headed for Guadalcanal, but at about 8:00 P.M. another flight of enemy planes appeared. At about the same time, a tropical rain shower also approached. These showers are heavy but fast moving, so all our ships headed for the shower's protection. None of us were ever discovered by the enemy, although one plane flew within eight hundred yards of the *Warrington*. Our orders were to not fire unless actually attacked, so as not to give away our positions.

The next morning the formation broke up, with the transports and cargo ships going their own way. We fell in at the tail end of a column of four destroyers and barreled down the slot at twenty-five knots, much to the consternation of my officers, who had never had the experience of steaming at high speed in close order. It took a lot of talking to convince them that they were not going to ram the ship ahead no matter how hard they tried. The powerful wake generated by ships steaming in column pushes the bow of a following ship aside so it cannot hit the ship in front.

Our temporary duty was completed on arrival off Guadalcanal, and we said good-bye to the destroyer division with a lot of regret. We had nothing to look forward to but more of the old grind.

A month earlier we had escorted an escort carrier, the USS *Prince William,* to Samoa, and had looked forward to a little liberty in a semi-civilized port. It did not pan out; after refueling, we turned around and headed back to Espíritu Santo. The ship and the crew were beginning to show signs of stress.

This type of operation is not good for either ships or men. The *Warrington* had not had a full, ninety-day overhaul since well before the outbreak of war, and things were beginning to wear out. Since leaving Panama in July, she had not had a two-week tender overhaul; and as things were developing, she could not see such an overhaul anywhere in the near future.

As for the crew, there were no good places for shore leave or liberty. We were in an area of "cannibal" islands. The natives were Melanesians, and if they spoke English at all, they used a very difficult to understand pidgin English. There were no towns or places of entertainment of any kind. The ships were allowed to carry a small stock of beer, to be issued whenever we could arrange a baseball game or a picnic ashore, but even these opportunities were few and far between. Much publicity was given, in the States, to the good deeds of the USO groups, and they deserved the praise; but no one ever saw a USO group aboard a destroyer, that I know of. Once in a while, a few men might be invited to attend a USO show aboard a larger ship, such as a cruiser, but this depended upon personal contacts, and, above all, time in port.

Our routine continued through the rest of November and well into December, when we bumped a propeller on a shoal for the second time. This time, the damage was too much for the repair facilities at Noumea, so we were ordered to sail to Pearl Harbor. This trip was uneventful, except that we crossed the International Date Line on Christmas Day, which gave us two Christmases. Celebrating two Christmases in the middle of nowhere does nothing for morale; it is not to be recommended.

At Pearl Harbor, things were better. It took about a week to repair the propeller, and during this time I granted as much liberty as possible. It was a vast improvement over the South Pacific, but even so, it had its drawbacks. The Royal Hawaiian Hotel had been taken over by the navy, so part of the crew was able to spend a day or two ashore; unfortunately, a very strict curfew was being enforced, along with a blackout, so evening activities were quite limited.

Repairs completed, we again put to sea and headed for the South Pacific with a new ship of a new type under our wing. This was the USS *Ashland* (LSD-1). She was a floating dry dock, capable of at least fifteen knots, and of carrying several smaller landing craft in her cavernous interior.

A few days after departure, the *Warrington* sonarmen picked up a good, solid, sound contact at about 10:00 A.M. I tried to warn the *Ashland,* with no success; TBS, flashing light, flaghoist, and even blowing our whistle had no effect. I not only had on my hands another ship whose people must have hated the TBS, but also, having just finished a long and luxurious cruise from the States to Hawaii, were in the mood to relax. And she was headed right for the presumed submarine contact.

Time was not on my side, so I had to make a fast decision—to attack or not to attack. I decided to attack, and at the proper moment we started dropping depth charges. The first charge exploded about 150 yards dead ahead of the *Ashland,* and probably turned out all her lights below decks. She made the fastest 45 degree turn I had seen in quite a while, and scampered away from the area where other depth charges were now exploding.

After the attack, we lost the contact; it may have been a false one. By that time, the *Ashland* was going over the horizon, so we speeded up and chased her down. I fully expected to get a tongue-lashing from her skipper for disturbing the peace, but we heard nothing until about two weeks later, when we received a copy of a letter addressed to ComSoPac, praising our alertness and aggressiveness. Maybe the skipper was embarrassed; in any event, we appreciated this letter, and just hoped his officer of the deck got the deserved tongue-lashing, and that the captain had learned something about the use of the TBS.

We were now into the early part of January 1944. After a few more Guadalcanal runs, we were directed, in early February, to escort a transport to the atoll of Funa Futi; there, we were to break off, enter the lagoon, fuel, be out by sunset, and rendezvous with a west-bound ship the following morning.

We arrived off Funa Futi at about 1:30 P.M. and quickly found out why our orders specified being out by sunset: the only entrance channel was narrow and twisting. I would not have dared to attempt it in the dark.

As we slowly moved through this channel, we felt a bump (somebody outside the lagoon had dropped a depth charge) and the chief engineer, Lt. (jg) William V. Keppel, was immediately on the telephone, wanting to know what we had hit. We calmed him down and went on into the lagoon. We discovered, first, that the lagoon was about fifty miles long, and second, as far as the eye could see, it was full of oil tankers. Not having any information as to where I should go for fuel, I stopped the engines and tried to signal the Harbor Control Post. As in the case of the *Ashland,* it was no go; I eventually lowered a boat and sent an officer ashore to get the information. It was a very long boat ride, so it was quite late when he returned to inform me that our fuel tanker was twenty miles up the lagoon. His good news was that a new entrance was being dredged at the south end of the lagoon, and it would be a straight channel through the reef. They reported that the new channel was almost finished and was usable as far as we were concerned.

With this news, I decided to make a run to our tanker and take on as much oil as possible by sunset, then tear back down the lagoon, hoping to get to the new channel by dark.

This plan worked pretty well until we were within ten minutes or so of the entrance channel. We ran into a patented tropical rainstorm; the skies literally opened, and we could hardly see our hands in front of our faces. One man, Quartermaster 1st Class John D. Martin, had eyes like a cat's, and could see landmarks invisible to the rest of us. He kept us on track until we could finally make out the lights of a dredge that was still working on the channel. About that time, the rain, true to tropical standards, stopped, so we had no trouble finding the channel entrance, but we were now in black darkness. For the first time since the war began, and for the last time in her life, we turned on *Warrington*'s running lights so the dredge would be able to see us, and eased into the new channel. We breathed a deep sigh of relief when we saw the surf breaking on both sides of the channel.

We made our rendezvous the next morning without difficulty, and headed back toward the Solomons, but our troubles were not yet over.

We had entered Lengo Channel, between Guadalcanal and the island of Malaita, at about 8:00 P.M., and I had left the bridge for a few minutes. As I started back up the ladder, the General Alarm started sounding, so I ran the rest of the way. On reaching the bridge, I found that the officer of the deck, Ens. Paul Pigman, had gotten us into trouble: the rudder was jammed hard right, and we were making helpless circles in the water, while our sonar was getting echoes off our own wake.

Efforts to break the rudder jam were fruitless, so the executive officer took a crew aft, to man the steering engine for hand steering. In the meantime, I had informed our convoy of the trouble, and she had sailed on; fortunately, she was only a few hours from her destination.

Steering by hand was a clumsy, difficult operation. It was made clumsy by the fact that the gyrocompass in the steering engineroom was mounted facing aft, so the helmsman had to apply rudder in the opposite direction from that which he was used to. It took a little while for the people in the steering engineroom to settle down on the course I wanted to steer, but we eventually made it in a sort of wavering fashion.

In our early days in that area, the only harbor we ever used was Tulagi, which was narrow and cramped to begin with, and was made more so by the wreck of a Japanese ship, lying in the middle of the fairway. But before our rudder-jamming episode, a new anchorage had been found, not far from Tulagi, named Purvis Bay. It had a narrow entrance, but otherwise it was a fine anchorage except in very strong winds; in some parts of the bay, the holding ground was not too good, so ships could drag their anchors.

After we got ourselves under some sort of control, we headed for Purvis Bay to employ the services of a tender to unjam the rudder. It was the first time that we had been in this bay, and we were impressed by a large sign, erected on a hill near the entrance, which said, "KILL JAPS, KILL JAPS, KILL MORE JAPS. IF YOU DO YOUR JOB WELL, YOU WILL HELP TO KILL THE LITTLE YELLOW BASTARDS. HALSEY."

Our boring operations began to seem a little more important with this idea in mind.

It took nearly a week to repair the rudder, during which time we tried to get a number of other jobs done by the tender, in particular closing a large crack in the deck along the starboard side of the stack. They tried; they filled it with cement. But it opened up again soon afterward, and became an important factor in the later tragedy.

I investigated the circumstances leading to the jamming, and found that when the sonarmen reported the submarine contact, Pigman had acted correctly in ordering full right rudder. He was standing on the port side of the bridge at the time, and as he hurried over to the starboard wing, he glanced at the rudder angle indicator—and misread it. Standard procedure called for an angle of 35° as "full rudder"; this left about 2° to spare, as a safety factor. The helmsman had turned the rudder to 35° as ordered, but Pigman, misreading it, snapped, "God damn it! I said FULL right rudder!" The helmsman, thinking Pigman had said "God damn you!" angrily spun the wheel as far as it would go.

Obviously, both men were at fault, but the important thing to remember, in light of what came later, was that there was nothing wrong with the steering system itself.

For some time previously, I had been aware of the fact that the crew was beginning to show signs of stress from the long days of work and no play; and this episode was a significant sign of it. As Quartermaster Bill Greene put it many years later, "It paid to be very polite to your shipmates, or you might find yourself picking yourself up off the deck."[1]

In addition to the stress, however, I felt that this incident indicated a need for further training in antisubmarine tactics, using a "tame" submarine as a target. Accordingly, I wrote a letter to ComSoPac, requesting two weeks of such training whenever operations would permit. More or less reluctantly, he granted this request a few weeks later, sending us to Havannah Harbour, on the island of Efate, where there was a small training facility.

On our arrival, we found that Havannah Harbour is a splendid anchorage, almost completely landlocked. Aside from the small facility ashore, and our tame submarine, there was nobody there but a single oil tanker. We had our training session to ourselves.

Two days before our time ended, however, we had company. A Task Group, consisting of three old battleships (survivors of the Pearl Harbor attack) and about fifteen destroyers, including the *Balch,* came steaming in. We were ordered to report to the Task Group commander, Rear Admiral Griffin, for duty. It turned out that the Task Group was headed for Sydney,

Australia, for ten days of rest and recreation. We were to have our time off at last.

The voyage to Sydney was pleasant and uneventful. All the ships went into Wooloomooloo Basin (pronounced "Wolla-Maloo") in Sydney Harbour, where the *Warrington* moored alongside the USS *Pennsylvania.* During the voyage, it occurred to me that with a crew that had been deprived of relaxation for some months, there might be some danger of an unpleasant reaction to too much freedom all at once. So I passed the word that I intended to grant all the liberty the law allowed in Sydney, but I wanted to remind all hands of two things: they would be subject to Australian laws, therefore they must avoid any trouble with Australian police; and they would be guests of the Australian people and should behave as they would want a guest to behave in their own homes.

As it turned out, their behavior was exemplary. They came back to the ship in various stages of dilapidation, but we had no trouble with police or anyone else. When we left, we left one man behind; whether he jumped ship or merely overslept, we never knew. We reported his absence to the flagship, and we never heard of him again. But my pride in this crew was reenforced.

It was about this time that our gunnery officer, Phil Koelsch, was transferred; his duties were taken over by Lt. (jg) Coleman S. Pack, USNR.

Shortly after leaving Australia, the *Balch* and *Warrington* were detached and ordered to join another Task Group, consisting of three escort carriers and about sixteen destroyers. This Task Group, acting in support of Task Force 37, was supposed to make threats against Kavieng, a Japanese post on the island of New Ireland. We closed in on the island one sunny morning, launched a few planes, and departed. What the Japanese thought of this is anybody's guess.

It was with this Task Group that we got our first taste of what it was like to operate with the USS *Balch.* The captain of the *Balch* was a pleasant officer named Coffin, who, to all appearances had not a care in the world about what was going on around him. The *Balch* and *Warrington,* being weak sisters in the antiaircraft department, were stationed side by side at the rear of the circular screen around the carriers. On our first night with this group, the *Warrington* received a TBS message from the flagship, ordering us to get in position. At the moment, we were exactly in position, but the *Balch,* our next-door neighbor, was fully five hundred yards inside her assigned position. Signals like this always irritate ship captains, whether deserved or not, so I merely answered that I was in position, and let it go at that. From then on, the flagship tried periodically to wake the *Balch* up, without success—she had her TBS turned off. She was still out of position when I finally gave up and went to bed.

We were with this Task Group only a short time, then we and the *Balch* were detached from the South Pacific Force and ordered to report to the commander, Seventh Fleet, in the Southwest Pacific Force. We were becoming part of MacArthur's navy.

We were not sorry to leave the South Pacific Force, which was being disbanded, in any case, although we were not overjoyed at our destination. At least, the change promised a variation from the old, soul-killing runs from Espíritu Santo to Guadalcanal.

We had at least two unsettling incidents indicating that all was not well with our crew and officers. The first involved the chief engineer and one of the mess attendants. The chief, having a watch to stand on a particular afternoon, had left orders with the mess attendant to keep his supper for him. When he came off watch, there was no supper, and the mess attendant admitted that he had thrown it out. Furious, the chief ordered the attendant to produce some supper immediately, or he would kick his rear end. The attendant put up his fists and dared the chief to carry out his threat, which the chief then did, and the attendant hit him back.

The chief came steaming into my cabin, demanding that the attendant be court-martialed for striking an officer. When I untangled the story, I told the chief that, if I got the mess attendant court-martialed for that offense, I would have to have him court-martialed as well, for striking another person in the navy. He had put himself into an impossible situation. I finally gave the mess attendant a summary court-martial for disobedience to orders, without saying anything about anyone doing any striking, but I told the chief engineer that if he ever repeated this performance, I would not hesitate to recommend him for a general court-martial.

The second incident was not officially reported and I did not hear of it until years later. The quartermaster and an officer were in the charthouse, looking at a chart, when another officer entered the charthouse behind the quartermaster and gave him a very painful kick, then turned and walked out without a word. The officer in the charthouse recommended that the quartermaster report the incident to me, but he preferred not to do so.[2]

The only other incident of which I was aware involved two seamen who engaged in a scuffle outside my cabin one afternoon. I stopped them, then arranged for them to put on a boxing exhibition for the rest of the crew. Some survivors still recall that "happy hour."

We received our orders to report to SoWesPac in early May 1944. The *Warrington* had been out of U.S. waters since early January 1942—about twenty-nine months altogether, and many of the crew had been aboard the whole time. They had also been away from home for a substantial time before that; her last real visit to the homeland was in November 1941, when she had started a much-needed overhaul at Charleston, South Carolina—an overhaul that was abbreviated by the attack on Pearl Harbor.

Consequently, the ship was in a run-down condition, and the crew was not at all enthusiastic about its immediate prospects. Those of us who served in the South Pacific area tended to look down our noses at our brethren in SoWesPac, although we realized that the Army Ground Forces in that area were having a very rough go of it. Our attitude was fairly well expressed by a wartime song, part of which went as follows:

> Admiral Nimitz said, "Let's take Tulagi,"
> But General MacArthur said, "No!"
> He gave as his reason "This isn't the season—
> Besides, there's no USO!"

Our low opinion was more or less concentrated on MacArthur's Army Air Corps people. We sometimes intercepted radio messages not intended for us, and one of these turned out to be a report from Halsey to Nimitz regarding a SoPac air attack on a Japanese convoy. It ended with the words, "WE HOPE MACARTHUR'S BOYS GET THE CRIPPLES THIS TIME."

chapter two

MacARTHUR'S NAVY

The *Balch* and *Warrington* arrived off the coast of New Guinea on 13 May 1944. Before we arrived, we had been asked by the commander of the Seventh Fleet to report any needed repairs. This was the only query of its kind that the *Warrington* received during my entire time on board; other superiors did not seem to care, or perhaps just assumed we were in top shape. However, although we had a long list of things to be done by a navy yard, we knew there were no such yards anywhere nearer than Australia or Pearl Harbor, thousands of miles away, so we just submitted a few minor things, principally complaints about the functioning of our radars. We were greeted by an officer and one enlisted man, who took care of these problems in a day.

The ships then sailed to Milne Bay, where we lay at anchor for about two days. One of our neighbors in the bay was a merchant ship, lying a few hundred yards from us.

One day, a single Japanese plane made a reconnaissance flight over the bay; a few days later, the rumor went around the ship that the crew of the merchant ship was demanding "hazardous duty" pay as a result of this "attack." This rumor was fervently believed by sailors who had little love for merchant mariners, with their high rates of pay and their tendency to go on strike whenever the spirit moved.

We heard a story, which may or may not be true, about a merchant ship berthed in an Australian port, whose crew went on strike and refused to unload the ship, which was carrying munitions and supplies for the marines. As the story went, an army officer appeared on the pier, armed with a .45 pistol. He confronted the crew members, demanding to speak to their spokesman. When the latter came forward, the officer demanded that he send his men back to work. The spokesman refused, whereupon the officer drew his pistol and shot him. He then called for the next man in authority, repeated this demand, and got instant action.

Our stay with MacArthur's navy was destined to be brief. I have already mentioned that we were attached to the Seventh Fleet; this was the result of some reorganization ordered by Admiral Ernest J. King. The various fleets, which had been designated by their areas of operation, had grown to such size and complexity that there might be more than one fleet operating in one area. The Atlantic fleets were given even numbers; those in the Pacific were odd numbered. The First Fleet was based on the West Coast, and was principally engaged in such activities as training. The Third and Fifth Fleets were a gigantic hoax; they were made up of the same individual ships, but the command rotated between Adm. William Halsey and Adm. Raymond A. Spruance, much to the mystification of the Japanese, who thought they were being confronted by two huge, separate fleets. The Seventh Fleet belonged to General MacArthur.

The Seventh Fleet consisted mainly of the old battleships—the veterans of Pearl Harbor—and a number of cruisers and destroyers including Australians. It also contained huge numbers of landing craft, since it would obviously be moving from island to island to fulfill MacArthur's famous promise to the Filipinos: "I shall return."

When we joined this outfit, the Army Ground Forces—the Sixth Army—had just captured the port of Hollandia, on the north coast of New Guinea. The marines were holding the southern half of the island of New Britain, thereby protecting the flank of any movement between New Britain and New Guinea, while isolating the big Japanese base at the northern end of that island. The base was further isolated by MacArthur's surprise invasion of the island of Manus, with its superb Seeadler Harbour, and by the massive air raids on Truk, in February.

After leaving Milne Bay, the *Warrington* and *Balch* (now beginning to operate like Siamese twins) arrived at Capes Sudest and Cretin, where we joined a convoy of LSTs headed for Hollandia. This was a new experience for former high-speed escorts. The maximum speed of a convoy of LSTs was about eight knots—hardly enough to stir up a breeze—so slow the destroyers had to patrol back and forth ahead of them just to keep from overheating their boilers. These flat-bottomed vessels were used for hauling troops and supplies for fairly short distances, into areas where there were no loading or unloading facilities; their bows were equipped with large doors with ramps, so that they could run right up on a shelving beach to unload. Because of their slow speed, it took this convoy three days to reach Hollandia.

Hollandia is located on Humboldt Bay, which is large and well protected, but it is a terrible place to lie at anchor, at least during May and June. The heat and humidity were almost unbearable. Air-conditioning was unknown then. There was seldom any breeze. On one day, the temperature in my cabin reached 138°. We welcomed our assignments to patrol duty outside the harbor; at least we could stir up a little breeze.

It was not long before we had work, however. Two days after our arrival, while the *Warrington* was steaming slowly back and forth on patrol, the *Balch* came racing out of the harbor at high speed. Curious, I signaled, "Where are you going?" The reply came back: "Come on!"

I requested and obtained a relief on my patrol station, and took off after the *Balch* at twenty-five knots; she was fast disappearing over the horizon, so it was a long chase before I finally caught up. When I did, I found that we were directed to go to a place called Wakde, where we were to assist the army by bombarding the Japanese troops in the area.

On arrival the next morning, we found that Wakde was a small island a short distance off the New Guinea coast; on the coast itself, where the army was having its problems, we could see nothing but jungle in every direction; there were no landmarks of any kind. We therefore sent a boat ashore to find out where we were supposed to shoot.

The word came back that the army would fire some white phosphorus shells (which create a heavy white smoke) as markers; we were to fire to the right of the smoke. There were no special communications set up between the land and naval forces to help keep us oriented, however.

The army did its part; we saw the white smoke blossom out of the trees about two miles away, so we opened up. Both ships commenced firing full six-gun salvos, as fast as we could. We felt speed was called for because the slight breeze that was blowing was moving and dissipating the target smoke. We ceased firing when all our five-inch AA ammunition had been expended. (The AA ammunition was used because it would explode on contact with any solid object when the fuse was set on "safe." This made it useful when firing on personnel.)

Ammunition gone, we returned to Hollandia, where we went alongside a New Zealand ammunition ship for replenishment. In the process, we learned a little about inter-Allied cooperation.

In those days, our provisions were rationed out to us on a standard allowance; that is, so much of this and so much of that on every replenishment. Among other things, our meat allowances always included a fixed amount of mutton, which our finicky Americans despised. On the other hand, the New Zealanders got plenty of beef, which they likewise did not think much of, so, as our ammunition replenishment went forward apace, so did our trading of provisions. Both we and the New Zealanders parted happy.

The next day we were sent back to Wakde to repeat the operation, and the army later thanked us profusely for the help in capturing a supply dump. While in the area we had noticed, on the island of Wakde, a small airfield with a number of wrecked American planes lying around. We were told that the Japanese had caught the Army Air Corps by surprise and wrecked the place before anyone could get off the ground. But we never saw any signs of life anywhere around Wakde, except for the army's smoke.

Back to Hollandia we went, and again replenished our supply of ammunition, then sat around for a couple of days, sweltering. On 28 May, we got orders to join a convoy of LSTs headed for the island of Biak off the "bird's head" at the western end of New Guinea. Allied forces had landed there a few days earlier, and heavy fighting was still going on.

Arriving on 30 May, we were ordered to join Shore Fire Control Group 1 to deliver call-fire in support of troops attacking an airfield known as Mokmer Airdome. A short time later, the army, suspecting that the Japanese were preparing a counterattack, asked us to patrol the western side of the island to see if we could spot any activity. Not finding any, we tried to stir some by spraying the jungle and anything resembling a target with our 40 mm and 20 mm guns. About the only thing we damaged was a Japanese landing barge lying on the beach, which had probably been put out of action earlier.

We did succeed in stirring up a little action, however; the Japanese had an AA gun hidden in a cave in the side of a coral ridge, and apparently we irritated the gun crew. They fired one shot, which burst about three-hundred feet directly over our heads. It did no harm, but our screen commander called us on TBS, saying "Bell Metal, Bell Metal [our voice call]! I wouldn't tweak his nose too hard if I were you. He's not bad." This, of course, put an end to our sport, and we returned to our normal station, after reporting our lack of information to the army.

A little later we were interested spectators when an LSMR (a rocket-armed landing craft) moved inside the reef and commenced a rocket bombardment against the cliff at our end of the island (see map 1). We had never seen one of these monsters in action, and found it very impressive. That night, we were named as fighter director ship, when the USS *Swanson*

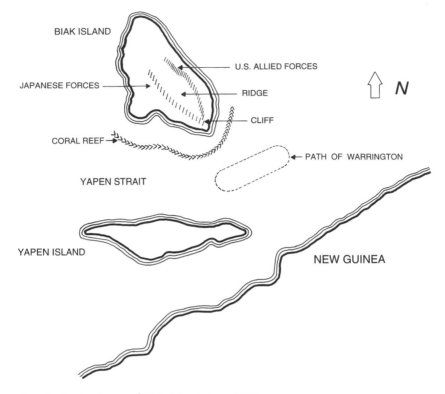

BIAK ISLAND

JAPANESE FORCES

U.S. ALLIED FORCES

RIDGE

CLIFF

CORAL REEF

↑ N

PATH OF WARRINGTON

YAPEN STRAIT

YAPEN ISLAND

NEW GUINEA

Map 1. Bombardment of Biak Island, June 1944

departed. It was just as well that we had no business to conduct that night; our only means of communicating with aircraft was by our TBY radio, which we had never been able to get working properly.

The following day, we returned to Hollandia. We made another trip to Biak on 3 June, and again we were called upon to assist the army. This time, we overheard the army calling our screen commander, asking for a destroyer to bombard the face of the cliff.

This cliff, at the end of a coral ridge running up the spine of the island, had been giving the army quite a lot of trouble. It contained many caves, most of which were inhabited by Japanese soldiers with machine guns. Some days earlier, the Americans had sent a force along the beach, past this cliff, in an attack; the Japanese had allowed a substantial number of troops to pass the cliff, then had opened fire on their rear, effectively cutting off their retreat. Because of the cliff's location, the army could not bring its own artillery to bear; hence, the request for naval help.

The screen commander asked us if we had heard the army's request, and, when we answered in the affirmative, he said, "Tag! You're it!" Whereupon, we headed in toward the island to pick up an army artillery officer as liaison. The organization here was much superior to that at Wakde; a major and an enlisted man came aboard, the latter carrying a walkie-talkie radio. The major—an impudent sort of character— immediately wanted to know if we thought we could hit anything, so I turned him over to Lieutenant (jg) Pack, with orders to Pack to give him a lesson in naval gunnery.

We were not to fire six-gun salvos this time; the army requested that we fire just one gun at a time, and allow time for an observer ashore to spot each one before firing the next. We closed in as near to the beach as we dared—about seven hundred yards from the cliff, which was point-blank range for five-inch guns, and then sailed slowly around in an ellipse, banging away. We had to be careful not to shoot low, for fear of hitting the trees fringing the shoreline; this would cause the shells to burst prematurely, and might endanger our own troops. We also had to be careful not to shoot high, because, so we were told, the army was trying to send troops up the ridge behind the cliff. After firing for some time, we asked the observer how we were doing, and he responded that we were doing just fine; Japanese soldiers, Korean laborers, and Biak natives were coming out of the caves in a dazed condition, and walking right into our front lines.

When we had expended all our ammunition, Pack and the major came down to the bridge, where I told the major that what we had just done was child's play, but I hoped he had learned from it. He seemed impressed, so I relented and offered him a shower, which he badly needed. The army's bathing facilities ashore were slightly less than those of the Ritz. We parted friends.

This operation took almost all afternoon. Late in the day, the LSTs finished unloading, so I left my station and lay to in the channel between Biak and New Guinea. I was waiting for them to form up when an army light bomber flew by, closely pursued by a Japanese Zero. I sounded General Quarters, in hope that the bomber would come back bringing his pursuer and we could get a shot at the latter, but he did not. We never knew if the bomber escaped. A little later, the convoy formed up and we returned to Hollandia.

After rearming, we awaited further orders. Several days later, the *Warrington* was on antisubmarine patrol outside the harbor, when we got a surprise dispatch that ordered us, and our old buddy, the *Bulch,* to sail to

Panama. We had no hint as to what was behind this order, but Panama was a lot closer to the United States than New Guinea, so we were happy—but then came trouble in paradise. Before I really had time to absorb the implications in this order, Lieutenant (jg) Keppel came to my cabin reporting that he had just discovered a strange noise in his port reduction gear.

This was serious news, indeed. Reduction gears are extremely important, and tender, pieces of machinery. They are designed to reduce the speed of the ship's turbines down to the speed of the propellers, and the gear teeth are machined to very close tolerances. If any foreign object gets into the gears and damages the gear teeth, the whole engine can be put out of commission until the ship can reach a navy yard. As mentioned earlier, the closest yards were thousands of miles away.

This presented a dilemma: should I report this problem, expecting the result would be a substantial delay in reaching Panama, or should I take the risk of carrying out my orders and reporting the casualty later? I calculated that the ship could make it to Panama on one engine, if necessary, so Keppel and I tried some experimenting, to see if we could run the port engine at all. We found that the noise disappeared at speeds under five knots, so we accepted that as a speed we felt would get us by, with the starboard engine making a speed of twelve knots (the ship's most economical speed). We would try to carry out our orders.

In the many years since that day, I have wondered if I made the right decision. If we had sailed for Pearl Harbor instead of Panama, our arrival on the East Coast would have been delayed by about two weeks—and this *might* have been sufficient to avoid the tragedy that came later. But not many of us have the ability to see into the future.

So the commander, Seventh Fleet, thanked us for our services and sent us on our way, first to the island of Manus, with its gorgeous harbor, where we joined the USS *Nashville*. We were to escort her as far as Espíritu Santo. We stopped there overnight, and then we were on our way.

The prospect of crossing the wide Pacific in company with the *Balch* did not particularly appeal to me, but I had no choice in the matter. On our last trip to Biak, we had almost had a collision with the *Balch*, when she failed to get a change of course signal. We had avoided disaster only by backing full speed on one engine, with full rudder; we were close enough to hear her blowers whining.

At Espíritu Santo, we said farewell to the *Nashville*, refueled, and set forth on the long haul to Panama at a sedate twelve knots.

The voyage was generally uneventful, and the weather was perfect all the way. The first lieutenant, Lt. (jg) Patrick B. Davis, feeling the spirit of

USS Warrington *(DD 383), July 1944.*

the occasion, became the author of *The Song of the Warrington,* to be sung to the tune of *The Strawberry Blonde:*

> Down to old Biak and back to the Hump* we go on and on,
> No matter what hits us, the tenders will fix us,
> We'll carry on!
> Oh, the *Sampson* got leave, while the *Warrington* got left
> Out in this ocean to roam,
> Now a new route we'll be taking, and knots we'll be making
> Toward home, sweet home!
>
> Smoky old hulks, hardly making eight knots,
> (It's a wonder how),
> Depth charges behind them we drop to remind them
> "You can't stop now!
> Though you're not worth a part of the ballast you cart
> We'll blast every sub in your way,
> Until this old can is in sight of Cape Ann,
> In the U.S.A.!" (*Humboldt Bay)

Our only problem on the voyage was another of the kind caused by months of stress. We had a fireman on board—a big man—who had not previously caused any problems but began picking fights, always with smaller men. When brought to Captain's Mast, he defended his actions with transparent lies, and increasingly heavy punishments appeared to have no effect. It therefore seemed to me that he must have a mental problem. I asked Lt. (jg) Robert Kennedy, the medical officer, to interview him for the purpose of making his own evaluation of the man's mental state. Dr. Kennedy was reluctant to do this, on the grounds that he was not a psychiatrist, but when I pointed out that he was the nearest thing we had to a psychiatrist, he talked to the man, and confirmed my own opinion.

This meant that I had to find some way to keep this man away from the rest of the crew. A destroyer does not have a brig, however, so we cleaned out a storeroom in the forecastle and put him in it. A sentry was stationed to keep guard over him, but he had authority to take the man out to go to meals or to the head when necessary. He could also let him out to exercise on the forecastle practically any time during the day; the object was not punishment but just segregation.

When we left Espíritu Santo, we were under the command of the commander in chief, Pacific Fleet (CinCPac) (Admiral Nimitz), until about a week before our arrival at Panama, when we came under the command of the commander in chief, Atlantic Fleet (CinCLant). This event was marked by the arrival of another dispatch, which directed us, upon arrival at Panama, to transit the canal, fuel, and proceed to the New York Navy Yard for fifteen days' overhaul. The captain of the *Balch* reacted to this news with a message to me: BROOKLYN IN JULY X WOW X PASS THE ICE CUBES PAPPY. Naturally, my crew was in seventh heaven; a seaman named Charlie Hutton proceeded to make a "Homeward Bound" pennant—one foot in length for every man on board— and everyone was talking about going home on leave. But on second, sober, thought, all was not as wonderful as it seemed. Fifteen days was not nearly long enough to accomplish all the repair work that needed to be done, and it was also not nearly long enough to allow all hands to go on leave.

I wrote a letter to the commander destroyers, Atlantic Fleet (ComDesLant) air mailed from Panama, outlining our repair problems (including, of course, the noise in the reduction gear), and recommending that the repair period be extended to ninety days. The reply from ComDesLant, which we received after arriving at New York, was "negative." Nobody seemed to have any interest in our state of health, so to speak.

We arrived in Panama on 8 July, with about a teaspoonful of oil left in our tanks, and moored at Colón overnight. I transferred our bad boy to the Naval Hospital and granted liberty—the first since Sydney—and the crew took full advantage of it. Leaving the next morning, we arrived at New York on the fifteenth and went directly into the yard.

Although the yard went to work on some of our more urgent repairs, it quickly became apparent that repairs were a distinctly secondary consideration. CinCLant had bigger and better things in store for us.

chapter three

THE FRANTIC ATLANTIC

 We were soon informed of the reason for our recall from the Pacific: we were slated to become a flagship for a convoy commodore. We never did learn the reason, however, for all the haste; after all, the Atlantic Fleet had gotten along pretty well for more than two years without such flagships, and reason suggested that efficiency would result from ensuring that the new flagships were in good operating condition. It was not to be.

Yard personnel swarmed aboard and commenced tearing apart our Combat Information Center and charthouse, installing FOXER gear (officially, FXR gear, which was designed to be towed astern, making noises like a ship's propeller, to deceive the enemy's acoustic torpedoes); installing Loran (electronic navigation equipment); and repainting the whole ship in a kind of camouflage known as "dazzle paint."

Most of this work was fine, as far as we were concerned; we were a bit unhappy when they painted out the little Japanese flags and silhouettes of planes and islands, representing our somewhat slim combat achievements. I fully intended to repaint them as soon as we got away from the yard.

I did the best I could, as far as crew leave was concerned; I granted ten days' leave to about one-third of the crew, but limited it to men whose homes were within five hundred miles of New York. The idea was to give them as much time at home as possible, without wasting time on travel. As usual, one or two people cheated a little; Ship's Cook George Finch, for example, took off for Chicago, where he got married. I discovered this bit of chicanery many years later.

The assignment of 1,850-ton destroyers as convoy flagships was a logical development. These ships, which included the *Warrington,* had been originally designed to serve as squadron commanders' flagships; therefore, they had more comfortable and spacious accommodations than the general run of destroyers. None of them were ever used for that purpose, however. I will go into more detail on this subject in chapter 12.

The denial of decent overhauls may have been the result of pure ignorance. I was to find that few people in the Atlantic area had a realistic concept of the nature of Pacific operations. In fact, the war in the Pacific was totally different from the war in the Atlantic.

We have already seen how the *Warrington* had been forced to operate for many months without proper overhauls, and how her crew had been deprived of much-needed liberty ashore. These conditions were not unusual in the Pacific; they affected everyone, and nobody really complained. In the Atlantic, on the other hand, there were navy yards on both sides of the ocean, and there were opportunities for a great deal of liberty, also. Ships paid frequent visits to navy yards, and were kept in good repair. When not on a convoy operation or in a navy yard, the ships were directly under the eagle eye of ComDesLant, conducting training exercises and undergoing inspections. In the Pacific, we never saw our bosses and whatever training we accomplished was done "on the fly"; inspections were almost unheard-of. Ships' crews were required to wear dungarees while at sea; white uniforms were supposedly too visible to aircraft. They also wore the same uniforms in port, except when in Pearl Harbor or some Australian or South American port. Atlantic sailors were much more uniform conscious. In the tropics, ship captains were encouraged to allow their engineers to sunbathe when off watch; it was the only chance they could have to cool off a little after four hours of the heat of enginerooms and firerooms. This was definitely frowned upon in the Atlantic.

The commander, Destroyers (ComDesLant), was Rear Adm. J. Cary Jones. I had known him when he was a commander, serving as division commander of Destroyer Division 19, and I considered him to be a fine officer. But he was as ignorant of the Pacific as anyone else.

He remembered me, and invited my wife and me to dinner one evening. I took the opportunity to bring him up to date on the Pacific, emphasizing the poor material condition of the *Warrington* in the process. He seemed surprised, and said he would see that we got a real overhaul as soon as operational requirements permitted. I had to be satisfied with this; it appeared that he was under pressure himself.

The efforts of the Brooklyn Navy Yard to meet our needs were generally commendable, but because of the short time, too much of the work turned out to be slipshod, and at least one job—the reduction gear work—was completely unsatisfactory, a fact we discovered several weeks later. They made no effort to accomplish many jobs, among them fixing the recurring crack in the deck on the starboard side of the stack.

I was informed that this yard had a reputation for doing shoddy work, and Admiral Jones had received so many complaints that he had finally issued strict orders that no one was to blame the yard for their troubles.

In due time, we left the yard for a trial run. As we built up speed, I began to get alarming reports from the engineers—the engineering spaces were being filled with live steam! It turned out that the yard, in its haste to do as much as possible, had dismantled many of our high-pressure steam lines, but, in reassembling them, had only set up the bolts hand tight. We aborted the trial and returned to the yard, where we spent another day or two tightening bolts. The second trial run was satisfactory; the noises from the reduction gears had disappeared.[1]

Now we were to experience the joys of being under the admiral's eagle eye, in what was known as the "Casco Fiasco." We were also about to become acquainted with our new commodore, Capt. William R. Headden, USN. Soon I would be longing for the good old days in the Pacific.

When we arrived in Casco Bay, Maine, I was told that the commodore would be coming aboard at about 6:00 P.M. that evening. As a matter of courtesy, I had the movies that evening delayed for his benefit, but, when he failed to show up by nine o'clock, I allowed them to be started. Twenty minutes later, the gangway messenger tapped me on the shoulder and informed me that the commodore was aboard, was in his cabin, and wanted to see me. I walked into the cabin, to be greeted by a stream of complaints ranging from the cleanliness of the ship to the way his bunk was made up.

The ship was dirty, having just come from the navy yard, but this was something that could and would be corrected quickly; likewise, the problem with his bunk could be quickly taken care of, but at that moment, I was tired, my crew was tired, and everyone was unhappy about the lack of a chance to get leave. We had left several men behind when we left the yard—a sure sign of poor morale. So when the commodore went into his long string of complaints, I blew my stack, as it were. I gave him chapter and verse of our problems ever since we had left the Pacific; I told him all these things were only temporary, that we would get things straightened out in the near future, but that at that particular moment, I was not in a mood to listen to carping and complaining. He glared at me, and asked, "Are you telling me?" I said I was, and that ended the discussion, but we had definitely gotten off on the wrong foot.

The next day, the DesLant training people came aboard, en masse, prepared to run all kinds of drills, especially damage control. They found us woefully deficient, of course, but professed to be interested only in helping us come up to whatever their standards were. Among other deficiencies, they made special note of the absence of our damage control markings. These were letters, X, Y, Z, and W, which were to be painted on all doors, hatches, and such, as indicators, showing which fixtures were to be closed at specific times. For instance, Damage Control Condition A required that practically everything be closed, but some might be opened when in use; others were closed at all times. Damage Control Condition B permitted some openings to be open at all times, and others at specified times. In the course of our years in the Pacific, and during our stay in the yard, many of these markings had been scrubbed off or otherwise removed, and not replaced. This made the DesLant people very unhappy, indeed. They were made unhappy by other things as well, such as the fact that, while we had held frequent drills, we had rarely, if ever, actually broken out equipment and tried to run it. Theoretically, this was something we should have been doing on a regular basis, but some of this required time in port, which we rarely had.

No sooner had the DesLant people left us, and before we could really digest what it was they required of us, we had to get under way for maneuvers with a group of about six DEs, with the commodore running things. The run home from Empress Augusta Bay the previous November was the only time any of my officers had ever maneuvered the ship in close order exercises, and they had forgotten what I had tried to teach them at that time. They now made a royal mess of close order exercises, and the commodore was gleeful in criticising the *Warrington*'s performance over the TBS, with much profanity and occasional obscenities.

At the close of these exercises, he announced that, on the next day, we would fire an antitorpedo plane AA practice. I objected; our single-purpose five-inch guns were not designed for antiaircraft firing, and our five-inch gun director could not keep up with the speed of a target plane. To try to fire such a practice would endanger the plane and its pilot, and would not prove anything, because our chances of hitting a target sleeve were practically zero.

My arguments got nowhere, so we went ahead and fired the practice the next day. After the first run, the pilot of the target plane turned around and returned to his base, reporting that we were a menace on the high seas, or words to that effect. Magnanimously, I forbore to point out to the commodore that I had told him so.

On our way back to port, Lieutenant (jg) Pack informed me that our number two five-inch turret had jammed in train, which meant it could not be moved right or left. I stepped into the charthouse and started to write a report of the casualty to ComDesLant, requesting the services of a tender to clear the jam. I had it about half written when the commodore came up behind me, reached over my shoulder, and commenced to rewrite my message. In so doing, he neglected to change the message heading, so it continued to read as though I had sent it. But then he did something I had not thought of doing—he blamed the yard for the casualty. As far as I knew, the yard had not worked on that turret.

Within ten minutes, we received a message from ComDesLant, directing us to return to port immediately, and for me, personally, to report to him aboard his flagship. This is the kind of message that invariably spells trouble, so I wasted no time getting over to the flagship on our return. As I walked aboard, one of the DesLant staff officers asked me if I was trying to get myself a general court-martial. I asked him why he asked, and he said the admiral was furious at my message, blaming the yard for my casualty. When I told him that Captain Headden had written the message, he just nodded his head and said, "Ah!" Headden was obviously well known in those precincts.

Going into the Admiral's quarters, I found that the staff officer was right; the admiral's eyes were blazing, and he started right out, wanting to know what I meant by sending such a message. Again I explained the circumstances, whereupon he merely nodded and told me to go back to my ship. As I left, I heard him calling the signal bridge, and as I went back to the *Warrington,* I passed the commodore, headed for the flagship. He never mentioned the incident afterward, but our mutual antipathy was not improved.

After a week or so of these activities, we were ordered to join a convoy then being made up in Norfolk, so we headed south. Some four or five hours before we arrived, the chief engineer came to the bridge and told me that the noise in the port reduction gear had reappeared. I had no alternative but to report this to the commodore, who, to my surprise, accepted the news calmly. I wrote a dispatch to ComDesLant (without interruption, this time), and the commodore wrote one addressed to one of the DEs, announcing that he would transfer his flag upon arrival in Norfolk. Soon thereafter, a message from ComDesLant directed us to go into the Norfolk Navy Yard for repairs.

On arrival, the commodore could not get off fast enough to suit either himself or me, as I came alongside his new flagship. The captain of the DE, leaning over the bridge rail, shook his fist at me.

We then went alongside a pier in the navy yard, where they started removing a section of the main deck right away, in order to gain access to the port reduction gear. When they had the gear opened up, I could see that the gear teeth were badly chewed up. I felt it was a miracle that we had been able to run that engine at all, and I still don't understand how we could have made a speed run out of New York without causing more damage.

The more I thought about that problem, the more puzzled I became. I felt sure that I had looked down into the *starboard* reduction gear while we were in New York and had seen nothing wrong, but when I spoke to Lieutenant Keppel about it, he sturdily maintained that no mistake had been made. I had every intention of making an in-depth investigation, to see if my recollection was correct, but for the moment I was too busy with other matters to press the point. It is appropriate to mention at this point, however, that then-ensign Luther T. Chesnut, USN, who was one of the assistant engineer officers (now lieutenant commander, Civil Engineer Corps, Ret.), when asked about this incident forty-five years later, confirmed my memory—the wrong gear had been opened in New York. Ensign Chesnut was detached the day the ship made her final voyage.

A day or so after the gear was opened, Keppel came to me, to show me what had been found beneath the damaged gear: a piece of steel, about two inches square and a quarter of an inch thick. This was clear evidence of sabotage, which definitely called for further investigation.

Again, I put it off because of the press of other matters, and before I could get to it, my relief showed up. I was glad to see him; the way things had been going, I was somewhat disheartened and angry, with a dull feeling that the worst was yet to come. My feeling of anger was partly due to the fact that ComDesLant had been transferring my men to other stations at almost a wholesale rate. It almost seemed that he was bent on breaking up a smoothly functioning team. The men we received as replacements were good men—no complaints there—but it would obviously take a little while to weld them into a new team. These transfers did, however, have one good result; it tended to improve our low morale a little, since many of these men were allowed to go on leave before reporting to their new stations, and of course the new men were not suffering from a feeling of having been mistreated.

My relief was Cdr. Samuel F. Quarles of the Naval Academy class of 1932. Most of his naval career had been in the old four-stack destroyers; except for one tour of duty in a battleship and two years on shore duty, that was the total of his experience. This was not to be sneezed at; one of my old skippers had once told me he felt that the old four-stackers were the best schools for both officers and men that the navy ever had. I agreed.

Quarles had only recently been relieved of command of such a ship, the USS *Babbitt,* which had been operating in the North Atlantic; therefore, he was no stranger to foul weather. On the other hand, he had had no experience in a ship the size of the *Warrington,* and it was plain he stood a little in awe of her.

In the course of going through the change of command procedure, I took him through the ship and tried to explain her little tricks and quirks. We did not hold the usual general drills—fire, collision, man overboard, and so on—so as not to interfere with the navy yard work going on, but otherwise, we covered everything the regulations required. I told him of a suspicion I had that the ship seemed a little top-heavy; I could not prove this, but she seemed a little slow-rolling, which is a sign of rather low stability. His response was, "Well, I guess she wouldn't last long in one of these Atlantic storms, would she?" To which I answered, "I'm afraid not." (My suspicion was later to be proved groundless, but I also found, much later, that I was not alone in feeling this way.)

We had not quite completed the change of command when the yard finished its work, and it came time to make a full-power run, to test the repairs. I took her out to sea, with Quarles riding along as an observer; when we came back in, I reported to ComDesLant that we were operational again, and then Quarles took over. I left, to go on leave before reporting to the Naval Academy, my new duty station. From this point on, the story is told by *Warrington* personnel and from the written record.

chapter four

RENDEZVOUS WITH DISASTER

Commander Quarles re-
lieved me on 30 August 1944, almost exactly one year from the day I
reported aboard the *Warrington*. According to his Action Report, he sailed
from Norfolk for Casco Bay very soon thereafter. To judge from his testimony before the subsequent Court of Inquiry, there followed a period of
intense activity.[1] Nevertheless, there seems to have been time enough to
permit a liberty party to become embroiled with the shore patrol, resulting
in a large number of men being placed under arrest. As in the earlier case
of men missing the ship after the navy yard overhaul in New York, here was
another indication of low morale.

After about a week at Casco Bay, the *Warrington* sailed back to Norfolk,
where she was assigned as escort for the USS *Hyades* (AF 28). This was a
reefer ship, brand new, about to sail on her maiden cruise with a captain
who had never commanded a ship before. He was Cdr. Morgan C. Wheyland, a member of the Naval Academy class of 1920, who had resigned
from the navy after four years' service, then entered the Naval Reserve.
Returning to active duty when war broke out, he now had a total of about
seven years of active duty, as compared to Quarles's ten years.[4]

The two ships were now placed under the operational control of the
commander, Service Force, Atlantic Fleet (ComServLant). Their orders
were to proceed to the Caribbean area, and, at a certain point, the *Hyades*
was to sail for the Panama Canal and transit it into the Pacific, while the
Warrington was to sail to Trinidad, join the USS *Alaska,* a battle cruiser, and
escort her back to the United States.

The two captains attended one or more conferences with the operations officer on the staff of ComServLant, to plan courses, speeds, and such, while their communications officers worked with the staff communications officer to develop a communications plan.[5] On 8 September 1944, weather advisories indicated that a hurricane was approaching, and was then to the east of the Bahamas. Nowhere in the record of the subsequent Court of Inquiry does it indicate that any of these officers took notice of this warning. In particular, there is no indication that any thought was given to the possibility that the hurricane might recurve to the north, placing the ships in severe jeopardy.

The normal track of a hurricane begins on a westerly, or northwesterly, course, but eventually nearly all hurricanes will change course to the north, usually increasing their speed of advance as they do so. This change is known as "recurving," and is particularly dangerous because the time when it makes this change is entirely unpredictable. Some will even cross land, such as Florida, before recurving; and a few have been known to describe complete circles when recurving. Appendix A goes into this subject in more detail (see also chart 2, p. 52).

While the captains conferred, the communications officers drew up their plan, one feature of which was the agreement on a radio frequency to be used in the event they became separated. The staff communications officer later testified that he had not *ordered* the others to agree on anything, but had merely "advised."[6] They chose 2885 kcs as their separation frequency; later, the staff communicator testified that, as far as he knew, nobody in the Continental United States used that frequency, but it was not illegal to use it.[7]

In the late afternoon or early evening of 10 September, the ships departed from Norfolk. Commander Wheyland, being senior to Commander Quarles, was designated as officer in tactical command (OTC) of the Task Unit.

The *Warrington* had on board 315 souls, two of whom were there on temporary duty. Lt. Kenneth S. Davis was acting as a substitute for Lt. (jg) Robert L. Jensen, the sound officer, who had been ordered to attend a sound school. And Ens. William L. Rogers was a passenger, on his way to a new duty station on Trinidad. He was married and had two infant sons.

Just before departure, the ship received a fairly large draft of enlisted men. They were good men, but young and inexperienced.[8]

On leaving Norfolk, the *Warrington* took station about 2,500 yards ahead of the *Hyades,* and as the latter zigzagged according to a prescribed plan, the *Warrington* patrolled her station; that is, she moved back and forth across the path of the *Hyades* in such a way as to search with her sonar the water that the *Hyades* would sail through on her next zig.[9]

Machinists Mate John J. Latronica recalled that things began to go wrong in the Engineering Department within four hours of the ships' departure. Most of these were small problems that the engineers were used to handling, but they all appeared to be the result of inadequate maintenance and repair in the past. One problem, however, was a recurring matter, which had given trouble off and on for at least the past year; one of the engineroom ventilation blowers failed. It was still out of commission the following morning when Lieutenant (jg) Keppel asked the captain to sign a letter to the Bureau of Engineering, asking for the replacement of all the blowers with a more reliable type. Quarles agreed to do so.[10] Apparently, Keppel had only recently learned that better blowers were installed in other destroyers. This letter was never mailed. Otherwise, the first evening at sea passed without incident.

The next day, the eleventh, was also more or less uneventful. Quarles reported that the two ships spent a good deal of time testing their TBS and TBY radios, with mixed results; the TBS worked reasonably well, but the TBY was unreliable.[11] This was not news to the *Warrington;* her TBY was always unreliable.

The weather had begun to deteriorate on the morning of the twelfth and grew worse rapidly throughout the day. Quarles says that the *Warrington* received the first storm warning at about the time the ships left Norfolk, and that the storm's position was plotted on her chart.[12] Using this single plot, he estimated that the ships would pass to the west of the storm—that is, they would cross its path ahead of the storm center.[13]

This is a dangerous thing to do; the movements of such storms are frequently only estimates, and can never be counted upon to remain constant. Rear Adm. Philip C. Koelsch, USNR, the former gunnery officer of the *Warrington,* had considerable experience with hurricanes while operating in the Gulf of Mexico with a reserve destroyer division. He developed his own rule: when near a hurricane, *RUN! Run FAST! and run EARLY!!*[14] I might suggest another rule: NEVER UNDERESTIMATE A HURRICANE!

In retrospect, it seems strange that neither of the ship captains nor the staff operations officer with whom they conferred made any special note of the fact that the course these two ships would have to follow would inevitably take them across the hurricane's path, and the determination of whether they would be ahead of or behind the eye of the storm would become a matter of crucial importance. Had they taken this into consideration, it is likely that they would have chosen movements that would have kept them well clear. As it was, all three officers share responsibility for what followed.

In its findings, the Court of Inquiry criticized Quarles for not protesting the course finally decided upon.[15] This was not fair to Quarles; as the junior of three officers in conference, a protest would not have been appropriate, but he could have called attention to the danger, if he had thought of it. As things transpired, Commander Wheyland, as OTC, had sufficient authority to adjust the unit's course to avoid danger, but he failed to use his authority.

As the weather worsened, the ships began to roll heavily; the wind was from the east-southeast (about 110°), and the seas were about 15° to 20° further south (about 125°). The ships were steering a course of 183°, and making good about 180°; and they were steaming at fifteen knots, making good about twelve. Therefore, both wind and sea were coming from points somewhat forward of their port beams, thereby contributing to their rolling. The *Warrington,* being the smaller of the two, was doing the most rolling; the sea is far less kind to the smaller vessels.

Early in the day, the rolling did not seem too bad; the breeze was light, and the swells, though large, were not steep. Nevertheless, even this slight rolling had an effect that no one seemed aware of: crew fatigue. In discussing the effects of rolling on the crews of deep-sea racing yachts, C. A. Marchaj noted that even moderate rolling, if kept up long enough, will wear down a crew, and rolling as much as 30° has been known to completely incapacitate a crew. Ens. Donald W. Schultz has informed me that the *Warrington* was rolling at least 30° during that afternoon.[16]

Late in the afternoon, Quarles received a report that some ammunition had broken loose from its storage racks in one of the forward five-inch magazines, and was rolling around. Alarmed, he authorized Lieutenant (jg) Pack to round up every available man on the ship to help restow it.[17] This was accomplished at the cost of very heavy labor; the ventilation to the magazine had been shut down, due to the weather, and men had to come topside frequently for fresh air.

By the crew's suppertime, around 5:00 P.M., the situation was so bad that few men were able to get anything to eat; Arel B. Smith, radarman, was finally reduced to a fistful of crackers—which he lost when a large sea smashed down on him.[18]

As more weather advisories came in, it appears that Quarles began to get uneasy about his earlier belief that the ships would pass ahead of the storm, but Wheyland did not seem to agree. One possible reason for this difference in viewpoint came out during the course of the inquiry, but was not specifically noted by the court: the *Hyades*'s radio log showed that she had received fourteen warnings, *but only five had been plotted on her chart!*

Evidently, the *Warrington* had received and plotted all, or nearly all, of these warnings, so her captain had a better picture of the situation.[19] (See tracks of ship and storm in Chart 1.)

Quarles's remedy for his uneasiness, however, was to signal the *Hyades,* recommending that the ships cease zigzagging and increase speed, in order to ensure passing ahead of the storm.[20] Bearing in mind that he initially thought they would pass ahead of it, this recommendation is good evidence of his indecision. At this time, the sea was about to carry away his port bulwark.

Later, Quarles said that he had only been trying to "provoke" a discussion.[21] Had he called the *Hyades* and asked for a TBS conference, this course of action would not have been ambiguous and open to misinterpretation.

Wheyland rejected his recommendation, saying he thought the storm was stationary, and ordered the ships to hold course and speed. Then only a few minutes later, he changed his mind and ordered them to cease zigzagging and to increase speed about one-half knot.[22] We do not know the reason for this change of heart; perhaps he chanced to look at his chart as an entry was being plotted. The court did not delve into this question, so we will never know.

In any event, it was not long after that when Quarles, becoming increasingly aware of his danger, informed the *Hyades* that he was forced to heave to.[23] Wheyland told him to heave to at discretion, but Quarles was already changing course to 110°, and reducing his speed to about five knots.[24]

At this point, Wheyland asked Quarles if he wanted the *Hyades* to stand by. In so doing, he put Quarles in a bad position. As OTC, Wheyland had a responsibility for both ships in his unit. Part of his responsibility was to keep his unit together, functioning as a unit as long as possible; therefore, when Quarles hove to, Wheyland should have conformed to his movements without questions or discussion. But by asking Quarles if he wanted the *Hyades* to stand by, Wheyland put Quarles in the invidious position of appearing timid if he said "yes" and rash if he said "no." Quarles chose to reject the offer, signaling, "NEGAT X WILL PICK YOU UP AFTER THE STORM."[25] He followed this with another, which proved to be very important later: "IN CASE WE SEPARATE WILL COMMUNICATE WITH YOU ON TWO EIGHT EIGHT FIVE KCS."

These incidents occurred at about 6:00 P.M., 12 September. This time, and those that follow, except the times of radio messages, which can be verified, are estimates, and are subject to considerable error. The court tried to establish times as definitely as possible, but for obvious reasons, people aboard the *Warrington* were not watching clocks that night. For

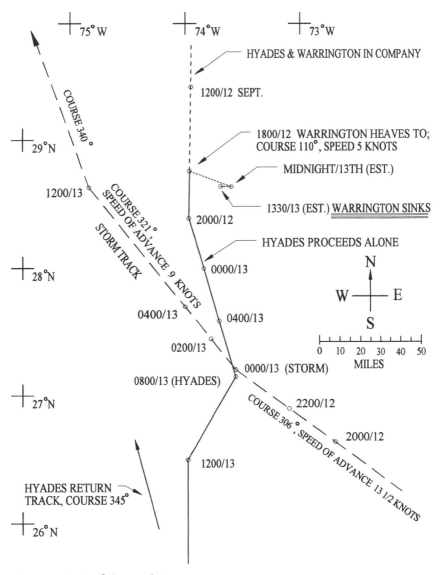

75°W

74°W

73°W

HYADES & WARRINGTON IN COMPANY

1200/12 SEPT.

COURSE 340°

29°N

1800/12 WARRINGTON HEAVES TO;
COURSE 110°, SPEED 5 KNOTS

MIDNIGHT/13TH (EST.)

1200/13

COURSE 321°
SPEED OF ADVANCE 9 KNOTS

STORM TRACK

1330/13 (EST.) <u>WARRINGTON SINKS</u>

2000/12

HYADES PROCEEDS ALONE

28°N

0000/13

N

W —|— E

S

0400/13

0400/13

0 10 20 30 40 50
MILES

0200/13

0000/13 (STORM)

0800/13 (HYADES)

27°N

COURSE 306°, SPEED OF ADVANCE 13 1/2 KNOTS

2200/12

2000/12

1200/13

HYADES RETURN
TRACK, COURSE 345°

26°N

Chart 1. Tracks of ships and storm

hours, the *Warrington* fought to stay on course 110°, at a speed of five knots. She experienced great difficulty in doing so; the wind and sea combined to keep throwing her bow off to the starboard (the south).[26] This would indicate that the wind was actually coming from a direction somewhat north of 110° (perhaps 100° or even 095°); this would result in the high bow of the *Warrington* acting like a sail. There is nothing in the testimony, however, to show that Quarles made any attempt to experiment with minor changes in course or speed, to help his helmsman stay on course.

At 6:15 P.M. Wheyland decided that he, too, should heave to, but the result had nothing to do with the *Warrington*. In fact, as soon as Quarles hove to, Wheyland reduced his speed to eleven knots and changed course to 137°, thereby continuing to move away from the *Warrington*. (See chart 1.)[27] He did not inform the *Warrington* of this new course and speed, nor did Quarles inform the *Hyades* of his course and speed.[28] There has been some speculation as to what the relationship between these two captains might have been; no one can be sure, at this late date, but the relationship does not appear to have been amicable. On the other hand, it might be that neither captain had a deep understanding of the importance of communications.

As the ships moved apart, the *Warrington's* radarmen tracked the *Hyades* out to about fifty-five thousand yards (a phenomenal distance, under the circumstances), then lost contact.[29] This was enough to have given Quarles a good idea of what the *Hyades* was doing, if he had wanted to know; apparently, he was too engrossed in his own troubles to worry about the *Hyades*. And if Wheyland felt he had any further responsibility for the *Warrington*, his actions did not show it.

With the approach of the storm center, the weather continued to worsen. Quarles began receiving a stream of more or less alarming reports from the engineers, of casualties large and small, and of water entering those spaces—but so far, still being controlled by the pumps. His response was to keep repeating to the chief engineer that he had better keep his engines running if he wanted to live.[30] At one point, Keppel apparently sent his assistant, Lt. (jg) Robert B. Moore, to Quarles with a list of engineering problems. Quarles, by his own testimony, brushed him off; "I was not accustomed to paying attention to Assistant Engineers," said he.[31] Ironically, the court later criticized both Lt. Wesley U. Williams and Lt. (jg) J. Marvin Pennington for not making enough reports to the captain. It would be instructive to know what Quarles would have done with another stream of reports.

Quarles was also concerned with the pounding, or "slamming," the ship was undergoing as she bucked the mountainous seas. She would rise to the top of a huge sea, balance for a moment, then "mush down" (Quarles's words) briefly, followed by the bow slamming into the next wave with a jar that could shake the whole ship. He feared that this might either break the

Lt. (jg) Robert B. Moore, USNR, assistant engineer officer, lost at sea 13–15 September 1944. (Courtesy of Sarah Moore Traylor)

ship's back or cave in the bottom. Actually, there was little danger of caving in the bottom, but there was some danger of her back being broken; the repeated up-and-down strains on the hull could conceivably have created sufficient metal fatigue to allow the bow to break off. This had happened to other ships.[32]

One of the most serious reports from the engineers related to the lack of ventilation in the enginerooms. They reported that most of the water coming in came through the ventilation ducts; the blowers had been put out of commission some time earlier. They reported that some or all of the blower intake covers were missing, and water was entering in larger quantities; but although the pumps were still handling it, the temperatures in the enginerooms had risen to the point that men could remain in those spaces only five to ten minutes. Quarles later told the court he thought he could walk into an engineroom and say, "This isn't bad; I've seen worse than this a hundred times."[33] He was to learn better.

There can be little doubt that this stream of reports, and concern about the "slamming" must have had an effect on Quarles's thinking. At about 9:30 P.M., he held a conference with his navigator, Lt. Patrick Davis, in which they discussed the idea of reversing course and running before the storm.[34] Quarles said that he had done this once before, against his better judgment, and that it had worked so well that now he was willing to think about it again. However, the earlier incident did not involve a hurricane. They came to the conclusion that it would be too dangerous to try at this time. He therefore held his course and speed. As far as we can tell from the testimony, they based this conclusion on a fear of what might happen as the ship made the 180° turn, not on what might happen afterward.

Surviving engineers are unanimous in their belief that the ship could have survived, had she maintained this course and speed, but fate intervened. At about 11:00 P.M., Keppel reported that incoming water was getting ahead of the pumps. Almost simultaneously, there occurred a machinery derangement in one of the enginerooms (for which the court blamed poor operating procedures) and Keppel stopped the engines.[35] For the next half hour, without engine or electrical power, the ship lay in the trough of seas. In a few minutes, however, the diesel-driven emergency generators tripped in, giving her electrical power. Number 2 emergency generator lasted only a short time, however. It was found later, on inspection, that its motor had been ruined by salt water. Number 1 generator continued delivering electrical power until main power was restored.

In the meantime, for unexplained reasons, noting that the ship had lost steering control on the bridge (after all, she was going nowhere), Quarles ordered steering control to be shifted to hand control. This meant that a crew had to be sent aft to the Steering Engineroom to man cranks for turning the rudder—a slow and clumsy method of steering, as we had discovered in February, in Lengo Channel. When engine power was restored, he elected to keep steering control aft, and for a while the result was confusion. As I mentioned regarding Lengo Channel, the helmsman tended to apply his rudder changes in directions opposite to the way the ship was supposed to go, because the compass was mounted facing aft. The testimony reveals that pandemonium reigned on the bridge at that time, with practically everyone yelling loudly at the helmsman. Quarles later blamed all this on unreliability of the steering system, a perception that was rooted in stories of the Lengo Channel incident told to him by one of his officers.[36] The court failed to check on Quarles's assertion, which it could have done by questioning surviving officers and helmsmen. It accepted

Quarles's claims without question. Incidentally, Quarles reported witnessing my handling of a steering failure.[37] However, I did not experience such a failure in my *Warrington* days.

The ship regained power in about thirty minutes, and, with difficulty, was brought back to her original course of 110°. The casualty, however, reminded Quarles that he had confidentially directed the communications officer to contact the *Hyades* and call her back. Now he discovered "to his horror," that Lt. (jg) John P. Hart, the communications officer, had been unable to get any response from the *Hyades*.[38] When he asked Hart what circuits he had used, Hart replied hastily, "all of them."[39] The *Warrington* was truly alone.

Alarming reports continued to come from the engineroom, so, with no sign of letup in the weather, Quarles finally decided to reverse his course in an effort to let the ship ride easier. He called Keppel on the sound-powered telephone and asked him if he thought the enginerooms could make fifteen knots when he reversed course. Keppel "despaired" of doing so, but Quarles told him he would have to, then rang up the speed change, followed by an order to put the rudder to the right. The ship came around without difficulty, picking up speed as she turned.[40]

For some minutes, Quarles remained on the bridge, observing the ship's behavior on the new course. Her motion was greatly eased, but he noted that she began yawing, and required increasing amounts of rudder to stay on course.[41]

Those who have been at sea for any length of time know that steering is made much more difficult in a following sea, because the effectiveness of the rudder is reduced, sometimes to a point where its effect is the opposite of what it is supposed to be. This is a matter of common sense, but there is still a school of thought that holds that running before a storm is preferable to fighting it.

One needs only to realize that the effectiveness of a rudder depends on the amount of water pressure that is brought to bear on its forward face. For instance, if a vessel is moving into a head sea, and applies right rudder, the effect will be instant and dramatic: the stern will swing to the left, and the bow will go the right quickly. If the vessel is sitting in still water, there will be no effect at all; and if the vessel and the water are moving in the same direction at the same speed, there will be no effect. On the other hand, if the ship and the water are moving in the same direction, but the water is moving faster than the ship, the pressure will come on the *after* face of the rudder, and will produce an effect opposite to that desired. With a following sea, but one moving slightly slower than the ship, rudder effect is reduced, and the vessel reacts slowly and sluggishly to rudder changes.

When Quarles reversed course, it was black dark—close to midnight—so he had no way of judging the speed of the waves. Because he had done it once before with a speed of fifteen knots, he calculated that fifteen knots would be adequate again. However, he had very little rudder control.

He warned the helmsman to be sure to stay on course, then he left the bridge, accompanied by Lieutenant Davis. This left the bridge in charge of Lieutenant (jg) Hart, a capable enough officer, who had been earlier trying to send messages to the *Hyades*. Quarles said he took Davis with him to find Lieutenant (jg) Keppel because Davis had a flashlight and Quarles did not.

The two officers battled their way aft and found Keppel lying on deck outside the entrance to the Forward Engineroom, in a state of collapse caused by the heat down below. Quarles asked him if he thought his ship's force would be able to effect repairs to the damage already suffered. Keppel was astounded by the question and emphatically denied the possibility. He suggested that Quarles come below and see the situation for himself.[42]

This Quarles did, and the first thing he noticed was the awful heat, which he later described as "deplorable."[43] The Engineroom was filled with steam, to the point where it was difficult to recognize the men's faces. But Quarles did not suffer the heat for long. As the three officers stood on the gratings before the throttles, the ship suddenly took a very deep and long roll to starboard, simultaneously swerving to port, and great quantities of seawater cascaded into the engineering spaces "from everywhere," as survivors described it.

Electric power was immediately lost, and the starboard engine stopped. Keppel asked permission to close the throttles to both engines, and permission was granted. It is not clear why this action was taken, since the port engine was still turning over at fifteen knots, and was the only source of ship control still available.[44] Within a few minutes, the After Fireroom was flooded and abandoned.

Quarles started back to the bridge. By this time, the ship was lying dead in the water, wallowing in the trough of the seas, and the trip forward was far more dangerous than the trip aft had been.

What had happened is known to seamen as "broaching to." This is defined as follows: "When running with a high quarterly sea, to turn toward it broadside on by accident, force of elements, or fault of a helmsman, thus exposing a vessel to danger of capsizing or shipping heavy water."[45]

It is clear from his testimony that Quarles may never have understood what had happened; throughout the hearings, he continued to blame failure of the steering system. Several writers, including C. A. Marchaj, have pointed out the dangers in trying to run before a following sea, some even claiming that speed makes no difference; safety depends entirely on the expertise of the helmsman. There seems to be little doubt that it is a course of action that should be taken only as a last resort and with great caution.

As Quarles fought his way back to the bridge, he passed Lieutenant Williams and a small group of men engaged in cutting away the motor whaleboat, which had been swamped and damaged when the ship broached to. He noted what they were doing, but said nothing, and when he reached the bridge he ordered all hands to jettison topside weights; after the broaching (which came to be known as the Big Roll), the ship had a permanent list of about 15° to starboard.

Following his orders, men began firing the torpedoes and throwing ammunition overboard, eventually adding the barrels of 20 mm guns and anything else they could detach. The battle for life was in full swing.

chapter five

THE DRAGON BREATHES

It was now about one
o'clock on the morning of 13 September 1944. Richard J. Reynolds has
calculated that the hurricane reached its peak during the night of 12–13
September, so we can safely infer that the *Warrington* was feeling its full
fury. (See appendix A.)

Lying dead in the water, with no lights, no heat, no sounds but the roar
of the wind and the breaking seas, the crew did not give up hope for hours.
Since it is impossible to pinpoint when various actions took place, I will
disregard chronology and describe what occurred in each section of the
ship, always remembering that many of these actions happened at the same
time.

I will start with the midships section—the four largest compartments
on the ship. If these four compartments could have been saved, in all
probability the ship would have survived. In order, from forward to aft,
they were the Forward (or Number 1) Fireroom; the After (Number 2)
Fireroom; the Forward (Number 1, or Starboard) Engineroom; and the
After (Number 2, or Port) Engineroom.

All of these compartments extended from the keel up to the main
deck, and all the way across the ship. The two firerooms each contained
two boilers, each of which was semisealed into its own boxlike container
(see appendix B); they were not quite watertight because of small openings
through which the oil burners were inserted, but at least they would not
completely fill instantaneously.

The ship could survive if one of these firerooms became flooded. If two
were flooded, she might survive, but would be helpless, unable to make

44

steam. But they had an Achilles heel, which nobody recognized until it was too late. To make steam, the boilers needed fresh water, and, if the forward fireroom ran out of feed water, its source of supply—a set of manifold valves—was deep in the bowels of the After Fireroom. If the Forward Fireroom was flooded, the After Fireroom did not have this problem.

The two enginerooms were wide-open spaces. Once flooding started, the only way it could be overcome was by pumps, some of which were operated by steam and others by electricity. These all took suction from the bilges; but the fire and bilge pumps, true to their names, could also take suction from the sea, to fight fires. All four compartments contained a fire and bilge pump.

Theoretically, the bulkheads between these compartments were watertight; therefore, it should have been possible to prevent water from moving from one compartment to the next. It should have been, but was not. At some time in the past, an unknown navy yard had cut a hole through the bulkhead between the After Fireroom and the Forward Engineroom in order to pass some pipes and cables through. A steel plate had been welded over the opening, but the points where the pipes and cables went through were not sealed with watertight fittings. This became a second Achilles heel. There was no way to set a flooding boundary, a point beyond which flooding was not permitted.

The After Engineroom had no known weak points.

All of these compartments depended, for livability, on high-pressure blowers, forcing air down below. Even with the blowers running, these spaces were very warm; without them, the heat built up quickly to an unbearable level. This situation already existed at the time of the Big Roll.

I mentioned earlier a crack was present in the deck on the starboard side of the stack. With seas coming over the tops of the deckhouses, a constant stream of water came into the After Fireroom through this crack, but until the moment of the Big Role, the fire and bilge pump took care of it.

With the Big Roll, tons of water flooded into the After Fireroom; the lights went out, and, in total darkness, men shut off the oil burners. In the space of ten or fifteen minutes, they secured the fireroom and abandoned it, with the water up to their necks. Their heroism in remaining at their posts long enough to secure the fireroom has never been recognized. The first of the four compartments was now wide open to the sea.

The Forward Engineroom, where Keppel, Quarles, and Davis were standing, also took a large amount of water, stopping the starboard engine and shorting out all power. The forward diesel emergency generator tripped in and ran for a short time, so the lights came back on. As related

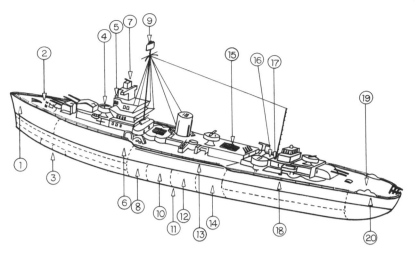

(Not to scale)

1. Storerooms
2. Forecastle deck
3. Five-inch magazine
4. 40-mm gun mount
5. Bridge
6. Crew's living compartment
7. Five-inch gun director
8. Forward Fireroom
9. Radar array
10. After Fireroom

11. Holes through watertight bulkhead
12. Forward Engineroom
13. Bulwark
14. After Engineroom
15. Torpedo tube mounts
16. Passageway
17. After Deckhouse
18. Crew's living compartment
19. Main deck
20. Steering Engineroom

Figure 1. General layout of the USS Warrington (DD 383)

earlier, Keppel asked and received permission to stop *both* engines; then, after Quarles left, Keppel ordered the engineroom abandoned.

The testimony before the court does not tell us where Keppel was during the next hours, but it is fairly certain he was not in the After Engineroom. A group of men, without orders from anyone, went down into the engineroom and tried to restart the port engine.[1] They were unsuccessful; some say there were not enough of them, others say there was not enough steam, but two things are certain: first, that these were brave men, and second, that the After Engineroom was not flooded at that time.

Inadequate steam pressure seems likely. There was no telephone connection between the engineroom and either fireroom, so they were unable to call for more steam; and if the supply of boiler feed water was running low, the fireroom would have been unable to supply the steam if asked. But lacking the means to communicate, the question could not be asked.

Some time after daylight, Watertender Bill Sapp, who was then the petty officer in charge of the forward fireroom, decided to go for more boiler feed water. At the risk of his life, he crawled on his stomach to the after fireroom, only to discover that it was flooded and had been abandoned; the manifold valves were under about twenty feet of water, inaccessible. He then crawled aft to the Forward Engineroom hatch, where he found Lieutenant (jg) Moore, to whom he reported his dilemma. There was nothing Moore could do to help, so Sapp crawled forward again, against Moore's advice. Reaching the Forward Fireroom, Sapp entered, and ordered his men to douse the fires and abandon the place. He was the last man out, with water up to his neck. He left the fire and bilge pump running, on residual steam.[2] The ship's situation was now hopeless.

After abandoning his fireroom, Sapp went forward to the wardroom. There he found a number of men lying on the deck, sloshing back and forth in about six inches of water as the ship rolled. They were exhausted and had no other shelter.

Also during the morning, Fireman Clarence Strunk, whose station had been in the After Fireroom, went up on top of the deckhouse abreast the stack. He had been greatly disturbed by the water coming down through the crack in the deck on the starboard side, and now he wanted to see what the port side looked like. He found another crack—a new one.[3]

While all this was going on amidships, the men in the after part of the ship were also having troubles. These men were completely cut off from the rest of the ship; the seas were coming over the tops of the deckhouses, and it was worth one's life to try to pass forward. (Yet, strangely enough, Lieutenant (jg) Kroll seemed to be able to go wherever he wished. Several men reported "he was all over the ship.") All telephones were out of commission. The crew's living compartment was taking water through the ventilation system; efforts to plug the ends of the pipes with pillows and blankets were ineffectual; with every sea, a gush of seawater would push the plug out. After the water level reached about eighteen inches, the men formed a bucket brigade, but found that as much, or more, water was coming in as was being taken out, so the effort was abandoned.

Most of the men congregated in the crew's head; but this comparatively small space soon became overcrowded, hot, and stuffy to the point where a few took their chances in the open.[4]

The only officer in this part of the ship was Lt. (jg) Louis R. Kroll,

USNR. He earned the undying respect of all the survivors in that area, for his unflagging efforts to save the ship and his efforts to maintain the morale of the crew. At one point, he asked Boatswains Mate Lewis Parrillo to help him stuff mattresses in ventilation intakes. Parrillo describes their action in his own words:

> Skipper, Mr. Kroll has a lot of credit due him. I for one had no use for him at all, but he sure gained my respect in a short time. He asked me for some assistance and in my mind I thought I was crazy for complying. He was doing the impossible. We secured ourselves to vents and he was stuffing mattresses in the vents. We were under water most of the time. We abandoned ship and he went on the same raft as I. He gave his life jacket to somebody and swam away. That was the last time I saw Mr. Kroll.[5]

In the course of the subsequent inquiry, several witnesses were asked if everybody had been able to get off the ship when she was abandoned. Most witnesses did not know, and said so, but a few were sure all hands had gotten off. They were wrong; there is definite evidence that one man committed suicide, and the story of the medical officer will be told shortly. Both Parrillo and Radioman Robert B. Ralph have told me that some of the new men were so terrified that they lay on the deck in a fetal position and refused to move when the word came to abandon ship.

All this while, the *Warrington* was listing farther and farther to starboard. By midmorning, the fire and bilge pump in the After Engineroom was no longer able to take suction from the bilge.

Forward of the engineering spaces, the emergency diesel generator made a valiant effort to supply electricity; but when Machinists Mate John J. Latronica went to inspect it, he found water in the oil sump, while a group of men of the forward repair party, under the supervision of Lieutenant (jg) Pennington and Shipfitter Howard T. Reynolds, were trying desperately to start a gasoline handy-billy pump. Continued running would ruin the engine, so Latronica obtained permission from Lieutenant (jg) Keppel to stop the generator.[6] Now the ship had no electrical power of any kind.

On the bridge, Captain Quarles, returning from his foray to the engineroom, told Lieutenant (jg) Hart to broadcast a distress signal. Over the 21MC (a kind of interoffice communication set), he quickly dictated a message to the Main Radio Room, to be sent in plain English, but he did not include the name of the ship (he later said he had omitted it deliberately, relying on the ship's call sign to remedy the omission). Hart obtained an estimated ship's position from Ensign Denny, the assistant navigator.[7]

The radiomen tried a number of radio circuits, but could get no response until they tried an unauthorized circuit, intended for the use of ships entering or leaving port. Paul Klingen, radioman 2d class, was on watch that night. The following is his version of what happened:

> At approx. 2330 [12 September], the bridge informed us that due to the storm we would not be relieved and we were to remain on watch until further notice.
>
> Approx. 0100–0200 the bridge instructed us to break radio silence and contact the *Hyades*. . . . When we received no response on the primary frequency, we shifted to the alternate frequency. During our 3rd or 4th attempt to contact the *Hyades,* with no reply, ship's power was lost.
>
> Both main and emergency transmitters depend on ship's power to run their generators, but they are on different circuits and it was possible to lose power in either shack and still have power in the other.
>
> I mention this only so someone would understand why the trip back to the Emergency Radio Shack was made. . . . Shortly after returning to the Main Radio Shack power was restored (approx. 0300). We continued trying to contact the *Hyades* on both frequencies she should have been guarding.
>
> After notifying the bridge / Communications Officer that we were unable to contact the *Hyades,* we were instructed to continue trying on the same frequencies and we would receive additional instructions shortly.
>
> The Communications Officer came to the Radio Shack with a list of approx. 16–18 frequencies we were to try. From here on, things got a little hectic. With Pirtle at the receiver and sending key, he tuned in the first frequency to check on any traffic on this circuit (nothing). I tuned the TBK to the same frequency and we sent out our signal (no response). We continued this operation for at least 6 or 7 of these frequencies, and allowing a reasonable time for anyone to answer, still no response.
>
> At this time, I noticed sparks were emitting from the generator, due to salt water entering the "dog house" in which it was located. Knowing we had only a limited time to get any message out, Pirtle and I decided to go to a frequency which we knew had traffic, to give us a better chance of someone hearing us, even if it wasn't on the list. We picked the Harbor Frequency. . . . we had to break into considerable traffic. . . . Pirtle then sent out our message; our call went out to "CQ" (any or all ships or stations on this frequency). Our first call was not answered. I'm sure everyone received and copied the message, but due to the fact that we were unable to authenticate our call and the message was in plain language, they must have been reluctant to answer. . . . we broke in again. . . . This time, Radio New York gave us a receipt. Pirtle then informed us he was receiving another message from New York, but at that time all power was lost. Power never returned.[8]

Klingen does not mention it here, but his reference to a trip back to the Emergency Radio Shack covers a tragic story.

The *Warrington*'s chief radioman was Arthur B. Tolman. When they first lost power, he and the other radiomen were trying to contact the *Hyades*. Losing power in the Main Radio Shack made it necessary for someone to go aft to the Emergency Radio Shack, to see if there was power there. Tolman called Klingen to accompany him aft. This was an extremely dangerous trip, but both men made it without mishap, only to find that there was no power in the Emergency Shack. As they fought their way back forward, Tolman missed his grip at one point, and was washed overboard. Klingen, unable to help, continued battling his way forward.

A short time later, he and Pirtle were astounded, when some men brought Tolman into the Main Radio Shack. He had been washed back on board again, but in the process, had broken a hip. The other men laid him out on some chairs, and Dr. Kennedy made him as comfortable as possible. He was in great pain. Dr. Kennedy's Sick Bay was inaccessible, so he was restricted in what he could do. We will return to this story later.

Two other men were also washed overboard that night. One of them, a seaman named William L. Zwick, was rescued, partly by the executive officer, who threw him a line and helped haul him aboard. Zwick eventually became one of the survivors. The other, a machinists mate named Benjamin E. Redhead, was one of the new men; he went overboard on the starboard side on or near the forecastle. Torpedoman Lawrence D. Allphin threw him a line, which, he says, landed within easy reach, but Redhead was apparently in such deep shock that he didn't see it; he disregarded it, and slowly drifted around the bow and out of sight.[9]

Jettisoning topside weights rapidly became a problem as candidates for heaving overboard became scarce. On the bridge, a discussion arose as to the feasibility of cutting down the fore topmast, with its heavy radar array. It was decided to give it a try, so Quartermaster John D. Martin, with the help of some others including the executive officer, climbed up and cut away the stays. The mast hesitated, then fell to starboard, hanging there by its various wires. As it hung, it swung back and forth with the roll of the ship, banging against the hull every time. This led the court to believe it had punched a hole in the hull, but it was never able to establish any real proof. This action had no appreciable effect on the ship's list, which by then, had reached a dangerous angle.

Another desperate action occurred when the chief boatswains mate, "Bull" Johnson, with the first lieutenant, Lt. (jg) Marvin Pennington, and two seamen, crawled out on the forecastle and cast lose the starboard anchor. Although all four men survived this attempt, only Johnson later survived the sinking.

At about 10:00 A.M., according to Ens. Donald W. Schultz, the emergency occurred in the five-inch magazines, described earlier. In describing the incident to me, Schultz added, "If we had known we were going to abandon ship just a couple of hours later, we sure wouldn't have put so much effort into restowing the ammunition." It was this remark that caused me to wonder when, exactly, this problem occurred. That, and the second remark made by Schultz, to the effect that, when he came up for a breather, he found a line of exhausted men sitting on the deck outside the captain's cabin, and Quarles standing in the doorway, watching the water rise around his feet.[10]

Around 11:30 A.M., Quarles had led everyone off the bridge and down to the vicinity of his cabin, "in order to reduce topside weight." Lt. Wesley Williams and Ensign James Dicken remained behind.[11] By his own account, he then stood in the doorway, watching the water rise with every roll. No one knows what went through his head at this time, but when he finally decided the situation was hopeless, and ordered the ship to be abandoned, the list was approaching 70°, and all the starboard life rafts and floater nets were under water.[12] At this point, the ship had about ten minutes of life left.

During the night of 12–13 September, the storm had started to recurve and was approaching the *Warrington* at a slightly increased speed (Chart 2). Richard Reynolds believes it had started to decay at this time, but if it had, there was not enough decay to be noticeable (see appendix A). Shortly before 7:00 A.M. on the thirteenth, it reached its closest point to the ship, but because it followed a curved path, it stayed close to the ship longer than it would have otherwise. Moreover, it was such a large storm that its effects would be felt in that area for days to come.

Nevertheless, by the morning of the thirteenth, it had passed the *Warrington* and was headed north, looking for more victims. It found them on the fourteenth, as it roared past Cape Hatteras. A small group of ships consisting of a merchant ship, the SS *George Ade,* being towed by another vessel, and two Coast Guard cutters, the USCGC *Jackson* and the USCGC *Bedloe,* were proceeding to Norfolk. The *George Ade* had been torpedoed by a German submarine, and had suffered considerable damage in her stern, but had not taken in much water.[13] The storm drove this ship aground, where she suffered more damage, but she was eventually salvaged.

The storm wreaked havoc with the two cutters. Both were sunk, with heavy loss of life. Fragmentary information indicates that the *Bedloe* was struck several times in succession by mountainous waves; although nearly all hands were able to get off the ship and onto a raft, there were only

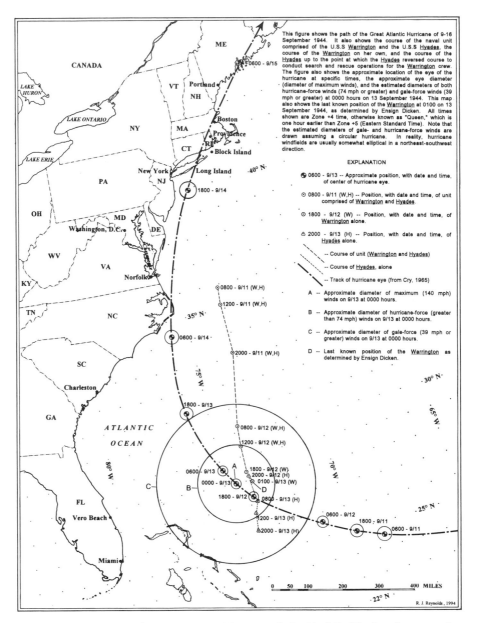

This figure shows the path of the Great Atlantic Hurricane of 9-16 September 1944. It also shows the course of the naval unit comprised of the U.S.S. Warrington and the U.S.S Hyades, the course of the Warrington on her own, and the course of the Hyades up to the point at which the Hyades reversed course to conduct search and rescue operations for the Warrington crew. The figure also shows the approximate location of the eye of the hurricane at specific times, the approximate eye diameter (diameter of maximum winds), and the estimated diameters of both hurricane-force winds (74 mph or greater) and gale-force winds (39 mph or greater) at 0000 hours on 13 September 1944. This map also shows the last known position of the Warrington at 0100 on 13 September 1944, as determined by Ensign Dicken. All times shown are Zone +4 time, otherwise known as "Queen," which is one hour earlier than Zone +5 (Eastern Standard Time). Note that the estimated diameters of gale- and hurricane-force winds are drawn assuming a circular hurricane. In reality, hurricane windfields are usually somewhat elliptical in a northeast-southwest direction.

EXPLANATION

⊛ 0600 - 9/13 -- Approximate position, with date and time, of center of hurricane eye.

⊙ 0800 - 9/11 (W,H) -- Position, with date and time, of unit comprised of Warrington and Hyades.

⊙ 1800 - 9/12 (W) -- Position, with date and time, of Warrington alone.

△ 2000 - 9/13 (H) -- Position, with date and time, of Hyades alone.

-- Course of unit (Warrington and Hyades)

-- Course of Hyades, alone

-- Track of hurricane eye (from Cry, 1965)

A -- Approximate diameter of maximum (140 mph) winds on 9/13 at 0000 hours.

B -- Approximate diameter of hurricane-force (greater than 74 mph) winds on 9/13 at 0000 hours.

C -- Approximate diameter of gale-force (39 mph or greater) winds on 9/13 at 0000 hours.

D -- Last known position of the Warrington as determined by Ensign Dicken.

R. J. Reynolds, 1994

Chart 2. Recurving of the hurricane (Courtesy of the Norfolk Weather Service and Richard J. Reynolds)

twelve survivors out of a ship's company of thirty-eight. The *Jackson* rolled completely over; she had twenty survivors out of a ship's company of forty-one. The survivors spent fifty-eight hours in their rafts before rescue.

Still not satisfied, the storm headed north, increasing speed all the time. Its next, and last, victim was the *Vineyard Sound,* Lightship No. 73, anchored about two miles off Cuttyhunk Island, guarding the Sow and Pigs reef at the entrance to Buzzards Bay, Massachusetts (Map 2). This vessel had a crew of twenty-two men of whom five were on leave when the hurricane arrived. They were unable to get back to their ship, so they lived to tell the tale. Lightship No. 86 was guarding the Hen and Chickens Reef, about four miles away. Both lightships had weathered numerous hurricanes in the past.[14]

Nothing is known about the conditions aboard the No. 73. The crew of No. 86 saw a series of red and white flares in the direction of No. 73, and residents of Westport, Massachusetts, also saw flares, but were unable to get to the beach to make identification.[15] By morning, there was no sign of the No. 73 or of any of her crew. Two days later, her battered dory washed ashore, and the bodies of two of her men were found. A search of the sea bottom about a week later found her wreck in seventy feet of water.[16]

Senior Chief Boatswains Mate Harold W. Flagg, USCG, Ret., was one of the lucky five that night. He and his surviving mates walked the beaches looking for signs of their shipmates. They found the two mentioned above. No more have ever been found.[17]

The storm went on and decayed into a tropical disturbance; it found no more victims.

Before returning to the trials of the *Warrington,* I would like to discuss a few points about hurricanes in general. When Quarles and Wheyland held their conferences with the ServLant operations officer, it appears that no one made any mention of "recurving."

Atlantic hurricanes are born off the coast of Africa. They move, usually quite slowly, in a westerly direction as they build up their power. There is no way to predict just when or where they will reach their maximum power. It is advisable to stay as far away from their fronts as possible, and because their winds circulate in a counterclockwise direction, it is also advisable to stay to the south of them. The forward speed of the storm is subtracted from the velocity of the wind. If staying to the south is not possible, one can run for safety ahead of the storm, but this should be done with great caution, and the run should be early enough and fast enough to ensure the storm will not overtake the ship. Otherwise, common sense dictates staying as far north of the storm track as one can get, and trying to steer an easterly course, in order to pass the danger as soon as possible.

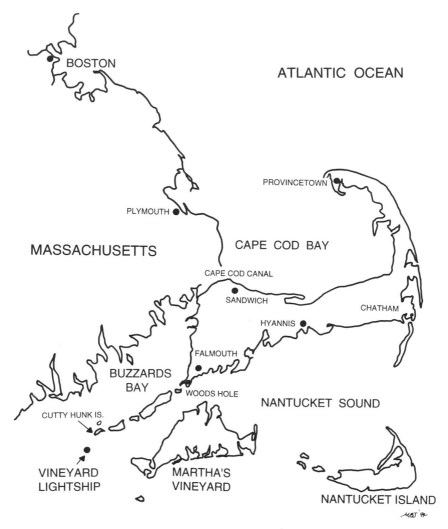

Map 2. Site of Vineyard Sound *sinking (Courtesy of Harold W. Flagg)*

But, as mentioned in chapter 4, these storms have another nasty, unpredictable habit. Sooner or later almost all of them change course from westerly to northerly. There is no telling when this will happen; therefore, a ship to the north of the track should always be alert for this change and be ready to act accordingly. This change of direction is known as "recurving."

But to return to the *Warrington,* the word "recurve" does not appear anywhere in the record of this disaster—and that circumstance may have a great deal to do with the fact that she found herself in the worst possible situation—inside the knuckle of the recurve.

c h a p t e r   s i x

THE SHOUTS OF MEN

Lying on her starboard side, the *Warrington* had only a few minutes to live. A bucket brigade had tried to bail out the After Fireroom, but had given up when it became evident that, with the access hatch open, the ship was taking far more water than was being removed. All this labor had achieved only one thing—more crew fatigue. Men began to sit down and wait for the signal to abandon ship; they had done all they humanly could.

Some men started casting off the lashings of the port-side rafts and floater nets. This process alerted the men in the Main Radio Shack; they never did receive any direct order to abandon. Paul Klingen opened the door, saw what was going on, and returned to warn Pirtle and the doctor; unconfirmed reports say he also helped Coxswain Claire Raymer out on deck. Raymer had suffered a broken leg and a severe injury to his nose, which was almost cut off. He was later seen on a floater net, but did not survive.

When Klingen notified the doctor, he and some other men volunteered to help Tolman get to a raft or net, but Tolman was in such pain that he begged to be left where he was. Dr. Kennedy announced that he would stay with Tolman. The subsequent Court of Inquiry went out of its way to find that Dr. Kennedy did not know the ship was being abandoned; for this reason, the doctor has never received the recognition he deserved for his heroic decision to stay with his patient.[1]

The topmast had broken free and fallen into the sea by this time, and the stack began slapping the water as the ship rolled.[2]

Quarles climbed up on the bridge structure and signaled with his arms to abandon ship; the roar of the wind was so great that no voice could be heard for more than a few feet. Chief Boatswain's Mate Johnson, standing near the stack on the midships deckhouse, saw the signal and passed the order to men in his vicinity. Men in other parts of the ship, "clinging like squirrels to the rigging," to use Quarles's description, saw the activity and followed suit.

There was no organization or order to the way people left the ship—a fact made much of, by the Court of Inquiry. The formal abandon ship drill provided for having the crew fall in at designated stations, take a muster to ensure that no one was being left behind, and embark in boats, rafts, or floater nets previously assigned. With the ship lying at an angle of approximately 75°, simply standing on the decks became impossible; it would have been necessary to stand on the bulkheads. Likewise, with the after part of the ship isolated from the fore part, an accurate muster was also impossible. The court, however, was highly critical of Lieutenant Williams, the executive officer, for not carrying out the formal drill.[3]

Williams has this to say about his own part in abandoning ship:

I was on the side of the main deck trying to decide the best course of action when a huge wave made the decision for me. It washed me forward, and in so doing I hit about six or seven stanchions with my face and arms. My injuries were not apparent at first . . . but I soon noticed the hole in my lower lip from four teeth being broken off; my first and second fingers on the left hand were torn about one inch apart and my left arm had about a six-inch laceration. . . . A raft was noticed on the starboard side and forward of the ship. . . . I noticed someone in the water. . . . [I] realized it was the captain . . . we both swam over and climbed aboard [the raft]. . . . The mountainous waves continually turned the raft over . . . it was exhausting and sometimes we would just hang on to the lines attached to the raft until we were somewhat recuperated. This exhausting experience lasted until the next day, when the waves subsided slightly.[4]

Radioman Robert B. Ralph, who was in the after part of the ship, adds:

Somebody looked out and said, "They are abandoning ship!" There were quite a few "boots" on board and they were very frightened. Most of them would not go topside, so we had to leave them. . . . I managed to reach [a] raft and grabbed a trailing line. We counted 61 personnel that afternoon. . . . We attempted to keep the injured and frightened in the raft and the rest hung on to the trailing lines. Due to waves tossing the raft around and turning it upside down, we lost half the men the first night. After the first night, the losses were from swallowing salt water or fatigue. . . . By the second day, we were down to seven.

Quartermaster Bill Greene jumped overboard on the starboard side and joined eight or nine men on a floater net, which had drifted around the bow and was slowly passing down the starboard side. Just as it reached the stack, the ship rolled to port, allowing the net to pass. There were twenty-nine men on the net by the time it reached amidships, one of whom was Bill Sapp. He says, "A few minutes later, the ship's bow went up into the air. She went down fast. She sucked us down, but let us go in a few seconds . . . then, there was an explosion, probably depth charges. No one was injured, but we were bumped to the surface." He goes on to describe how men got tangled in the net as the seas broke over them; they tried to help each other until they became too tired to do anything. "Some drank sea water and died. Others didn't know what they were doing and swam away from the net and sharks got them. When my net was picked up, there were four of us left."[5]

Boatswains Mate Lew Parrillo relates,

We had Mr. Pennington aboard and thought he survived, but guess he also drifted off. We had incidents where someone would go real ape and we had to fight them off. We were all about ready to go deep six, for we were begging to have meals and going down under, suck on hand lines, thinking we were in a soda parlor.[6]

Nineteen-year-old Radarman 3d Class Arel B. Smith, whose incredible experiences are related in chapter 7, gathered some of the new "boots" in the Radar Room, where he tried to keep them calm after the Big Roll. He tells of this experience in his own unique fashion:

We got into the serious part of the storm and he [the sonar officer, Lt. K. S. Davis] realized we were getting into some serious trouble, and I remember he told me, "When we get into that main part of the storm I want you to stay close to the hatch because these young men are not experienced and they're going to try to get out." . . . So he asked me to be sure and stand guard on the hatch. . . . Shortly before all this he came to me and told me we had one jug of water left for the radar crew . . . and that son of a gun went whopping across the compartment and broke all to pieces and therefore we had no more water. . . . This storm was monstrous. It swept men off the deck. One man was swept off the deck up forward—midship—and was washed back aboard at the back. I think he was the Chief Radioman if I remember right—broke his leg when he did this. . . . And the waves were way high. They got to 40 to 100 feet high, maybe up to 120. . . . So all of a sudden we hit a lurch . . . about that time we capsized sure enough. This was horrid. It was unbelievable. Believe me, I had to fight everything in my power to keep from opening that hatch . . . I wanted to get out of there. . . . I kept the other men and they headed for the hatch and were trying their best to get to it, but I got 'em off and we did not open the hatch. And then when we came back up—we didn't come back up all the way—we just kept having one trouble after another, and the bilge pump [the handy-billy pump] swept off the side of the ship and it swept into the sea. . . . The wind and water just stripped the side of that ship just as clean as what we used to strip . . . with triphammers.

After going to volunteer their help in a bucket brigade, only to find that the effort to bail out the engineroom had failed, he and his men went back to the Radar Room and just waited. It was at this time that he reports,

These young people that come aboard ship they—before the storm hit they were seasick; oh! they were terribly seasick. But I'm saying this— that fear overcomes seasickness. When we got into that storm and . . . had problems, there was no more seasickness. It just went away. . . . It was a terrible waiting period . . . we sat at the mercies of that storm from 11 o'clock at night until 1 o'clock in the day . . . we just continued to rock and roll in the waves, and somewhere in the vicinity of 1 o'clock in the day on 13 September 1944, Captain Quarles told us to abandon ship. I came out of the Radar Shack and I could of walked down to the water by going on the port side . . . I don't know why I didn't, but there was a whole bunch of guys doing the same thing that I did. I went around the superstructure . . . the guys were jumping off the starboard side—we were laying on the starboard side. I just made a lunge and I jumped into the water and I sank down quite a bit, and when I came back up a wave caught me and whopped me against the lifeline and hurt my back real bad . . . I'm still having trouble with my back even all these years away.[7]

Some men never did reach a raft or a net, and a few of those who did were without life jackets or belt. Those who survived without jacket or belt say that they had been issued such gear, but had removed it in order to help with bucket brigades or for other reasons.[8]

As Radioman Robert Ralph has observed, a very large number of men was lost during the first twenty-four hours in the water. This is confirmed by Watertender Bill Sapp, who says fully half of the men on his floater net (twenty-nine, originally) were tangled in the net or taken by sharks on that first terrible night. In fact, there is good reason to believe that at least half of the *Warrington*'s entire ship's company died that night.

Many survivors mention the bitter cold, probably the result of wind chill. The constant, unremitting pressure of the wind must have aggravated the already-severe fatigue afflicting these men. Moreover, as men would lose their holds on rafts when they capsized, or when trying to escape the entangling nets, they would almost instantly lose sight of their raft or net in the inky darkness, and then be unable to find them again. No cries for help could be heard. Ensign Donald W. Schultz said, "If you once lost your raft, your chances were pretty slim."[9]

Escaping from the sinking ship, Quartermaster Bill Greene writes,

> I glanced over at the ship a minute or two after we cleared the stack. The ship had turned turtle and was upside down with her keel showing. It struck me as being funny, as there was a man standing all alone on the keel near the stern. I looked away for a moment and when I turned back the ship was perfectly perpendicular with the bow high in the air and the stern sliding under. The man was gone.[10]

Shortly after the ship disappeared, there were two or three depth charge explosions. The stern at that time would have been at least four hundred feet deep, so these explosions should have been harmless; as a matter of fact, only one man claimed he was injured.[11] One or two more claim they heard of injuries, but can name no victims. Men on the raft with the one claimant say they saw no signs of injuries.

Greene goes on to describe what happened during that first night: "With the coming of night came hell. I do not ever expect to witness anything half as bad. . . . I don't know if anyone got tangled in the net and drowned, but I do know that every man was screaming and trying to hang on for dear life and trying to avoid being trapped beneath."[12]

With morning came an improvement in the weather; the wind subsided in the small hours, and the sun came out at dawn, but the seas remained high. But with this improvement came two more problems: sharks and thirst.

For some unknown reason, the sharks seem to have been fairly selective. Some survivors never saw any, but others say there were many around. At least two survivors claim they drove curious sharks away with blows of their fists (perhaps the sharks were small). On the other hand, Torpedoman Lawrence Allphin saw a shark attack a man next to him on a raft. He states that he saw a ten- or twelve-foot shark approaching his raft, so he drew up his legs, and, as the shark went by, he kicked it with all his strength. The shark, undeterred by the kick, went by and seized the man next to Allphin at about waist level. It took him down so fast he made no outcry, but only looked terribly surprised and somewhat indignant.

Experts on shark behavior say these animals are more active at night than in the daytime.[13] George Burgess, curator of the International Shark

Attack File at the University of Florida at Gainesville, says that attacks in deep water are most likely to be the "bump and bite" type, in which the shark circles the victim for some time, then closes in and bumps against the victim, then follows with repeated attacks.[14] Search and rescue aircraft later noted a number of mutilated bodies still in the floater nets.

Some of the groups on the rafts experienced crumbling discipline, particularly when men started to hallucinate. Lt. Patrick Davis mentions a man on his raft who threatened to kill him.[15] Machinists Mate John Latronica had to quell what he describes as a "free-for-all," which ended when he confiscated all weapons and dropped them into the sea. (Latronica is one of the men who deserved a commendation, but never received it.) He followed his action by conducting a prayer service for the men who had died.[16]

The court appeared to make no allowances for those men who went out of their heads. The simple fact of indiscipline was enough to give the court excuse for criticism.

Most cases of hallucination ended in death. The case of John I. Richards, BM2c, is one in which the man survived. In most cases, hallucinations followed heavy drinking of seawater. If the drinker was unable to vomit what he had drunk, he was fairly sure to be doomed. Lieutenant Pack, for example, had been drinking seawater when he announced to his raftmates that "the girls" were coming down from New York in a canoe to join them, and that he was going to meet them. He was never seen again.[17]

At one time on the fourteenth, a plane passed by the survivors but did not see them. After it passed, Lieutenant (jg) Hart also left his raft, accompanied by one of his radiomen, in search of a freshwater geyser he insisted was close by. Latronica recalls,

> He was about half a mile out, I would say, all the time. When the waves would take us up to a certain point, we could see him out there with this other fellow. Before he left . . . he told me to go over to this airfield and find out why these planes didn't stop, and while I was over there bring back some sandwiches.[18]

Latronica believes the passing of the plane caused several other men to just give up hope and die.

Actually, during the fourteenth, several planes and ships were sighted, but none came close enough to make contact. What none of the survivors realized was that no one knew the *Warrington* had sunk, so no one was searching for them. Had they known they would have lost all hope.

Although her distress signal had been picked up, and action was being taken, the identity of the ship in distress was still not known, and, as far as anyone knew, she was still afloat. The men all knew that a message had been sent and received, so they assumed a search was under way.

It was also during the fourteenth that men began to notice some flaws in their lifesaving equipment. First, the kapok-filled life jackets became waterlogged and heavy—as much as forty pounds, according to Walter Teague. Of course, they were useless from then on. There were also complaints that the canvas covers rubbed faces and necks raw, opening the way for infections; also, the jackets tended to cut the men under their arms. A few men were equipped with inflatable rubber belts, which proved to be far preferable, provided they had received the proper care. Supposedly, these belts had to be worn whenever the crew went to General Quarters: unfortunately the belts got badly worn where they were creased and often developed small leaks. A small leak was a serious problem; the belts had to be inflated by the owner's breath, and once he was in the water, he had difficulty keeping the belt inflated. Generally speaking, the Mae West type of inflatable jacket was by far the best, but was not available to mere sailors.

During the first night, some water casks ("breakers") were lost when rafts capsized. Others were damaged, allowing the fresh water within to become contaminated with salt water or to leak out. Consequently, fresh water became scarce, although the men on one raft, who had managed to save their supply, were generous in sharing with others. Even so, there were some men who never tasted fresh water during the time they were in the rafts. This led to more drinking of salt water.

Food also became scarce. The men on Quarles's raft lived on malted milk tablets, and one raft had a supply of hardtack (which it traded for water). But others had no food, and many had had no food since noon of the twelfth.

Thus, 14 September dragged on. As the hurricane was attacking the Coast Guard cutters, the sun had come out over the *Warrington* wreck. At first men reveled in its warmth after the viciously cold night; but soon they began to suffer from sunburn, and some, especially bald-headed men, died from this cause.

The second night arrived. The weather this night was reasonably comfortable, but the sharks were still on watch. This became another night of terror, combined with fatigue, hunger, and thirst. Some men managed to sleep, and thus ease their fatigue a little.

It is interesting to note, however, that some members of the subsequent courts-martial found it hard to believe that anyone could sleep under such conditions. One officer asked Paul Klingen how he could sleep in the water with so much going on, to which Paul replied, with understatement,

"Sir, I was kind of tired."[19] The questioners clearly had no concept of what these men had to go through.

The clear night foretold a clear day for the fifteenth, with seas still abating, but fairly rough. By this time, a formal search had begun, although no one yet knew that the *Warrington* had gone down. Searchers were looking for the ship, not for survivors. For the latter, it looked like another deadly day.

But change was on hand. At about 4:50 A.M. on the fifteenth, the raft commanded by Lt. Patrick Davis was rammed by a ship. Ens. Eugene E. Archer was aboard that raft, and says he happened to be awake, when he thought he saw the silhouette of a large ship bearing down on them in the darkness. He sounded the alarm, which his raftmates derided as being the results of delirium—until the ship hit them. At this time, there were only seven or eight men on the raft from the original thirty-five to fifty. They jumped from the raft to escape the ship's propellers, and as she passed by, they screamed up at her. "It seemed like fifty feet of freeboard," says Archer. Then they swam back to their raft. Gene Archer helped the injured Pat Davis get back to the raft, but Chief Storekeeper Edward J. LaBuda disappeared at this time.[20]

The ship was the *Hyades*. Her people heard the screams, stopped their engines, located the raft with a searchlight, and then lowered a whaleboat to pick up the first group of survivors.

Their ordeal was almost over.

chapter seven

IN THE CRADLE OF THE DEEP

Arel Boney Smith enlisted
in the navy in late 1942, at the age of seventeen, having grown up in a poor
Texas family during the Great Depression. Following recruit training at
Great Lakes Naval Training Station, Illinois, he went that same year to the
Warrington. The ship was then in Panama, which, in itself, provided an
adventure for the young landlubber. But by 1944, he was a veteran of two
years' service, with a rating of radarman 3d class, and a personal love for
the navy.

During the afternoon of 12 September 1944, as the weather grew
progressively worse, Smith spent most of his time in the Radar Room,
located just below the bridge. At about 5:00 P.M., he went below to get
some supper, but found that the violent rolling made it impossible to keep
even a bowl of chili on the table, so he repaired to the gallery, where he
obtained a handful of crackers. Starting back up to the Radar Room, a huge
wave hit the ship and "flopped" down on him, leaving him with only a few
soggy crackers. This was the last food he would get for the next sixty
hours.

He and his group of "boots" sat in the Radar Room for many hours,
hearing the storm outside, but not really knowing what was going on. It is
interesting, and a bit touching, to hear a nineteen-year-old "Smitty" referring to these men as "young"; he almost sounds fatherly to boys of his own
age.

When the Big Roll occurred, and the ship broached to, there was panic
in the Radar Room, and Smith had his hands full for a while, keeping his
group from running off.

After volunteering for the failed bucket brigade, and finding they could do nothing, they sat in the Radar Room from about midnight to 1:00 P.M., waiting until the time came to abandon ship.

Smith had heard that sinking ships suck men down. He got away from the ship suffering a back injury in the process (see chapter 6), and swam desperately to get as far as possible but found that the seas were so high he couldn't make much headway. Looking up, he saw the fire-control radar antenna (mounted on top of the five-inch gun director) coming directly down upon him. Just before it hit him, the ship rolled to port, allowing him to escape.

Finally getting clear, he looked for a raft, but every one he saw was already overloaded (one of the consequences of not launching the starboard-side rafts while they were still accessible). He mentions speaking to Howard Reynolds, shipfitter 1st class, and meeting a pair of men who were hysterical. He had to fight one of them "like a tiger" to get away and keep from being drowned. He then passed some men who were apparently deep in shock.

Two years earlier, when Smith had first reported to the *Warrington*, he had been issued an inflatable rubber life belt instead of the usual kapok-filled jacket. These belts were a fairly recent innovation, and they were known to develop small holes where the belts were creased. Smith's shipmates took pleasure in assuring him that his belt would develop a leak sooner or later and then he would truly be sunk. Smith took this razzing to heart, and took great care of his belt, never wearing it unless ordered to do so, and always keeping a small amount of air in it. It was a type of belt that required one to blow into it for inflation.

Once in the water and free of danger from the sinking ship, Smith worked the belt up under his armpits, finding it more comfortable in that position. This simple act helped save his life later.

Having given up the attempt to find a raft, Smith just drifted. He had no reason to swim—there was nothing to swim to. Soon there were no other men in sight. Accompanied only by a roaring wind and murderous seas, he drifted off alone.

The powerful wind made the air seem much colder than it really was. The day passed and as daylight waned, this sensation increased. Several survivors have mentioned the intense cold that awful night. Smith remembers, "Laying in that water was so cold—oh! God, that was cold!" During the night, he passed out twice from the cold, and his belt saved him. As he lost consciousness, his head fell forward, and the belt served as a pillow, keeping his face out of the water. In time, he made good use of this arrangement; whenever he felt sleepy, he folded his arms on the belt and drifted off to sleep.

During the afternoon of the thirteenth and the following night, Smith gave up hope of being rescued. But not having any destination to swim to, he simply relaxed and drifted, thereby saving vital energy. He says that in the evening he noticed what looked like a small wake behind him, as though he were actually moving somewhere under the influence of some unknown power. The very idea of moving gave him a little hope and he gained some confidence that the good Lord would see him through.

"I didn't hear no voice," he says. "I just *knew*. It was there. And I just knew that God was gonna save me. And there wasn't any other way." He continues,

> So I rocked on and on, and then I got delirious. You know, hallucinations came to me, and I thought I was coming up on this island and—I was gonna get picked up. . . . They were firing shells all around me. And this is the things that happened to me while I was out there; and then, I got hallucinations that the Japs had sank us and that the ships they were in were going around us. And believe me, people, these hallucinations can be real. I still see them . . . I lost all my friends. I lost my personal buddies. . . . Thank God, old Rice [Kenneth Rice, another radarman] missed the ship when we started out from New York there, and he got in the brig—he was in the brig when we sank. Some of the others did, too, and I thank God that they did. . . . This thing of facing all these boys being killed—we were like brothers. . . . All of them were gone. They weren't there any more.

He lay there for about forty-two hours, then he says he heard a huge noise. "I opened my eyes and there sat the USS *Hyades*!" He started calling for them to come and pick him up; apparently, he had been awakened by the sound of the ship's engines backing. She stopped near him, because he was heard. They "hollered back and told me to be calm and they would be right there. They came out in this little old whaleboat, and when they came by me, they throwed me a line."

At the time, Smith did not realize his body was at all sore, but when he hit the end of that line, it jerked so hard he says he thought every bone in his body was broken. He lost his grip on the line, and the boat crew had to throw it to him again. This time, he held on, and they dragged him over the side of the boat, "and I want you to know they almost killed me."

Before taking him back to the ship, the boat crew picked up some other survivors from a nearby raft. Evidently, Smith had not been far from his friends, but had not seen them because of the high seas. According to

Smith, the men on the rafts "had been crawling on and off those rafts until they were miserable."

This remark points up the fact that, as men suffered minor scratches and bruises, these injuries festered in the salt water, or caused flesh to die and fall off. His back injury did not bother him greatly at this time; as far as he was concerned, his only injury was a small scratch on one ankle, which "ate a place out plumb to the bone with salt water before they picked me up." Machinists Mate 1st Class Alfred "Moon" Hanson suffered a similar injury, when he stumbled between two rafts, bruising an ankle. His injury was so serious that it was months before he could return to duty.

On reaching the ship, most of the survivors were hoisted aboard and placed in stretchers, but Smith, the last to be hoisted aboard, said, "I don't need that," and stepped out on the deck. It was the last thing he remembers until he came to in a bunk down below, with someone trying to pour coffee and brandy down his throat.

He didn't like the taste, so he tried to fight them off, asking them to just give him coffee or something to eat. An old bosun mate nearby was begging for what the others refused. "He was about half tight there just after they picked us up."

Late in the day of 15 September, the survivors were all taken aboard the aircraft carrier USS *Croatan,* the flagship of the task group commander who had been assigned the job of coordinating the search for survivors.[1] Smith remembers being extremely hungry. All they had fed him aboard the *Hyades* was some green pea soup "that was the most delicious I ever eat in my life." Aboard the *Croatan* things improved; they were given plain meat-and-bread sandwiches, and "Oh, God, I was so hungry and I was in this compartment that had bunks in it . . . the minute they passed me, I rolled out over the other side and the other aisle, and went down past the guys . . . I got three sandwiches before it was over with, because, boy, I was so hungry that I was about to die."

Some of the men picked up were in very bad shape. Smith describes one of them: "he was just as purple or blue or something as anything I ever seen in my life. I don't think he ever realized that he was picked up . . . he died later on and . . . was a good friend of mine."

The *Croatan* eventually transferred all but one or two of the survivors to one of the DEs for transportation to the naval hospital at Norfolk. Moon Hanson was kept aboard for a while longer because of the nature of his injury. He was later sent to the naval hospital at Bermuda. At the hospital, they did not X-ray Smith's back, because they allowed him to move about with virtually no supervision. He was the only one allowed this freedom. In addition to his unbelievable luck in being picked up at all, his being alone, with his belt, had aided him in avoiding the various injuries suffered by the majority of those on the rafts or nets. Even his back did not bother him much—yet.

He was sunburned down to his toes even though he had been submerged for days. He recalls that the sun came out on the morning of the fourteenth, and "it was just as hot out there in that water as it was cold to begin with. . . . You wouldn't believe how brown I was . . . it cooked my feet plumb down through the water, the sunshine did." For a short period, he could not stand because of the sunburn, but did regain total mobility.

After his work as a witness at the Court of Inquiry and the courts-martial, he was recommended for advancement to radarman 2d class. Like his shipmates, he did not enjoy duty as a witness. His reaction was fairly standard:

> I was sitting there about half scared to death and they said, "What did you do with that life belt that you had on that carried you over that period of time?" As far as I know at that time I had the record on life belt alone in the ocean and I think I still do. And so they said, "why, I'd have fought the whole Navy to keep that life belt if it'd been me." And I said, "Sir, . . . I wasn't looking for no souvenirs."

After the courts-martial, Smith was ordered to report for duty to a net tender in Boston Harbor. This practically amounted to shore duty, because net tenders seldom go anywhere, and Smith enjoyed it. But net tenders roll heavily, and this rolling aggravated Smith's back injury to the point where he had to be transferred to the naval hospital in Chelsea. There examination revealed that he had broken a vertebra when he was slammed against the lifeline of the *Warrington*. Doctors told him they could and would operate, if he wished, but warned him that they could not guarantee the outcome: he might end up paralyzed.

This was a terrible blow to Smith, who felt that the navy had been good to him, and his ambition was a navy career; either way, his navy career was ended. He rejected the operation, and thus made himself eligible for an honorable discharge by reason of disability.

Anyone who has ever served aboard a rescue ship knows that sighting men in the water is extremely difficult, even in moderate seas. But Smith was found and had survived some forty-two hours in shark-infested waters with no molestation. His luck seems unbelievable. His unflappable nature allowed him to face his ordeal calmly, thereby conserving both physical and mental energy. It may also have helped him to avoid the attention of the sharks, since he did not create a disturbance in the water.

chapter eight

THE USS *HYADES*

 How did the *Hyades* happen
to appear so fortuitously, after disappearing from view on the evening of
the twelfth and remaining incommunicado until ramming Davis's raft and
waking Radarman Smith from his slumbers? The answer is interesting, and
it adds to the understanding of this tragic episode.

At about 9:25 A.M. on 12 September, Quarles made his somewhat silly
recommendation to cease zigzagging and to increase speed. In rejecting this
recommendation, Wheyland said that information received from Miami at
8:30 A.M. indicated that the storm was stationary. The Court of Inquiry
was unable to locate this, or any other message indicating that the storm
was stationary in the communication files of the *Hyades*.[1]

At 11:53 A.M., the *Hyades* ordered, "Cease zigzag and resume base
course."[2] She had already increased speed by one-half knot.

At 12:22 P.M., she received the following warning from commander
Gulf Sea Frontier (ComGulfSeaFron):

THE HURRICANE WAS CENTERED NEAR 26 DEGREES NORTH
AND 72 DEGREES WEST AT 1200 ZEBRA [8:00 a.m., local time]
MOVING WESTWARD AT ABOUT EIGHT KNOTS X THIS IS A
LARGE AND SEVERE STORM X WINDS OF FULL HURRICANE
FORCE EXISTING WITHIN 75 MILES OF CENTER AND WINDS OF
FORCE EIGHT OR GREATER HAVING A RADIUS OF 200 MILES
FROM CENTER.[3]

One should note that the time on this message is only about thirty minutes
earlier than the time when Wheyland thought the storm was stationary.

By early afternoon, the advisories on hand aboard the *Hyades* indicated that the eye of the storm was within two hundred miles of the ships, bearing about 160° to 165°.[4] And after receiving the advisory above, the two ships continued at a speed of fifteen and a half knots on course 183°, which was a collision course with the storm center.[5] As the afternoon advanced, the weather became progressively worse, with a constantly dropping barometer. At about 6:10 P.M., the *Warrington* hove to, followed shortly by the *Hyades,* as we saw earlier.

When last seen, the *Hyades* was disappearing from the *Warrington*'s radar screen at a distance of some 55,000 yards.[6] Her course was 137°, speed eleven knots (see chart 1). One gets the impression that *Hyades* may have considered herself released by the *Warrington*'s negative response to her offer to stand by.[7] Whether the relations between Quarles and Wheyland were less than cordial is not really relevant unless this relationship affected the behavior of either or both captains, and there is little evidence to this effect.

Both ships were too close to the storm center for safety. I have already mentioned that Quarles was slow to heave to. Wheyland did not change the course of the *Hyades* until *after* he had parted from the *Warrington.* Why he picked that particular moment to change course and speed, we will never know; the court did not ask him, and his navigator was not called upon to testify.

This takes us back to the recommendation made by Quarles to try to get ahead of the storm.[8] To cease zigzagging was logical enough; the purpose of zigzagging was antisubmarine protection, but no submarine could have attacked under the prevailing weather conditions. The idea of trying to get ahead of the storm, however, remains controversial. Initially, Wheyland insisted on continuing the zigzag and maintaining course and speed. Then, at 11:53 A.M., he acted as Quarles recommended.[9]

When the ships separated, neither ship informed the other of her course and speed. The *Warrington* radarmen tracked the *Hyades* for about twenty-seven and a half miles. Quarles made no use of this information, nor did he plot the movements of the *Hyades.* Had he done so, and had the *Warrington* survived the storm, Quarles would have had some idea of where the *Hyades* was so that he could rejoin without delay, the ships then being under radio silence. The *Hyades* should have obtained the same information from the *Warrington.* During the time the *Warrington* radarmen were tracking the *Hyades,* the latter's chief radioman, Edwin G. Doyle, heard "someone" tuning a transmitter to 2885 kcs—the unusual frequency selected to be used in event of separation.[10] He assumed this was the *Warrington,* but did not attempt to establish communication.

Before the court, Doyle gave several reasons for this lapse, one of which was that he had been without sleep for three days.[11] The court failed to note that the ships had been feeling the effects of the storm for about twenty-four hours before separation, and there was no emergency before that. Doyle also explained that not only did he not have his full complement of radiomen, but that of those radiomen he did have, only one was fully qualified to stand a watch. Moreover, most of the others were seasick.[12] He produced documentary evidence to prove that his radio gang was badly undermanned and that both he and Captain Wheyland had made efforts to rectify this shortage long before the ship arrived in Norfolk. He also showed that the situation was not improved until the ship reached Majuro, in the far Pacific.[13] He claimed to have known when the ships separated and said that he set up his loudspeaker on 2885 kcs. He does not mention setting up any transmitters on that frequency, nor did the court raise this question.[14] The court also never raised the possibility that some watch-stander, trying to guard another frequency, became distracted by the loud-speaker and turned its volume down, forgetting to raise the volume again later.

When the ships separated, the following signals were exchanged by flashing light:

Warrington to *Hyades*: AM FORCED TO HEAVE TO.
Hyades to *Warrington*: HEAVE TO AT DISCRETION.
Hyades to *Warrington*: DO YOU WISH US TO STAND BY YOU?
Warrington to *Hyades*: NEGAT X WILL PICK YOU UP AFTER THE STORM.
Warrington to *Hyades*: IN CASE WE SEPARATE WILL COMMUNI-CATE WITH YOU ON 2885 KCS.[15]

Although these messages were exchanged by flashing light, and there was no question as to their receipt by either ship, subsequent attempts by the *Warrington* to contact the *Hyades* on 2885 kcs met with complete failure. This situation probably influenced Quarles in his decision to reverse course later and try to run before the storm.

As chart 1 shows, the *Hyades* circled around behind the storm (but was still dangerously close to the center) and then resumed her voyage to the Caribbean.[16] She sent no information to the *Warrington,* nor did she try to obtain any from her.

The trials of the *Warrington* have been told. At approximately 2:00 A.M. on 13 September, she finally made contact with Radio New York and sent the following distress message, as receipted for by New York: "URGENT X

IN DISTRESS X 27-57 NORTH X 73-44 WEST X WE NEED ASSIS-TANCE."[17] Quarles said that the message he sent was different (see his action report, appendix C).

This message was sent and received on 2716 kcs, not on 2885, as planned. This 2716 kcs is known to radiomen as the "harbor circuit," inasmuch as it is supposed to be used only by ships approaching or leaving a harbor.[18] For this reason, it was not being guarded by the *Hyades*. The *Warrington* radiomen on watch, Paul Klingen and Linder G. Pirtle, had broken into this circuit without authority, realizing that time was short; power was gone, and batteries were running down. They deserve high praise for their initiative and intelligence.

Radio New York immediately retransmitted the distress message to the Navy Department and to the commander Eastern Sea Frontier.[19] It developed later that the message was also picked up by Radio Honolulu and Radio Balboa (Canal Zone), both of whom tried to reach the *Warrington*. At about 3:27 A.M., ComGulfSeaFron sent a plain-language message directing two seagoing tugs, the ATR-9 and the ATR-62, to proceed to the assistance of a vessel in distress.[20] This message was broadcast on a wide network and was picked up by the *Hyades*. This was the first inkling that the *Hyades* had that anyone was in distress, but since the ship's position was garbled, the message was filed and forgotten.[21] Both CinCLant and ComServLant received this message and because the reported position lay on the track followed by the *Warrington* and *Hyades,* ComServLant radioed the following to the *Hyades:* "REPORT IMMEDIATELY CONDITION OF YOUR UNIT AND WEATHER."[22] At this moment on 13 September, the *Warrington* was in her final agony. Not knowing this, the *Hyades* replied: "CONDITION OF UNIT GOOD X WEATHER HEAVY BUT ABATING X PROCEEDING AT REDUCED SPEED."[23]

Commander Wheyland's message, like the one from ComServLant, was addressed to CinCLant, Commanders Eastern and Gulf Sea Frontiers, the ATR-9, ATR-62, ComInCh, and the *Warrington,* for information. But by this time, the *Hyades* had been out of communication with the *Warrington* for some seventeen hours.[24]

Now CinCLant entered the picture, addressing the following message to the *Hyades:* "ARE YOU IN COMPANY WITH WARRINGTON X IF NOT PROCEED IMMEDIATELY TO HER ASSISTANCE X STAND GUARD ON 400 KCS OR OTHER LOW FREQUENCY FOR INTER-SHIP COMMUNICATIONS AND SEND MIKE OBOES ON REQUEST TO ASSIST ATR-9 TO MAKE CONTACT."[25] The term "Mike Oboes" refers to the Morse Code letters "M" and "O," consisting of two and three long dashes, respectively, which a receiving ship can use to adjust a radio direction finder.

At 8:45 P.M. on the thirteenth, four hours and fifteen minutes after receiving CinCLant's message, the *Hyades* replied, stating that the *Warrington* was not in company and that the *Hyades* was proceeding at her best speed to the aid of the *Warrington*. Her estimated time of contact was eight hours and she requested the *Warrington*'s position.[26] This was the first time that anyone knew the ships had separated.

When this story was first initiated, the Judge Advocate General's Office in the Navy Department was requested to furnish the record of the Court of Inquiry but was most reluctant to do so. Only after several attempts to obtain the information, even with the aid of Sen. Tom Harkin, the JAG Office finally released all but the first 451 pages of the record of the Court of Inquiry. A request for the records of the courts-martial was met with the statement that these records could not be located. Unfortunately, the first 451 pages of the record undoubtedly contain the narratives of all the survivors. It is likely that practically all of Commander Wheyland's testimony is in these pages; certainly, there is very little in the pages available, and this does not explain his reasons for the long delay in responding to CinCLant's message. The court later noted this delay and expressed the opinion that it contributed to the heavy loss of life, but went no farther.[27]

The reason for this delay is subject to much speculation. There are some who believe Commander Wheyland was cautious about returning to the storm area, although the storm had already moved north and was still moving at a high rate of speed (about forty knots, according to the Norfolk Weather Bureau).[28] Others believe the fault lay within the operations of the *Hyades*'s Communications Department. In support of this theory is the testimony of Chief Radioman Edwin G. Doyle, Jr. According to him, incoming messages had to be taken directly to either the communications officer or his assistant, who would designate to whom the messages were to be routed. Thus far the system was fairly normal, but after that either of these two officers could initial the message for the captain, if he saw fit to do so; he could then deliver it to the captain whenever he felt it desirable. Doyle admitted that he had no assurance that messages were ever delivered to the proper officer.[29] The court remarked on this irregularity but made no recommendations for improvement.

In his closing argument, Commander Wheyland had this to say:

As to the period of time which elapsed from the time that Radio New York started sending out messages on the FOX schedule: The *Hyades's* log which is of record here indicates that the Commanding Officer put about within a few moments of receiving the message which was indicated in that log and which seems to be the only message that the Commanding Officer has any knowledge of, and it was at that time that the *Hyades* went to the assistance or began the search for the *Warrington*.

I wish to say at this time that there is no evidence of any kind whatsoever that the Commanding Officer of the *Hyades* did not act upon any message *that he was given personally*.[30] [Emphasis added]

This argument goes on to insist that it would be inconceivable to require that the commanding officer go to the Radio Room in person to ensure that he saw every message.

The court missed another important point. The argument does not mention the CinCLant message, which was addressed directly to the *Hyades*, not broadcast over the FOX schedules, and it leaves the door open for the possibility that the commanding officer could have failed to see the CinCLant message due to mishandling of the radio traffic by his communications personnel. The court made no effort to determine whether or not Wheyland knew of the irregular procedures; it simply indicated that he *should* have known, and let it go at that.

In the record of the weather advisories received by the *Hyades* (and presumably received by the *Warrington* as well), the radio log showed receipt of fourteen advisories, but only five were plotted on the navigator's chart. No one knows what became of the other nine advisories, because neither the communications officer nor his assistant nor the navigator were called upon to testify. There seems little doubt that the commanding officer was being deprived of crucial information, which might account for his insistence on holding his course and speed early in this episode, as well as accounting for his delay in responding to CinCLant's order. Doyle also testified that his radio messengers were seasick. Perhaps they were, and perhaps they failed to deliver their messages promptly. This possibility, and the possibility that the two communications officers were also seasick, was not explored.

After coming to a course of 345°, the *Hyades* held this course for several hours, then changed to course 077° (east-northeast) in order to sweep through what Wheyland thought was the most likely area for searching. She was still looking for the *Warrington*, and not for survivors, being unaware that the ship had gone down. She may, therefore, have passed by some men in the darkness. Some survivors later reported seeing a "merchant-type" vessel apparently searching the area.[31] She finally met with success at about 4:50 A.M. on the fifteenth, when she rammed the raft commanded by Lt. Patrick B. Davis. At that point Wheyland knew what to look for, and the search was on.

A few hours earlier CinCLant had ordered the commander, Task Group 22.5, aboard the aircraft carrier *Croatan* to organize and conduct a combined air and surface search. Soon seven DEs, two fleet tugs, and the rescue ship *Cherokee* had joined the search for the *Warrington,* but not for her crew.[32]

After picking up Davis and his men, Wheyland, for reasons of his own, waited another two hours before reporting, at 7:07 A.M., to commander Task Group 22.5 that the *Warrington* had sunk and that the *Hyades* had rescued some survivors.[33] This delay may also have cost some lives.

During the day—the fifteenth of September—the *Hyades* picked up three officers, fifty-eight enlisted survivors, and one body identified as a seaman named William DeLee. At about 7:00 P.M., she transferred all but three survivors (subsequently buried at sea) and the one body to the USS *Huse* for further transfer to the *Croatan,* and then proceeded on toward Guantánamo, as ordered.[34] A total of five officers and sixty-three men were eventually rescued and transferred to naval hospitals.

On arrival at Guantánamo, the *Hyades* was met by Captain R. S. Wentworth, USN, who had been ordered to conduct a preliminary investigation into the disaster. Captain Wentworth's report is not available, but we do know that he must have recommended a Court of Inquiry, and we know

Above and right: Burial at sea, 15 September 1944. (Courtesy of John L. Eichman)

that Commander Wheyland was relieved of his command by his executive officer. Wheyland was then ordered to report to the Court of Inquiry. The *Hyades* sailed for Majuro, in the far Pacific, and Chief Radioman Doyle was flown back from that atoll. We hear no more about the *Hyades*.

Wheyland, Quarles, and Williams were subsequently tried by general court-martial, and were all acquitted. Wheyland was promoted to captain; Williams was promoted to lieutenant-commander; but Quarles never received another promotion. He never again commanded a ship. The secretary of the navy saw fit to order the chief of naval personnel to attach the record of the court-martial to Quarles's record "as a matter of interest." He did not take similar action with regard to the other two officers.

Wheyland survived the incident unscathed; the secretary of the navy was silent in his regard.

The story of the *Warrington* is near its end. She and most of her crew share a common grave, some fourteen thousand feet deep. It only remains to tell of an incident that occurred after the sinking, and to tell the story of the Court of Inquiry.

Shortly after the *Warrington* survivors began arriving at the Portsmouth Naval Hospital, broadcaster Walter Winchell made the following announcement over nationwide radio: "I have scooped the Navy! The USS *Warrington* has been sunk with all hands!"[35] As we have seen, the navy was well aware of the loss of the ship by that time, and the survivors were already safely ashore. But Winchell's irresponsible action surely hurt feelings and caused distress, pain, and unnecessary grief for family members to whom this was the first news of the disaster. Under wartime secrecy restrictions, the navy gave out a minimum of information, but efforts to notify the families began at once.

We must not leave the story of the *Hyades,* however, without rendering proper honors to the crew of the whaleboat that went to the rescue of the survivors in the high seas. This was a dangerous operation; the men who manned that boat were all volunteers who deserve being remembered for their courage. There were four of them: Ens. Paul Riggs, USNR; Seaman Michael Vuono; Seaman Eustace White; and engineer Burley Clayton. Ensign Riggs was later awarded a certificate by the Veterans of Foreign Wars, which stated in part, "Through his outstanding efforts and disregard for personal safety, 41 members of the U.S.S. *Warrington* were rescued."[36] Vuono says they picked up fifty-eight men, which agrees with the official tally. Mike adds, "It was a good thing they screamed, because we would have passed them."

This last statement gives rise to a certain amount of speculation. There is no doubt that the *Hyades* delayed returning to assist the *Warrington* for about four hours after receiving CinCLant's order. The court found that this delay contributed heavily to the loss of life.

But is this true? A close examination of all the known facts presents a somewhat different picture. The *Hyades* rammed Davis's raft at about 4:50 A.M. on the fifteenth.[37] This was the first indication that the *Hyades* had that the *Warrington* (or some other ship) had sunk in that vicinity. The process of stopping the engines, sending out the whaleboat, and hoisting the survivors aboard could easily have taken half an hour or more—while daylight was steadily approaching. In fact, Ens. Eugene Archer specifically states: "I was hauled up over the side to the deck of the *Hyades* just as daylight broke." What better time could there be to initiate a search for survivors?[38]

Let us examine the scenario that might have existed had there been no delay. The *Hyades* would have arrived in the area about four hours earlier—in black darkness; she could easily have missed Davis's raft, which means she could have been many miles away by daylight, still looking for the *Warrington*. There is a possibility that she might never have found any of the survivors. The court's view of this situation might, therefore, be in error, and the delay of the *Hyades* just might have been a blessing in disguise.

But what if earlier messages had been heeded? *Warrington* men such as Watertender Bill Sapp reported that a large number of men were lost during the afternoon and night of the thirteenth, and more were lost during the fourteenth. The *Hyades* received two or three messages on the thirteenth and fourteenth regarding the ATRs being sent to assist the ship in distress, with the *Warrington* named as information addressee, but did nothing about them. As the court noted, "an intelligent evaluation"[39] of those dispatches should have alerted the *Hyades* to the fact that the ship in distress was very likely to be her escort—and she would have had no trouble figuring out the position. This could have led to the *Hyades*'s arrival in the area *fourteen* hours earlier than she actually arrived. This would have been in the late afternoon, but still in daylight, and would almost certainly have resulted in saving many lives.

chapter nine

THE COURT OF INQUIRY

Soon after the loss of the
Warrington became known, Fleet Adm. Ernest J. King, commander in chief,
U.S. Fleet and Chief of Naval Operations (ComInCh), ordered a preliminary investigation to be carried out by Captain R. S. Wentworth, USN, as
mentioned in the previous chapter. As a result of Wentworth's investigation, Admiral King ordered a full-scale Court of Inquiry to be conducted by
a board of three officers.

The officers named to this board were Capt. W. H. Mays, USN, Naval
Academy class of 1919; Capt. R. D. Edwards, USN, class of 1921; and
Capt. R. L. Swart, class of 1924. Commander Wheyland, a member of the
class of 1920, was a contemporary of all three members of the court. The
judge advocate was Cdr. Norman K. Roberts, USNR.

While the *Warrington* men were still in the hospital and within days of
the sinking, a rumor began to circulate to the effect that Admiral King had
made the remark that "No modern warship should ever be lost to weather,"
and had ordered the court to "bear down" on the survivors. The truth of
this rumor has never been established, but it exists to this day; and if true,
it was characteristic of Admiral King, who gave short shrift to fools who
made mistakes. To some extent, the actions of this court lend credence to
this rumor.

Whether or not King ordered the court to bear down will never be
known with certainty, but bear down it did. If he did order this action, it
was an error on his part, since he did not have all the facts at his fingertips;
furthermore, he should have known that none of the enlisted personnel,
and very few of the officers, could have had any responsibility for what had

happened. But from the first day, the court persisted in referring to Quarles and Wheyland (and later, Williams) as "defendants," although none had been charged with any offenses requiring defense. Although this was perfectly legal, it illustrates a mind-set that was not appropriate to the circumstances. Moreover, the court's attitude toward some of the enlisted men indicated they were thought of as being guilty of a crime. The court badgered some witnesses (Latronica and Wright, especially) unmercifully. At no time throughout the proceedings did the court manifest the slightest compassion for, or under standing of, the sufferings undergone by these men, living or dead.

In their final report, they even went out of their way to blacken the names of Lieutenants (jg) Keppel and Pennington, who could no longer defend themselves, and who had both literally worked themselves to death trying to save the ship. Nothing that either officer did, or failed to do, contributed to the loss of the ship, but the court accused them of dereliction of duty.

Some of Keppel's activities have been described earlier; Pennington, after helping Pack restow the ammunition, conferred with Pack on the question of whether or not to inspect the after magazines to see if their ammunition storage was intact; they decided it was too dangerous to go aft to make an inspection, so they went to Quarles for further orders. Quarles himself testifies that they repeated this several times in the course of the night. Pennington also took part in the efforts to start the handy-billy pump in the Emergency Diesel Generator Room, and risked his life, with several others, to release the starboard anchor.

The court's action with respect to these two officers seems arbitrary and inexcusable. On the other side of the coin, the court took little interest in the actions of Dr. Kennedy, beyond expressing disbelief that he knew the ship was being abandoned. The heroic behavior of a number of enlisted men went unnoticed and unremarked, even when witnesses such as Quarles named them individually at the express wish of the court.

The only *Warrington* man whose actions met with the approval of the court was Lt. (jg) Louis B. Kroll. There is no question but that Kroll deserved special praise, but so did others.

The members of the court, although unfailingly courteous to Quarles, clearly regarded his testimony with a good deal of skepticism. Quarles presented matters that had nothing to do with the loss of the ship, but the court delved into each subject in great detail. For instance, Quarles discussed crew morale, training exercises held in Casco Bay, changes in the ship's organization, and Lieutenant Williams's qualifications as a shiphandler (but not as an executive officer). It is difficult to say how much of this the court believed, but it seemed to believe at least some of it. Some of these subjects can be found in Quarles's action report (appendix C).

The court's attitude toward Commander Wheyland was markedly different. Unfortunately, most of Wheyland's testimony is in the 451 pages not released by the Judge Advocate General's Office. But in Wheyland's brief closing argument, he does not try to put blame on others for the tragic four-hour delay. Instead, he denies delaying, claiming that he turned his ship around within minutes of receiving CinCLant's orders.[1] The court did not press the matter.

There was a reason for this. The court had made strong efforts to obtain the presence of the *Hyades*'s navigator and communications officer as witnesses, but without success. It was thus hampered in developing all the evidence needed. As a matter of historical interest, the problems faced by the court in this matter are worth explaining, through the statement made by the judge advocate:

> Insofar as the two officers from the *Hyades* are concerned, they have not appeared and whether they will within the reasonably near future, I don't know . . . they are the Communications Officer and the Navigator. Under date of 3 October their presence was requested of the Bureau. Under date of 7 October the Bureau advised us that so far as the two officers were concerned, they referred us to CinCPac. They agreed to send the Chief Radioman back immediately, however. Under date of 10 October Commander Service Force referred the matter to CinCPac. Under date of 11 October CinCPac replied to CinCLant stating that the presence of those two officers in the Pacific was essential. . . . On 12 October we informed CinCLant we would first examine the Chief Radioman and see if his presence was sufficient. On 13 October the Bureau, acting on our original request, ordered those two officers returned to this command, and advised us that they should report on or about 25 October. We received copies of the orders on these two officers (Bureau Orders to the *Hyades*). On October 30th Commander Service Force Atlantic Fleet sent a dispatch to Commander Service Force Pacific Fleet, making the Bureau and CinCPac and the *Hyades* as well as ComTwelve [Commandant, 12th Naval District (San Francisco)] information addressees, requesting information relative to the date of detachment and probable date of arrival of the two officers. To date, we have received no reply to that dispatch. While the Chief Radioman has returned, I still believe it is desirable to have those two officers testify before this court. In order not to delay the proceedings I suggest that we go ahead without waiting for the determination of their availability, with the right being reserved by the judge advocate to put them on the stand should they be available.[2]

This statement was made on 6 November; the two officers never did appear.

The court could have prepared written interrogatories for all three *Hyades* officers (including the assistant communications officer) and mailed them to the new commanding officer of the *Hyades,* with the request that they be answered, under oath, by the officers concerned. This is not an unusual procedure, and the captain would no doubt not have refused such a request. The court, however, let the matter drop, simply listing Wheyland's failures as proposed charges against him.

In dealing with Williams, the court at times acted as though he were invisible. It must be remembered that Williams was sitting in the courtroom, along with both the other "defendants," so he would be fully aware of anything said by Quarles in his regard. This didn't bother the court; they asked questions of Quarles that seemed deliberately designed to make Williams look bad no matter what Quarles's response might be. This may be the reason why Quarles's answers were sometimes evasive.

As previously noted, Williams was not one of the original interested parties to this inquiry. It is not clear why the court made him a party, but he appears to have thought the court might have felt that he had not been where he was supposed to be. As far as the testimony reveals, the court seemed to think he should have been in closer proximity to Quarles throughout the storm.

Actually, there is nothing in navy regulations that requires the executive officer to be in any particular spot in such an emergency. His duties are, mainly, to be of maximum assistance to the commanding officer. To accomplish this, he must rove around the ship, going from one trouble spot to another, giving guidance, directing operations, and so on. This Williams was doing; apparently his sin in the eyes of the court was that he made few, if any, reports to the captain.

This raises another question: what was the personal relationship between the captain and the executive officer? Shortly after Quarles took command, Williams went to him to find out what Quarles's wishes were with regard to some of Williams's duties. Quarles replied: "Read *Navy Regulations.*"[3] This reply did not endear the captain to the executive officer. When Quarles then took away Williams's duties as navigator and gave them to Lt. Pat Davis, it may have had a bad effect on Williams. In any event, it appears that Williams thenceforth immersed himself in the paperwork of his job and stayed as far away from Quarles as he could. We do know that when Quarles led the men down from the bridge at about 11:00 A.M. on the thirteenth, Williams and Dicken remained on the bridge; therefore he had been within easy reach of Quarles for a while, and we know he took part in the debate about what to do with the fore topmast.

During the storm, however, the record clearly shows that Quarles bypassed Williams on several occasions.[4] Nevertheless, Williams assisted in jettisoning the whaleboat and he helped rescue a man overboard. He assisted in cutting down the foremast, and with a line lashed around his waist, he was lowered from the superstructure to the starboard side of the main deck, where he tried desperately to tie down the open cover on the access hatch to Number 2 Fireroom, where the seas continued to flood into the ship.

In short, although his captain had bypassed him in the chain of command by summoning Lieutenant Davis to the bridge for assistance, Lieutenant Williams did in fact carry out the duties of a ship's executive officer throughout this ordeal. If the court felt that, while the captain's job was to make the overall command decisions and the exec's job was to be the doer, using his own initiative, the court should have commended Williams for a job well done. Instead, the court recommended that Williams lose his commission, without even the benefit of a trial in which to mount a defense of his actions.

His failure to make reports was a minor fault, as things turned out. The worst mistake Quarles made was to reverse course, and he himself confessed that it was the numerous gloomy reports he had received from Keppel that influenced this decision. Would similar reports from Williams, or anyone else, have changed this decision?

Quarles seems to have felt that his crew let him down in some way; he was unsympathetic toward their disappointment at not getting the leave they expected (and had earned) on arrival on the East Coast (they were "feeling sorry for themselves") and he disparaged them as being "fair-weather sailors," although some of the men still aboard had more hurricane experience than he did.[5] These attitudes could not have helped Quarles before the court. There is an old saying, "There is no such thing as a poor crew; there are only poor officers."

The court wasted time on several matters. For instance, it called as a witness Lt. Cdr. Charles N. Mayo, the staff communications officer for ComServLant, who had been instrumental in preparing the communications plan used by the two ships. He testified that he did not *order* the ships to use the plan, but merely suggested parts of it. With respect to the use of 2885 kcs as a separation frequency, he testified that "to the best of my knowledge it is not used by anyone in the Continental United States," which could imply that the men should not have used it. But he did not suggest an alternative. He acknowledged that the ships' communications officers had agreed to the use of 2885 kcs.

Although much of Quarles's testimony is fairly verbose and rambling, one point may have had some bearing on the actions of the court. When the court asked him about his relationship with Williams as of 12 September, Quarles replied, "as prescribed by *Navy Regulations, which was the last word I gave to the Executive Officer*" [emphasis added]. And later, "I have no recollection of [giving him] any specific orders." He says he sent for Williams at least once, but cannot recall giving him any orders.[6] The court then asked Quarles to comment on Williams's actions on the night of 12 September. As Williams sat and listened, Quarles offered his assessment of Williams's abilities as a shiphandler and concluded:

> I knew that he had not been on the ship long, and that while he had been on the ship he had been devoting himself primarily to the personnel . . . therefore, in an emergency involving material matters, I had a tendency to turn to the officers who had been on the ship longest, *which was by no means by-passing Williams* [emphasis added]. It was such an emergency that I turned to the nearest officer at hand whom I thought could be of assistance.[7]

We do not have the specific orders given to the court by Admiral King, but it probably was directed to determine the causes of the disaster and the responsibilities of the people concerned, and to make appropriate recommendations for further action. The court did a pretty thorough job in those areas, within the limits of its capabilities.

1. Causes of the disaster.

The court found that the loss of the *Warrington* was the direct result of Quarles's reversal of course, which led to broaching to and subsequent flooding.

An indirect cause was the insistence on the part of Wheyland to maintain a course and speed that were essentially a collision course with the center of the storm, thereby hazarding both ships.

The heavy loss of life was partly the consequence of Wheyland's delay in returning to the scene and partly due to the disorganized manner in which the *Warrington* was abandoned.

2. Responsibilities.

In the opinion of the court, both Quarles and Wheyland were negligent in the performance of their duties; Quarles, for causing the loss of the ship, and Wheyland for not only hazarding both ships, but also contributing to the loss of life. It held Williams responsible for the disorganized abandonment of the *Warrington*.

3. Recommendations.

The court recommended that Wheyland and Quarles stand trial by general court-martial on the basic charge of neglect of duty. It recommended that Lieutenant Williams's commission be revoked, and further recommended that a suitable award be provided, posthumously, to Lieutenant (jg) Kroll. It then went on to make a number of recommendations for the improvement of lifesaving and other equipment.

AREAS THE COURT DID NOT ADDRESS

Except for the assignment of responsibility to Williams, the court's final judgment seems fairly reasonable. In this case, however, the court overlooked some significant factors, which seems to have resulted in a biased outcome.

First, no executive officer would have ordered the ship to be abandoned without at least a preliminary order from his captain. Quarles said that he gave orders for men to line up on the port side. If he did, why did he wait until his starboard-side rafts and nets were inaccessible? When he finally did order abandonment, it was far too late to organize any preparatory steps.[8]

The court quite properly expressed the opinion that Lt. (jg) Louis R. Kroll had acted in the highest traditions of the navy, but failed to recognize that Lt. (jg) Robert M. Kennedy, Medical Corps, had also acted in the highest traditions of not only the navy, but also the medical profession. It also failed to take notice of any recommendations made by *Warrington* survivors of meritorious behavior by any other *Warrington* personnel, living or dead.

Second, the court failed to make any recommendations for rectifying the system of handling communications aboard the *Hyades*.

Third, the court's thoroughness may have resulted in some injustice to *Warrington* personnel. It only examined two witnesses from the *Hyades,* as against sixty-eight from the *Warrington;* this discrepancy alone would give the court far more opportunity to be critical of the *Warrington* than the *Hyades*; it simply had more information to work with.

Accidents at sea, like accidents ashore, frequently have more than one cause; as noted, the court found several causes for the loss of the *Warrington*. But, because both the captain and the executive officer were new to the ship and the majority of the remaining knowledgeable officers were dead, the court was not completely or accurately informed on matters that had developed during the previous year.

Fourth, in bullying and intimidating the witnesses, the court, to some extent, defeated its own purposes. Witnesses became hostile and would volunteer nothing.

Intimidation was apparently not limited to the witnesses. Lieutenant Williams's counsel seemed afraid of the court, and he was somewhat handicapped by a lack of real knowledge of naval matters.

Quarles's counsel was quite skillful, except that he allowed Quarles to talk too much, without necessarily adding relevant information.

Fifth, I have previously mentioned two factors that were not mentioned by the court. Neither led directly to the loss of the ship but may have contributed to it. Both were matters of personal judgment based on the observable facts as Quarles could have seen them; but he was not in a position to see their consequences as we can today.

I refer, first, to what may have been unnecessary delay in heaving to on the evening of the twelfth. Quarles was in a bad situation in this, however; like any commanding officer, he wanted to carry out his orders, which tied him to the *Hyades.*

It has long been understood that a commanding officer's first concern is for the safety of his ship and his crew, and that he must be ready to accept reprimand, if necessary, to ensure their safety. Therefore, he must be ready to use his own judgment and initiative in taking appropriate action, regardless of what any superiors might think.

Quarles followed this precept, but may have held off too long. If he had hove to earlier, he might have been able to run before the storm to safety, but he says himself that this "would be like running away from a battle." The *Warrington,* under such circumstances, could have easily run ahead of the slower *Hyades.* So he delayed—until the *Hyades* separated from him.

The second instance came when Quarles was standing in the doorway, watching the water rise around his feet with each roll of the ship. He may have stood there for about two hours. The ship listed farther and farther to starboard, until all the starboard rafts and nets were no longer accessible. No one but Quarles could make the decision to abandon ship. The chief boatswains mate, Johnson, stood near the stack, watching the bridge, clearly expecting orders to abandon ship, and probably wondering why Quarles delayed. Whatever the cause, half of his lifesaving equipment was lost. And Williams, who could do nothing until Quarles made his decision, was blamed by the court for the lack of organization.

No one made the court aware of the long months of continuous operations in the Pacific, which almost wore the ship out. Neither did anyone inform the court of the lack of opportunity for training, for the

Warrington survivors *John Lawrence Eichman, S1c (left) and Paul Klingen, RM2c. (Courtesy of John L. Eichman)*

same reasons. Few ships train specifically for hurricanes, so lack of training was hardly a contributory factor in the loss of the ship, but Quarles brought up this subject himself, emphasizing ComDesLant's criticisms, and the court seized upon this information in a sort of "feeding frenzy."

The court did not note the strange statements occasionally made by Quarles. For instance, Quarles's testimony relative to his distress messages as he sent them differed considerably from how they were received, and when Quarles testified that he had "deliberately exaggerated" his situation, in order to expedite rescue operations (see appendix C), the court should have taken notice. After being rescued, he says he exaggerated the number of rafts and nets in order to ensure a maximum search effort by Commander Task Group 22.5.[9] This may have been taken as an insult to CTG 22.5, or perhaps the court felt that it was not worth bothering with.

Based upon this record, then, it looks as if this court was out to get someone; unfortunately, the system is such that a court with this mind-set will inevitably find a victim. Why the court chose to include Williams is difficult to understand, when it had two ready-made victims close at hand. And why would it bother to smear the names of Keppel and Pennington?

Quarles may have antagonized the court to some extent with some of his testimony. For instance, when the court asked him why he had not used a sea anchor, he replied,

> I know of no suitable material on the ship for a sea anchor. . . . I do not think that any sea anchor could have helped the situation, because a ship with the length to beam ratio of the *Warrington* . . . it would require the most tremendous force imaginable to hold the ship's head up to the wind. The ship did not drift fast enough to have caused the sea anchor to exert a great deal of pull. In other words, the sea anchor would have drifted through the water with the same speed that the ship was drifting through.[10]

By definition, a sea anchor does not exert pull; it is simply a drag, or drogue, which *resists* the pull of the ship as the latter drifts, holding the bow while allowing the stern to swing freely. Being largely under water, it is not affected by the wind, so all the pull on a sea anchor is caused by the effect of the wind on the hull of the ship. Perhaps the court knew this but just let it go.

Boatswains Mate Lewis Parrillo quoted the judge advocate as saying that the members of the court would never understand what the men of the *Warrington* went through.[11] In fact, there is no indication in the record that any member of the court even tried to visualize what happened. They evidently saw the tragedy through the eyes of the *Navy Regulations,* and perhaps through the eyes of Admiral King, who was well known for terrorizing his subordinates.

I have mentioned the hostility of witnesses. An excellent example of this and the reasons for it can be found in the testimony of Shipfitter 3d Class Walter Wright, who was helmsman from 9:00 P.M. to 11:00 P.M. on the night of the twelfth, when such difficulty was encountered in keeping the ship on course, and the first serious water came on board.[12] This man's testimony was critical, but under the court's aggressive questioning, his attitude became defiant to the point where he just quit talking.

In the course of the hearings, the court asked Quarles and Latronica to name any members of the ship's company who, they believed, deserved special mention for meritorious behavior. Why they picked just these two witnesses is a mystery—obviously, many people, equally deserving, would be omitted. Their list contained fourteen names.[13] The court ignored this list, except for Lieutenant Kroll, whom it cited. As pointed out earlier, it accused Lt. (jg) Jesse Pennington, also on the list, of dereliction of duty.

Except for the testimony of the missing *Hyades* officers, the court finished its work in November 1944. The witnesses were then scattered to other duty stations.

COURT-MARTIAL

In December, pursuant to the court's recommendations, courts-martial were ordered for Wheyland, Quarles, and Williams. The recommendation that Williams's commission be revoked was evidently considered inappropriate. Whether they were tried separately or together is uncertain; the Navy Department cannot locate the court-martial records. In any case, all three officers were acquitted, and all three are now dead.

The enlisted survivors had been recalled to serve as witnesses before these new courts. There seems to have been a bit of badgering going on here, too, although not as much as with the Court of Inquiry. Two incidents will serve to present the picture.

Fireman Clarence Strunk was the man who discovered the new crack, on the port side of the stack. Apparently the court took his testimony with a grain of salt, because at one point Strunk is reported to have pushed his chair back with a crash, angrily shouting, "I am not a liar!" The president of the court, a rear admiral, is said to have replied, "Son, do you know who you are talking to?" Strunk said he did, and repeated that he was not a liar, and no more was said.

The other incident involved Radioman Paul Klingen, who says that he was called into the courtroom to testify, only to find the members reading his Court of Inquiry testimony and laughing over the idea that anyone could go to sleep while in the water. Paul told them he was "kind of tired," as I related earlier, and gives this further report:

> Another stated he would like to know how I was so sure I was actually transmitting a signal if no one answered. They were not talking to me direct, just conversation between themselves. To them, I must have been invisible.
>
> When the Court convened, an officer at the head of the table asked for my name and rate. I faced him and answered his question. This was a long and narrow table, and I was approximately in the center. Another officer at the other end of the table said he did not hear my answer. I turned to face him and repeated my answer, at which, the first officer informed me that he asked the question and that I should answer to him.
>
> After it was established that I was the radioman on watch they asked questions about what frequencies were used, who authorized use of them, how could I be sure the signal was actually going out, was the transmitter in working order, and was the antenna still intact. All through this ques-

Some Warrington survivors, December 1944. Top row, from left: Andrew K. Thurston, S1c; Llewellyn V. Riley, MM1c; Alfred Hanson, MM1c; Benjamin H. Knabb, S2c; William C. Greene, QM2c; Paul Klingen, RM1C; Clarence Strunk, F2c; Deryl Rowell, GM2c; Walter Wright, SF3c; John J. Latronica, MoMM2c. Middle row, from left: Fred J. Kieser, F1c; "W J" Sapp, CWT; Walter C. Teague, CWT; Lt. (jg) Eugene E. Archer; Lt. Patrick B. Davis; Lt. (jg) Donald W. Schultz; Elmer R. Canaday, CMoMM; Willie G. Johnson, CBM; George H. Finch, SC2c; L. O. Jasmin, SoM3c. Front row, from left: Alfred D. Browning, F2c; Sterling R. Bussey, F2c; Howard D. Wallin, F1c; Garland S. Stewart, S1c; Lawrence D. Allphin, TM1c; Ray W. Padgett, TM2c; Robert B. Ralph, RM3c; William Schroerlucke, Jr., S1c; Ralph G. Lemon, EM1c; James J. Devitt, S2c. (Courtesy of William C. Greene)

tioning I still had the same problem between the two officers at each end of the table.

At one stage, through this questioning, either he did not like my answer, or I said something he didn't like, so the first officer informed me that a court-martial is a serious matter and if I wasn't careful, I could be facing one myself.

Needless to say, I was a little upset after that, and although I'm sure all my answers were as accurate as I could recall, I was left with the impression that they thought I was less than truthful.[14]

In that same month of December, while these courts were still in session, three destroyers were lost in a typhoon in the Pacific, with very heavy loss of life. Admiral Nimitz addressed some harsh remarks to the task force commander responsible, but no one was court-martialed. (Two of the commanding officers died.) Admiral King's reactions are not known, but the incident may have had some influence on the outcomes of the *Warrington* and *Hyades* trials. The connection, however, is speculative.

PART TWO
LOOKING BACK

chapter ten

THE WHOLE IS THE SUM OF ITS PARTS

In the words of Samuel Johnson (1709–84), "No man will be a sailor who has contrivance enough to get himself into jail, for being in a ship is being in jail, with the chance of being drowned."

The way a ship is built is crucial to the safety of its crew. In the case of the *Warrington,* a number of design problems became apparent as survivors told their experiences. In this section I will look at ship design, lifesaving equipment, station bills, communications, and damage control. This will provide insight into the makeup of this ship and what went wrong.

SHIP DESIGN

According to Rear Adm. Charles A. Curtze, USN (Ret), not much attention is given by ship designers to the factor of seaworthiness. Admiral Curtze was a member of the Naval Construction Corps, until the Corps was abolished, and is experienced in designing destroyers, but not those of the *Warrington* type. This lack of attention is not deliberate, he says, nor is it a result of lack of interest. It is caused by those who order vessels to be built. These people—and they are not just naval people—specify exactly what they want their vessels to be able to do or to carry. Such specifications might include armament, speed, cruising range, habitability, crew size, and so on. These demands often conflict with each other, so the designer has to make many trade-offs; and in the shuffle, seaworthiness may be lost.

There is no one definition of seaworthiness; even naval architects disagree on this definition, which is just one of the reasons why seaworthiness does not receive the attention it deserves. For our purposes, however, we will define it as "the ability of a vessel to withstand extremes of wind and sea, with a minimum of discomfort for the crew."

The designers of the *Warrington*, in common with all the designers of American destroyers of the 1930s, failed to meet this standard in several respects—particularly in the fashionable broken-deck design of the hull, which created a very low freeboard amidships, just where the access hatches to some of the engineering spaces were located. David H. Miller observes that the freeboard of one of the old 1,200-ton, four-stack destroyers was higher than that of the *Somers* class, which included the *Warrington*. (See appendix B.) As we shall see later, both in 1938 and in 1944, this low freeboard prevented safe access to these spaces when heavy seas were running. Two of the three destroyers lost in the Pacific in December 1944 were broken-deckers.

Another design flaw was the absence of a covered, safe, means of passage between the forward and after parts of the ship. An open passage-way across the ship between the midships deckhouse and the after deck-house served to isolate the after end of the ship when dangerous seas were sweeping across the deck, particularly after the *Warrington*'s Big Roll. There was no communication between the ends of the ship. In a telephone interview, Machinists Mate John J. Latronica complained that no leadership came from the bridge to those in the after section of the ship. But without communication, it is difficult to see how much leadership was possible.

A third flaw concerns the locations of the engineroom and fireroom blower intakes. These intakes were only about four feet above the deck, making them extremely vulnerable to even moderate seas. In some other types of destroyers, they were as much as twenty or thirty feet above the decks. After the loss of the *Warrington*, the Bureau of Ships authorized a modification to these intakes, raising them well above the deck.[1]

The General Board

The navy has an organization known as the General Board, made up of senior officers from about ten or eleven offices and bureaus, under the overall command of the chief of naval operations. This board meets from time to time, to discuss the design and characteristics of ships still on the drawing board. It appears that the chairman of the board at these meetings may be, and often is, a senior retired admiral.

We have reports of two of these meetings held in 1933, the first of which[2] was concerned with the design characteristics of the proposed 1,500-ton destroyers and was chaired by Adm. J. V. Chase, a former commander in chief, U.S. Fleet. The members present discussed in detail the torpedo armament versus a possible reduction in the gun armament, and a possible change in the type of guns. The amount of detail they discussed is astonishing as well as eye opening, but much of it is outside the bounds of our story. Of interest is the fact that a representative of the Bureau of Ordnance states that the 5-inch 38-caliber guns (5″/38), which was the standard AA gun on all ships during World War II, was just then coming into production.

To get the general flavor of this discussion, I will quote short excerpts:

Admiral Schofield: Having in mind the at times rather violent motion of the destroyer, would there be any loading difficulties with the 5-inch 38?

Captain Stott: We don't anticipate that.

Admiral Schofield: Is it more difficult to load for direct fire?

Captain Stott: It would be slightly more difficult [than the 5-inch 51] because the trunnions will be considerably higher.

Admiral Sexton: My inclination has been toward the single-purpose gun . . . better hitting accuracy.

Captain Reed: I favor the double purpose gun for the reason that I think that the ability to combat aircraft will make up for the estimated 50 percent loss in fighting at 5,000 yards. Going through a screen or repelling an attack through a screen the ranges will be much shorter than 6,000 yards. I think that a destroyer will be engaged at much less range than 6,000 yards except in a few cases. That is why they are engaged with similar vessels.[3]

This argument went on, with people about evenly divided in their opinions. Those of us who later served aboard the *Warrington* frequently wondered why we were afflicted with single-purpose guns in a war involving air defense. Some of the thinking sounds almost weird nowadays, but we have to consider the context of the times. For instance, Capt. R. L. Ghormley, Office of CNO (later a vice admiral), had this to say: "The 5-inch 25 is a very delicate gun as far as its mechanism is concerned. As soon as it begins to rain or as spray comes on board the guns have to be covered immediately or they won't work. . . . [The 5″/25 was then being carried by some cruisers and battleships.] We don't know whether destroyers can shoot at aircraft successfully."

Lieutenant Commander P. W. Fletcher, from the Bureau of Ordnance, had this to add: "If the destroyer is going to defend herself against aircraft, she could do it better with machine guns, .50 caliber or 1.1, than she could with a double purpose gun."

His views are not lonesome; several others liked the idea of .50-cal. machine guns or the 1.1's, which were subsequently found to be worthless.

Admiral Land makes one very telling comment: "All designs being a compromise, the reason, generally speaking, is increased gun battery as to size and weights, increased accommodations and *generally improved, we trust, seagoing qualities*" [emphasis added]. He then goes on to list the improvements in the 1,500-ton destroyers over the old 1,200-tonners. He lists ten improvements, of which number eight is "Improved behavior in a seaway due to improved freeboard and design of topsides." In the light of what happened to the *Warrington,* this last statement is particularly interesting.

Torpedoes were considered superior to guns.

> **Admiral Schofield:** The offensive weapon is the torpedo, and armament as far as it has been built [the 1,500-tonner] is on the idea of the offensive nature of the type.
>
> **Lieutenant Freseman:** I believe that the offensive weapon is the torpedo, that the guns should be taken off and we should add the four extra torpedo tubes.[4]

Passing on to the second meeting, this one chaired by Admiral George R. Marvell, we find these officers discussing some of the characteristics of the 1,850-tonner—the *Warrington* class.

Admiral Land refers to a model, sitting on the table in front of them, and says, "The guns, as you know, are 5-inch 38 *double purpose guns, single mounts*" [emphasis added]. He then goes on to say that the main reason for their meeting is to come to a decision regarding the substitution of four *double* mounts, *single purpose* guns. The model also has twelve broadside torpedo tubes, and he is suggesting the substitution of four triple torpedo mounts (six tubes on a broadside), or an alternative of one centerline and two broadside mounts, with the same number of tubes.

Admiral J. M. Robinson, chief of the Bureau of Engineering, says that the ship will be able to make thirty-five knots at 42,800 horsepower, with either setup, but cannot get more. There will be a fuel capacity of 614 tons of oil, and cruising range 6,300 miles with a foul bottom. This cruising range was proved by the cruise of the *Warrington* from New Guinea to Panama.

They then discuss the gunnery situation, especially with respect to antiaircraft defense. Captain Stott says that with single-purpose guns, "we would have available the 1.1″ or the .50-caliber. The 1.1 would be a better gun for this platform than the 5-inch." It is clear that these people place great faith in the 1.1. Admiral G. R. Marvell thinks their main problem is finding a compromise between guns and torpedoes, in order to remain within their weight limit. Admiral Watson asks, "Do you consider the double purpose is necessary?" To which Admiral Sexton replies, "No. Particularly when I get those 1.1's."

Then we come to one of the most amazing statements of all:

Admiral Cole: It is my feeling that these ships should be made as much like a cruiser as possible and that they should have a single purpose gun. I don't think they will be attacked by heavy bombers. They might be subjected to dive bombing attack in which the machine gun is sufficient.

Then Captain Stott says

I don't think anybody can definitely say that they [5-inch AA guns] will be particularly effective. A ship of that size is going to be a very lively gun platform. . . . It is really too big to be used primarily as a destroyer and torpedo-carrying craft. I think she should be armed to be as useful as possible as a cruiser.

Admiral A. J. Hepburn disagreed. He did not believe in trying to make this ship a menace to something outside its own category so far as cruiser characteristics were concerned. He ends by saying,

If we are contemplating these ships in anti-aircraft action for the protection of other parts of the fleet, or for an offensive against aircraft, or for a warning, then I still question the efficiency of a double purpose gun on this type of craft, so my choice would be for the single-purpose gun and the twin mount.[5]

So this is how the *Warrington* came to be armed with single-purpose guns. And this may be the primary reason why a ship originally intended to be a destroyer squadron commander's flagship was never used for that purpose.

Neither of these meetings covered the subject of hull design; apparently, this had been decided earlier, for both the 1,500 and 1,850-tonners. Both classes ended up with broken decks and highly vulnerable access hatches to their firerooms.

Admiral W. V. Pratt felt that destroyers should carry mines and a large number of depth charges, but he didn't feel there was much danger from air attack, therefore, he, like most of the others, felt a great affinity for the 1.1. Admiral Cole asked what the freeboard amidships would be, and when told it would be nine feet, he seemed satisfied.[6]

LIVESAVING EQUIPMENT

Warrington rafts were found to be easily capsized by strong winds and heavy seas as they rose to the crests of the waves. This caused the loss of men, water, food, and equipment. The Bureau of Ships (BuShips) was responsible for finding and solving such problems. BuShips stated it was studying the use of inflatable rubber rafts and rafts filled with fiberglass or plastic pellets instead of the standard balsa-wood types. These improvements would probably have saved weight, but it is hard to see how they would have much effect on capsizing. Today's rafts are of similar overall design. They carry homing devices and have better stowage for food and water.

Floater nets proved to be more of a menace than a help under hurricane conditions. A floater net was a rope net fifty feet in diameter and six feet deep. It was fitted with floats like buoys along the upper edge. In rough conditions it was not very effective. Out of some sixty men on two *Warrington* floater nets, only eight survived.

Kapok-filled life jackets were mentioned earlier as being subject to waterlogging; this, of course, depends on the length of time the wearer is in the water. It is notable that Quarles, who evidently spent a large part of the time inside the raft, thought favorably of the kapok-filled jacket until he had had an opportunity to compare notes with people who were not as fortunate as he; then he changed his mind. Others mentioned the discomfort caused by the rubbing of the canvas cover on faces and necks, and the cutting under the armpits. In those days, the Mae West jackets, issued to aviators, were much superior.

The stowage of food and water aboard the rafts came in for considerable criticism. With respect to water, the old standard wooden casks, or "breakers," were sometimes found to be leaking, probably due to old age, allowing the contents to be either lost or contaminated by salt water. They did not lend themselves to easy division of the water among the survivors, and when opened for use, they again became contaminated. Some breakers came adrift and were lost completely.[7]

Most survivors felt that water supplies should be kept in small containers—about the size of beer cans or smaller—so that they could be parceled out more easily and would be less susceptible to contamination, or that the breakers should be made of hard plastic (similar to football helmets), with built-in handles, or loops, for securing them to the raft.

Food stowage was generally thought to be satisfactory; it was in cans of individual, pint-sized capacity. Like the water, however, once it was opened, it had to be entirely consumed, or it would be contaminated. Therefore, the size of the cans became crucial. Of course, all containers of any kind should be capable of floating. The Bureau of Ships did not comment on these stowage problems.

WATCH, QUARTER, AND STATION BILLS

These bills are charts, or tables, which assign individuals to various stations around the ship for various purposes, including emergencies. They are posted on bulletin boards; they include information on battle stations, fire, collision, abandon ship, fire and rescue stations (when another ship needs assistance), and any others that the captain thinks necessary. They are used in drills held frequently.

At the time of this event in 1944, the Heavy Weather Bill was not generally required, but has become common since then. This bill provides instructions as to which doors, hatches, ventilation systems, and such are to be closed at the approach of severe weather, and who is designated to close them. Heavy weather is a common occurrence; theoretically, then, crews get plenty of practice at carrying out this drill, but the heavy weather at hand may not be anything like a hurricane or typhoon, so common sense tells us that the Heavy Weather Bill should be designed to protect the ship in even the very worst kind of weather.

Abandon Ship is not a drill that is carried out very frequently. Presumably, the thinking is that this is a purely desperation operation following battle, collision, or grounding, and that there will be adequate time to line up all hands and count noses before leaving the ship; furthermore, all rafts, boats, and nets will be available and manned by designated personnel, with an officer or senior petty officer in charge of each. While this may be the case fairly frequently, it still remains up to chance. There have been cases of torpedoed ships sinking within two minutes; and the destroyers lost in December 1944 all capsized without warning. The formal Abandon Ship Bill in these cases was worthless.

COMMUNICATIONS

Here we come to what appears to have been the real, fundamental cause of the sinking of the *Warrington:* poor communications. Here is a list of the times when communications failed:

1. When the commanding officers conferred with the staff operations officer in Norfolk, nobody really discussed the presence of a hurricane, as far as the record shows; if it was discussed at all, the danger of its recurring was not recognized.
2. On Monday, 11 September, Quarles reported that the ships spent a good deal of time testing TBY and TBS. Evidently, these tests were not used for discussing the impending storm and proper actions to avoid it.
3. On the twelfth, Quarles made a recommendation to cease zigzag and increase speed, which Wheyland first rejected, then followed. An opportunity to discuss the problem was lost, leaving the door open to misinterpretation by Wheyland.

4. In early evening of 12 September, Wheyland failed to respond to Quarles's first message on TBS, indicating his need to heave to.

5. Quarles announces his need to heave to by a flashing-light signal. This is answered. After a further exchange of flashing-light signals the *Hyades* departs, giving Quarles no information as to her course or speed. Quarles fails to give the same information to the *Hyades.*

6. Efforts to recall the *Hyades* fail completely. This is a crucial failure of communications.

7. Efforts to communicate a distress signal fail on numerous frequencies.

8. The *Hyades* picks up two or three messages relating to a ship in distress, each naming the *Warrington* as an information addressee. These messages are filed without action.

9. When directed to report the condition of his unit to ComServLant, Wheyland seems to misunderstand the meaning of the word "Unit."

10. When directed by CinCLant to proceed to the assistance of the *Warrington,* the *Hyades* delayed for four hours before responding.

11. After picking up survivors from Davis's raft, the *Hyades* failed to report to CTG 22.5 for two hours, allowing a large group of ships to waste time looking for the *Warrington.*

12. During the storm there was a complete breakdown of communications between the forward and after parts of the *Warrington,* depriving the personnel aft of any direction and/or assistance.

13. The *Warrington* had no public address system, making it difficult to coordinate activities around the ship, especially when movements were restricted by heavy seas.

14. The sound-powered telephones eventually failed. They required men to wear headphones, and this required that men be stationed at important points around the ship where there were outlets. This was not done, nor could it be done in advance, when the important points were not known.

15. Whether or not any alleged ill feeling existed between the captains and affected their behavior is impossible to prove at this distance, but there is no doubt they did not give great consideration to each other.

As these fifteen points show, communications contributed mightily to the fate of the *Warrington.* All officers are exposed to intership communications, in varying degrees. Some are specialists; others learn more or less by osmosis, through daily observation and interofficer conversations. There is no special emphasis placed on this subject by the navy.

WEATHER PHENOMENA

The Court of Inquiry severely criticized both captains for failing to recognize and act upon the observable weather phenomena as they approached the storm. These phenomena are not always as easy to interpret as the court appears to have thought, but Wheyland did have enough information from weather advisories to enable him to take early action to avoid the storm without relying on visual observations. Therefore, what he did or did not observe personally is fairly irrelevant. Nevertheless, we have no indication that he looked at his barometer readings. Our records show that there was a slow but steady drop in the barometric readings for several hours, then the drop became precipitous.[8]

Quarles had the same information; he apparently did try to observe the weather,[9] but was somewhat deceived by the *apparently* steady readings early on the twelfth (he describes them as "relatively" steady). He failed to notice the significance of the very slow but steady drop. He does not mention the wind, except to remark once that it did not veer as he expected it to.

In the absence of specific testimony, we can only guess that the wind was light and variable at first, then settled into a steady but strengthening breeze from the east, finally developing into a gale from the east southeast. As long as the ships remained on a collision course with the storm center, this wind direction would remain about constant. Its comparatively steady direction, therefore, was a danger signal. Quarles may have had some inkling of this; if his testimony is correct, it seems he was worried about the course the ships were on for quite some time before he sent his message recommending a change in course and speed.

It is quite possible that ships can sail into a dangerous weather situation without benefit of weather advisories. When this happens, it becomes exceedingly difficult to tell in what direction a storm is moving, or its forward speed. About all a captain can do is make an educated guess as to the possible direction of the eye of the storm from his own position and apply historical knowledge of past storms to judge where it might be going, hoping it is not in the process of recurving at the time.

According to the testimony, the initial signs of this storm were fairly recognizable: high, thin, clouds; long, slow, swell *moving about parallel to the storm's movement,* but with the front of the swells at about right angles to the direction of their movement; and light, variable, breezes, slowly freshening and gradually steadying into a direction about 10° to 20° from that of the waves. (After all, it is the wind that creates the swells, so they follow the wind direction.)

Under these conditions and assuming a minimum of information, an alert captain should start observing his barometric readings carefully; in fact, I recommend that he start making a graph of those readings on the theory that "the picture works the problem." He should be prepared to put the Heavy Weather Bill into effect early, and if he wants to run from the storm, he should do so before danger strikes. Nothing will be gained by proving his "machismo" by continuing to stand into danger.

DAMAGE CONTROL

The subject of damage control dates back well before World War II. In the prewar years it was not given much attention, except by those officers whose functions included fire fighting, control of flooding, and such.[10] The experiences of the Royal Navy early in the war, however, brought out the immense importance of damage control, and the vital need for all hands to understand at least the rudiments of the problem and its solution. As time passed, the American Navy also began to learn, the hard way.

Damage control schools were established at a number of places, and gradually most officers and a great many enlisted men were sent to them. The curricula at these schools usually included case histories of ships that had been lost because of poor damage control procedures, and demonstrations of the ways effective damage control could be carried out. As the world situation grew more tense, however, the operational demands on the ships grew rapidly, so many ships found themselves in situations in which they could not spare people for schools.

The *Warrington* was one of these. Her rapid and somewhat unexpected moves, such as her sudden shift from the Hawaiian Detachment (see chapter 14) to the Atlantic, in 1941, and then back to the Southeast Pacific Force, made all but a few school assignments impractical. Moreover, as officers and men were transferred, their replacements came aboard without school training. By the time the ship arrived in the South Pacific, most of her school graduates were gone. By the time Quarles took command, there were no damage control experts on board but there were a few experienced petty officers.

The ship ran drills every morning during the dawn alert period, but these drills had a number of shortcomings: they were brief, usually an hour or less; they tended to become routine—that is, little or no imagination was used to visualize new situations; and very little of the damage control equipment was actually broken out and put to use. Maneuvering the ship, or putting essential equipment (such as steering gear) out of commission, was frequently impossible, because of the need to maintain station on one or more other ships.

It was little wonder, therefore, that the lack of training became obvious when the ship arrived in Casco Bay. As a result, the ship received unsatisfactory marks from ComDesLant's people. Numerous drills and inspections followed, and the response was gratifying, but Rome was not built in a day, and there was still a long way to go when Quarles came aboard.

The damage control schools taught that there are only two things that ever sink ships: fire and flooding. In the event a ship is faced with either, the first step is usually the same. Boundaries must be established, beyond which neither the fire nor the flood will be allowed to pass. Once this is done, the source of the danger can be combated.

The court questioned Quarles with regard to his actions to compensate for the flooding of the engineering compartments; but it did not question the setting of flooding boundaries, nor did Quarles mention them. Instead, the court showed great interest in Quarles's plans for counterflooding, a process in which empty compartments are deliberately flooded to counterbalance the weight of those already flooded. This can be a very intricate problem, usually suitable for large ships only. In the case of a destroyer with flooded engineering spaces, it is virtually impossible to achieve, because these compartments are so large, and because they extend all the way across a ship. The court apparently did not understand this, but gave serious attention to Quarles's discussion as to what might happen if he flooded other compartments, without indicating which compartments he had in mind.

After the Big Roll, the After Fireroom was immediately flooded, and the Forward Engineroom followed shortly thereafter, thanks to the holes at the bottom of the intervening bulkhead. The flooding of these two compartments created a 15° starboard list (aided by the wind); hence, the idea that counterflooding would eliminate the list. Quarles pointed out correctly that if other compartments were flooded, their weight, combined with a roll of the ship, could cause all the water on board to suddenly shift to the port side, creating a real risk of capsizing. The big problem, of course, was that there were no compartments available for counterflooding. Unfortunately for Quarles, the unfamiliarity of the court with destroyer construction led it to criticize him in its Opinions for not counterflooding.[11]

Had the crew been able to establish flooding boundaries at the after bulkhead of the Forward Fireroom and the forward bulkhead of the After Engineroom, there is a good possibility that the ship might have been saved. This would have meant that all entry points of water in the Forward Fireroom and the After Engineroom (such as ventilation systems and hatches) would have had to be sealed watertight to create two large watertight "boxes." The forward living spaces and storerooms remained dry almost to the end of the ship; possibly, a more organized effort could have sealed the after living spaces. Without the two middle engineering spaces, and without adequate boiler feed water, the ship would not go anywhere, but at least she might have floated until help arrived.

The testimony, however, leads the reader to believe that the hatches to all four compartments were open most of time; the end, therefore, was inevitable.

CONCLUSIONS

If later sailors learned some lessons from the loss of the *Warrington,* then this disaster would have had some limited purpose. The story itself is not unique except in the comparatively large number of survivors; most hurricanes or typhoons leave very few, if any survivors, making it difficult to obtain a reasonably clear and coherent picture of just what happened. For instance, who, without the testimony of Bill Sapp and Bill Greene, would have suspected that floater nets could be killers? Who would have suspected that the shortage of boiler feed water—and the reason for it—would ruin the ship's last hope for survival? Who would have envisioned rafts flipping over like pancakes as they rose to the crests of the seas?

We hope that knowing these things saves lives for those who come after.

chapter eleven

A LADY WITH A PAST

The USS *Warrington,* destroyer number 383, was the second ship of that name. The first was number 30, and the third was number 842.

The original *Warrington* (DD 30) was named for Lewis Warrington of the U.S. Navy. Lewis Warrington was born on November 3, 1782, in York County, Virginia. His mother, Rachel, who was the orphaned daughter of a minister, bore Lewis out of wedlock. Lewis's father, Joseph Rochambeau, a French nobleman, had deserted the expectant mother, and she later married another.

In 1800, at the age of eighteen, Lewis obtained an appointment as a midshipman in the navy, after briefly attending the College of William and Mary. He rose in rank with reasonable rapidity and in June 1814, as a lieutenant, he was appointed to the command of the corvette USS *Peacock*. Operating off the coast of Florida, he encountered the British brig HMS *Epervier,* whose captain, before leaving England, had boasted that he would capture an American ship. In a fight lasting more than an hour, Warrington defeated and captured *Epervier,* for which Congress voted him a gold medal, and the State of Virginia presented him with a gold-hilted sword.

A few months later, the *Peacock* was prowling for more British victims in Far Eastern waters. In January 1815, she encountered a small British ship, and Warrington promptly ordered her to strike her colors. The English captain protested, saying that the war was over, but Warrington, fearing a ruse, persisted in his demand, and the outgunned Englishman surrendered. He was right, however, and no doubt Warrington quickly discovered his error and released his captive. He goes down in history as competing with Andrew Jackson for the "honor" of firing the last shots of the War of 1812.

At about this time, Lewis's French father, who had gotten wind of Lewis's achievements, offered him the right to use the noble family name. Warrington rejected the offer and would have nothing to do with his father.

He married a Norfolk girl in 1817, and continued his naval career another thirty-four years until his death in 1851. He sailed in the Caribbean area for several years, helping the British and Spanish to suppress piracy. He had a pleasant personality and was well liked by his foreign allies.

He served temporarily as secretary of the navy in 1844, when Secretary Thomas Gilmer was killed in an accidental explosion of a gun aboard the USS *Princeton* during a firing demonstration. From 1846 until his death, he served as chief of the Bureau of Ordnance.[1]

Following the Civil War, and the epic battle between the *Monitor* and the *Merrimac,* the navies of the world began building ironclad ships. Among the new types were small, fast boats called "torpedo boats"; since these represented a threat, they called for countermeasures, so the "torpedo-boat destroyer" was born. In time, the small, fast ships grew larger and shed the word "torpedo" from their name, but retained their speed and general usefulness. They were the original "tin cans," the workhorses of the fleet. It became navy policy to name them after famous Americans, such as naval or marine corps heroes. In due time, destroyer number 30 was named for Lewis Warrington.

The first USS *Warrington* was a coal-burner of about one thousand tons, which carried four four-inch guns and twelve twenty-one inch torpedoes in four mounts. She was of a type known as "broken-decker," a term derived from the fact that the forecastle deck was some eight feet above the main deck. (It may help the reader to visualize this better, if I explain that the "main deck" on any naval ship is the highest continuous deck, from bow to stern. On destroyers, it is also the uppermost deck one sees, running from the superstructure area to the stern. Thus, it runs under the forecastle in a broken-decker.) The ship was laid down in Philadelphia in 1909, and was launched on 18 June 1910. She was commissioned on 20 March 1911, under the command of Lt. Walter M. Hunt, USN.

During most of 1911, the *Warrington* was engaged in training activities up and down the East Coast. In December of that year, she departed from Charleston, South Carolina, in company with the ships of Destroyer Divisions 8 and 9, bound for Hampton Roads, Virginia. Nearing the Virginia Capes at about midnight, in rainy and foggy weather, an unidentified schooner knifed out of the fog and chopped off about thirty feet of the *Warrington*'s stern. As far as we know, this seagoing hit-and-run driver was never apprehended. The *Warrington,* now bereft of propellers and rudder, had no choice but to drop an anchor. The other destroyers remained at the scene, vainly trying to get a towline across to the *Warrington.* For hours, the *Sterett, Walke,* and *Perkins* struggled in the increasingly heavy seas, but it was not until the arrival of the revenue cutter *Conondaga* that she was finally taken under tow and brought to Norfolk for repairs. These took about a year; in December 1912, she resumed her training activities with other ships of the Atlantic Torpedo Flotilla.

When the United States entered World War I in April 1917, the *Warrington* patrolled off Newport, Rhode Island, for about six weeks; then, on 21 May, she sailed for Europe. Arriving in Ireland on 1 June, she began six months of patrolling the southern approaches to the British Isles and escorting convoys on the final leg of their voyages across the Atlantic to Britain. In late November 1917, she was ordered to France.

Her new base of operations was Brest, where she resumed a grueling schedule of patrolling and convoying. She had only one brush with a German submarine, which occurred on the morning of 31 May 1918, while she was escorting a convoy along the French coast. She answered a distress call from the U.S. Navy transport *President Lincoln,* which had been torpedoed by the U-90 well out to sea that morning. Reaching the area of the sinking late that night, the *Warrington* rescued 443 survivors, while the USS *Smith* took aboard all but one of the remaining 688 survivors.

That one survivor was a Lieutenant Isaacs, who had the misfortune to be rescued by the U-90, which ended his war for the time being.

Enroute back to Brest, the *Warrington* and the *Smith* depth-charged the U-90 but did not sink her. Lieutenant Isaacs later escaped from a German POW camp and reported that the U-90 had been badly shaken up by the depth charge attacks.

The *Warrington* then went back to antisubmarine patrolling out of Brest until the end of the war, but remained in European waters until the spring of 1919. In March of that year, in company with other destroyers, she convoyed a group of submarine chasers and tugs to Bermuda. From Bermuda, she sailed to her last port, Philadelphia, where she was decommissioned on 31 January 1920. She was finally scrapped in 1935.[2]

During the last year of the war, and for the next two or three years, the United States built many more destroyers, all similar to the *Warrington* insofar as they sported four stacks, four four-inch guns, and twelve torpedoes, plus the usual armament of depth charges. They were slightly larger than their predecessors—about 1,300 tons—and had flush decks (their main decks formed a straight line from bow to stern, with no interruption). They also became oil burners.

The last of these fine little ships was the USS *Pruitt* (DD 347). The newcomers also carried a three-inch antiaircraft gun either on the after deckhouse or the fantail. These were very primitive antiaircraft weapons; the barrels were only sixty-nine inches long, so they did not have great range, and there was no sighting mechanism. They were manned by one person (in addition to loaders) who had to aim and fire the gun by himself. To do this, he had to fit his right shoulder into a curved bracket, and from this position he could, with some effort, move the gun in any direction. I have seen one of these so-called peashooters in action, when the counter recoil cylinders were not functioning. The pointer was driven to the deck by the recoil on each shot, but being a big, husky man, he struggled back to his feet each time and went on firing. The guns were never used for AA firing in my time, however; they were much more useful for firing star shells in night practices.

In 1936, Congress passed the Vinson-Trammel Act, which initiated a large shipbuilding program as the clouds of war began to gather again over Europe. Fortunately, planning for a new generation of destroyers had been going on for at least three years, and possibly for four or five. One of the ships included in this planning was another USS *Warrington,* destroyer number 383.

This book is the story of the second *Warrington,* but it is appropriate to mention that there was eventually a third *Warrington* (DD 843), which served honorably through the Vietnam War. By an interesting coincidence, one of the survivors of the 383 also served aboard the 843; this was William C. Greene, quartermaster 3d class.

Of all the thousands of ships at sea, only a comparative few ever feel the breath of the Dragon. The USS *Warrington* (DD 383) is unusual, in that she felt that breath not once, but twice.

chapter twelve

THE PEACETIME NAVY, 1920–1939

The four-stack destroyers built just after the end of World War I were very seaworthy little ships, capable of speeds up to thirty-five knots, even in their old age. It was said that they could be rolled until their stacks dipped water, and they would return to an even keel; and although this is a slight exaggeration, there is no doubt they could withstand a great deal in the way of foul weather. In the process, though, they could be extremely uncomfortable in a seaway, with a sort of corkscrew motion that was most unsettling to many stomachs. Nevertheless, there were many who claimed that these were among the best ships the navy ever owned, both from the standpoint of general usefulness and as schools for both officers and men. Small wonder that destroyermen—the "Tin Can Sailors"—were a prideful lot. Primarily de-signed to be the number one enemy of the submarine, they had a reputation for being able to do almost anything.

But after the *Pruitt* (DD 347) slid down the ways, the navy entered the usual postwar doldrums for which America is notorious. All the armed forces were starved during the 1920s, as the 1,200-tonners grew old gracefully. No new ships appeared until after the passage of the Vinson-Trammel Act.

We have seen how the planning for new ships began several years before they became real, and we must remember that, when the planning was going on, the world knew nothing of the kind of war that was to come. There were no wars of any real consequence until the Spanish Civil War in 1937, and although it provided some lessons in air warfare, the absence of any sizable naval activities left a gap that naval planners could not entirely fill.

The new destroyers—both 1,500- and 1,850-tonners—began to join the fleet in 1936. Because they were so radically different from the old 1,200-tonners, they became known as "gold platers," and were universally envied by the old-timers. The vast majority of these ships were the 1,500-tonners known as the *Mahan* class; there were several classes of the 1,850-tonners, most of which sported two stacks. The *Somers* class, of which the *Warrington* was one, had a single stack; since there were only six in this class, this made them quite distinctive.

The 1,850s were originally intended as squadron commanders' flagships; apparently, the idea of using them as cruisers did not get far, although that idea resulted in the single-purpose guns mentioned in chapter 10. They carried eight of these guns, in four twin turrets, or mounts; the 1,500-tonners carried four or five double-purpose guns. All of these ships carried one fairly new development: sonar.

Sonar, like radar, was first developed by the British, who called their version of it "ASDIC." Two divisions of American 1,200-tonners experimented with sonar as early as 1937, developing antisubmarine tactics.[1]

In the prewar navy, four destroyers comprised a division, two or three divisions made a squadron, and two or more squadrons made a flotilla. A squadron commander would live aboard a ship of the same type as the rest (a 1,200-tonner), and his staff would be divided up among the other ships. The same arrangement applied to division commanders, but the flotilla commander usually luxuriated, together with his staff, aboard a light cruiser. These organizations were somewhat modified during World War II, which may partially explain why the 1,850s were never used as squadron flagships.

As one may have gathered from the General Board discussions in chapter 10, the 1,850s were more heavily armed than the gold-platers. There seems to have been an idea afloat in those days that, in the coming war, the destroyers would participate in a great final all-out Armageddon-type battle, being led in a sort of Charge of the Light Brigade by these eight-gun "monsters." History shows that this concept died at Pearl Harbor on 7 December 1941.[2]

The antiaircraft armament was rudimentary. Originally, it consisted of a .50-caliber machine gun mounted on each wing of the bridge, and a 1.1-inch pom-pom just forward of, or above, the bridge. The latter soon proved to be worthless; it only deigned to fire when the spirit moved, and was cordially despised by all who had anything to do with it. Capt. "Fid"

Murray, a former *Warrington* officer, has said the 1.1-inch gun made a fine swab rack, when fully elevated.

The 1,850s all suffered from various design flaws, of which the lack of a realistic antiaircraft defense was only the most obvious. This flaw, however, had much to do with the fact that these ships seldom, if ever, were used to their best effect. For obvious reasons, they were usually kept out of situations where enemy air attack was likely; nevertheless, they did quite well on those rare occasions when they did come under air attack. Only one, the USS *Porter,* was lost to air attack, and then only because of a submarine torpedo following the air attack. Others, like the *Davis,* survived after being heavily damaged.

There were those who thought the 1,850s should be used as substitutes for light cruisers (see chapter 10) because the navy could not afford as many light cruisers as it wanted during the Great Depression, and who also may have believed that economy required the 1,850s to be shortchanged with substandard materials, and as many corners as possible to be cut. There is no proof of any of this, however.

There was also a widespread belief that the 1,850s—the *Warrington* in particular—were somewhat top-heavy. Although this belief persisted to her last days, there was never any proof other than a tendency to be a slow-roller (a sign of low stability in some cases). On the contrary, she was eventually to prove the falsity of this belief. Others of the type, such as the *Somers, Selfridge, Sampson,* and *Phelps,* had fine wartime records.

The USS *Warrington* (DD 383) was built by the Federal Shipbuilding and Drydock Company of Kearny, New Jersey; launched on 15 May 1937; sponsored by Miss Catherine Taft Chubb; and commissioned on 9 February 1938 at the New York Navy Yard. Her first captain was Cdr. Leighton Wood, USN, a member of the Naval Academy Class of 1915.[3]

Members of the original crew (the "plank-owners") are unanimous in agreeing that Captain Wood was a fine officer and commander. The comments of Fireman Alfred L. Simmons are typical:

> Commander Wood was small in stature but large in life. I remember him standing on the quarterdeck when the crew came aboard for the first time, and thinking that he was a mean-looking person, and nothing could have been farther from the truth. A very gentle person, and dedicated to a "happy ship." He encouraged us to wear tailor-made whites and "Bob Evans" hats, to really look like sailors. He was a master at handling the ship; always used lots of power when docking, and would slide into the dock as easily as a whaleboat.[4]

Commissioning ceremony, February 1938. Cdr. Leighton Wood (saluting) receives the ship from Rear Adm. Clark Woodward, commandant of the 3d Naval District. Capt. Jonas H. Ingram, commandant of the Brooklyn Navy Yard, stands at right. (Courtesy of Charles W. Pickering)

Unfortunately, Captain Wood was to lose his life during World War II, aboard the cruiser USS *Montpelier*.[5]

After commissioning, the *Warrington* made a leisurely shakedown cruise to the Caribbean. In those days, shakedown cruises seem to have been rather relaxed affairs, giving the new crew time to get acquainted with one another, and to start the process of developing teamwork. Before sailing, however, the *Warrington* underwent some engineering trials; these were conducted in the cold waters of Maine, where she achieved a speed of 41.8 knots on her full-power trial.[6] The captain found it necessary to slow down on a turn, though, because she had heeled so far over that her main battery guns were unable to fire. This may have been the origin of the top-heavy rumors.

Sailing south, she first visited Guantánamo Bay, Cuba, and then sailed to Santa Lucia, Cartagena, Willemstadt, and San Juan. The process of welding the crew into an effective unit had begun. On commissioning, the crew she received were mainly strangers to each other, and were a "mixed bag" in many respects. Some were old hands, with previous long service in the Asiatic Fleet; others were "boots" (recruits) fresh out of naval training stations. Altogether, they were a fine body of men, but possessed of some rowdy tendencies. The "Asiatics" tended to be rugged individualists, with a rather low opinion of regulations, but as teachers of seamanship they were superb.[7] All hands enjoyed the ports visited—especially the boots, many of whom had never seen the ocean before. All were impressed by the excellent but cheap meals obtainable in the Caribbean area.

When the shakedown was completed, the DD 383, like her predecessor, DD 30, operated up and down the East Coast, engaging in various types of training exercises for the next few months.[8] A real break in this routine occurred in September 1938, when the *Somers* and the *Warrington* received sealed orders directing them to take aboard a full load of provisions and fuel and sail on a specified course. The story is told that the captain of the *Somers*, being slightly senior to Captain Wood, appropriated the *Warrington*'s stores and set sail about twelve hours earlier than the *Warrington*.[9] This time difference was to have serious repercussions.

When well out to sea, Captain Wood opened his sealed orders, to find that the two ships had been ordered to sail to England, where they were to load British government gold, to be transferred to Fort Knox for safekeeping, in view of the threat of war. Almost halfway across the Atlantic, however, the *Warrington*'s orders were canceled and she was directed to return to New York; Prime Minister Neville Chamberlain had made his infamous deal with Hitler, abandoning Czechoslovakia; there would be "peace in our time." The *Somers*, having passed the "point of no return," sailed on to England and picked up a load of gold,[10] but now the twelve-hour delay imposed upon the *Warrington* had its first effect. Since she had not quite reached the point of no return, she turned around and headed back the way she had come.

On her way back, the *Warrington* ran head-on into the great hurricane of 1938, which devastated New England. This was to be her first encounter with the breath of the Dragon. Fireman David Miller recalls:

> When we hit the heavy weather, our skipper, Commander Wood, reduced speed to about 6 knots and headed our bow into the wind and seas. This took care of the situation for the first half-day or so, but as the weather grew worse, so did our situation. The wind was just a few points off our port bow, and heavy seas began to crash aboard amidships on the port side. Soon the battering of the seas began to break our motor launch loose from its moorings amidships.[11]

Efforts to secure the launch were unsuccessful; the boat became expendable after some men had been swept off their feet (but not overboard).

The heavy pitching and rolling made sleep impossible (see the comments on crew fatigue in chapter 4), and the galley was only able to furnish enough food for sandwiches; but even this ended when the heavy seas prevented anyone from obtaining even bread. These seas, sweeping across the decks amidships, not only prevented men from moving from the after living compartments to the messhall, but also prevented them from reaching the firerooms to relieve the watch; and one man, on watch on the after steering station, was unable to leave his post for three days.[12] Even if the men had been able to reach the fireroom hatches, they would not have been able to open them without causing the firerooms to be flooded. The isolation of these men in the after part of the ship was a design flaw that was never corrected, as we saw earlier.

The isolated men were unable to communicate with the officers or chief petty officers, who were quartered forward; the ship had no public address system, so they might as well have been aboard an entirely different ship. Hours after their appointed time to relieve the watch, Dave Miller and another fireman, "Bunker" Hill, made an attempt to get to the steaming fireroom by coming out on top of the After Deckhouse and crawling forward via the torpedo tubes.

This effort almost led to tragedy. There was an open space between the deckhouse and number 3 torpedo mount, with a stanchion of sorts about five feet from the deckhouse. The men made a dive for the stanchion, and almost immediately Bunker's feet were swept from under him to starboard by the ferocious wind and he flapped in the wind like a pennant. On the next hard roll to port, however, he got his feet back on deck and made a lunge toward the deckhouse, where Miller grabbed him. That ended any further attempts at heroism.[13]

They remained lying on top of the deckhouse for a while, fascinated by the storm. Rumor has it that the ship hit 69° on one of her rolls at this time. I cannot vouch for the truth of this claim, but can only say that, if it were true, it proved conclusively that the ship was not top-heavy.

There is seldom any way to measure accurately the wave heights; but Miller says that when the ship was in a trough between two waves, they appeared to be higher than the foremast. At times, as the ship crested one of these watery mountains and started down the other side, the screws would come out of the water and "race." At other times the ship would pick up speed when coming down the face of one of these monsters, somewhat as a surfboard might, and would dig her bow into the bottom of the next wave so deeply that she would come back out of it stern-first, like a stick thrown into a pond.[14] In fact, one authority claims that while waves move forward in a more or less regular train, the water on their rear faces sometimes moves in the opposite direction; thus, as a ship shoots down the forward face, it suddenly rams into what amounts to a head sea as it hits the wave ahead.

Returning to their living compartment, the men lay on their bunks and hung on, as surges of water began slopping in on them from the ventilating system overhead. Efforts to shut off the ventilating system were only partially successful, and this, too, would be repeated years later. Miller says he happened to be watching the ladders leading up to the main deck when there was a loud, heavy pounding overhead, and suddenly both ladders disappeared under a solid wall of water, pouring in for what seemed like a full minute. For the first time, he began to wonder if the ship would survive.

The doorways at the tops of the ladders led into the inside of the After Deckhouse; it would appear that the deckhouse itself must have been under water. When the water stopped coming down, several men jumped to close the doorways and to dog them tight. There was about a foot of water in the compartment, soaking all the bottom bunks; pillows and mattresses were sloshing around.[15]

At some time, Captain Wood took an action that may have saved the ship. Having been halfway to Europe and back, the *Warrington* was low on fuel; and being light, she rolled more than she normally would have, and rolled more slowly, occasionally hanging on a roll through several seas. To correct this, the captain ordered the deck manhole cover removed from one of the empty oil tanks on the starboard side, thereby allowing the sea to fill the tank. The water was then fed to other empty tanks until the ship was well ballasted.

In those days, there was little or no system of storm warnings in existence. Captain Wood, therefore, had no way of knowing where this storm came from or where it was going; he could only hang on and ride it out. Records show that this storm lasted from 10 through 22 September, and maintained its hurricane strength for seven days. When it came ashore in New England, it killed six hundred people. It had sustained winds of 121 mph, with gusts to 183 mph. It moved across the ocean at speeds of up to 56 mph. The *Warrington* was in the worst part of it for about two days.[16]

When the ship finally arrived in New York, she was a sorry sight, indeed. Her boats were gone; her steel ladders were twisted and broken beyond repair. The sea had stripped the paint off her sides down to the bare metal; and her hull numbers were gone. But she was still strong and solid, and no one had been hurt or killed. Miller closes his story this way:

In the Navy Yard, the storm damage was repaired, and later, steel bulwarks were installed on the main deck, beginning at the break of the deck under the bridge and extending aft beyond the hatches to the firerooms. These bulwarks could not fend off heavy seas, but they made good "splash guards." From then on, we could come up on deck in moderate seas without getting wet. We could also relieve the fireroom watch without taking water down the hatch with us.[17]

His account brings to light three more flaws in the ship's design. First, these new bulwarks should have been included in the original plans, and should have been more strongly built. We have already seen them stripped off by the seas while Commander Quarles watched them go. Second, the men in the after crew's compartment should have had the means to entirely shut off the ventilating system. This, too, we have seen causing trouble later. And third, the broken-deck construction created an area of low freeboard at a very critical point: the access hatches to the firerooms. A succeeding generation of destroyers, the 2,100-ton *Fletcher* class, all had flush decks. However, the high bows of both classes tended to make them difficult to handle at low speeds in strong winds.

Practically everyone who goes to sea has his own definition of seaworthiness. But, since we have defined it, in part, as the ability to withstand extremes of wind and sea conditions, with a minimum of discomfort for the crew, the flaws noted above all affected the ship's seaworthiness.

In New York, repairs were made and the ship resumed her former routine of training exercises for the next few weeks. Then, in company with the *Somers,* she sailed to Miami, Florida, to celebrate Navy Day. This was a holiday that no longer exists, thanks to political wire-pulling after World War II, aimed at unifying the armed forces. It was originally celebrated on Theodore Roosevelt's birthday, 27 October, and was intended to acquaint the general public with its navy, through parades, open houses, and the like.

Unable to see into the future, the men of the *Warrington* enjoyed their Navy Day in Miami to the fullest. The two destroyer landing forces put on a small parade, ending at the fifty-yard line in the Orange Bowl stadium. The town officials had arranged a brief ceremony and a ship's dance to be held after the parade. The *Miami Herald* reported that 150 local girls had been invited for the benefit of the "poor, neglected sailors," but for unexplained reasons, 2,000 actually showed up, making it necessary to rope off the pier.

Back to the serious business of training, the *Warrington* cruised up and down the East Coast for the rest of 1938. On one occasion, while operating out of Newport, Rhode Island, with a "tame" submarine, she accidentally scraped off the sub's radio antenna when the sub decided to surface a bit early.[18] No great harm resulted, luckily, and that evening the submariners and subhunters celebrated a narrow escape arm in arm, over their beer.

At another point in this period, it was discovered that the ship's auxiliary steam lines were designed too small and had to be replaced.[19] This meant that the firerooms had to be secured while the work was going on. In order to supply steam to the galley and for the crew's comfort, the Navy Yard furnished a small, coal-burning "donkey" boiler, which was set up on the pier alongside the ship. Fireman Al Simmons and his mates enjoyed standing their watches at this boiler:

> What a place to stand a watch! We had a canvas shelter behind the fire box. A great place to cook bacon and eggs and anything else we could get from the galley. I guess we were one of the last ships that had to resort to a coal-fired boiler for steam. We had one fireman, "Slice-Bar" Powell, that had served on a coal-fired ship, and he soon had us qualified in the use of a slice-bar to break up the fire. The cruiser *Brooklyn* was moored across the dock from us and was always complaining about our smoke.[20]

Navy ships of those days were always starved for manpower; 75 percent of the authorized strength was about normal. In order to conduct a gunnery exercise, it was necessary to borrow men from the engineers to help man the guns. Most of these men served as loaders; therefore, a good deal of their off-watch time was spent on the loading machines, perfecting their techniques until the gun crews could operate as gracefully and skillfully as a ballet.

In one type of practice, known as Short Range Battle Practice (SRBP), gun crews that achieved certain high scores were authorized to paint a large white letter "E" on or near their guns; the gun-pointers were allowed to wear a special insignia on their sleeves, all gun-crew members were granted a small pay bonus, and all were allowed to sew a letter "E" on their sleeves.[21] These marks of high achievement were good for one year, then had to be earned again. All gun-crew members, including the borrowed engineers, took great pride in these awards. The engineers, however, also had their own set of awards for excellence: A large red "E," painted on one of the ship's stacks, and a red "E" sewed on a jumper sleeve. Competition among the gun crews, and among the various ships as well, was keen. In the *Warrington*'s first year of gunnery competition, she earned the "E" on three of her four five-inch mounts, and the fourth earned it the next year. It was found, however, that after the first gunnery practices, many of the wash-basins in the officers' quarters had been cracked.

The winter of 1938–39 brought a navy yard overhaul period, during which all hands were granted Christmas leave, followed by a return to the

Southern Drill Grounds—the area around Puerto Rico and the Virgin
Islands—where she conducted the usual exercises and served as a plane
guard for the USS *Yorktown*. On 19 January 1939, she joined units of the
Battle Force, as they exited from Panama Canal, enroute to Gonaives,
Haiti.[22]

At this time in our history, before World War II, the United States
Fleet was divided, like all Gaul, into three parts: (1) in the Atlantic was the
Scouting Force, consisting mostly of cruisers, destroyers, and submarines;
(2) in the Pacific lay the Battle Force, containing most of the battleships,
with more cruisers, destroyers, and submarines; and (3) in the Far East was
the Asiatic Fleet, containing one or two cruisers and about thirteen destroyers. The *Warrington* was attached to the Scouting Force. These forces
had abbreviations, and so did the subdivisions within them. For example,
the commander, Battle Force, was known generally as ComBatFor; he was
in command, also, of Destroyers, Battle Force, or DesBatFor.

Occasionally, BatFor and ScoFor ships got together in one ocean or the
other, to hold joint maneuvers. In 1939, however, BatFor maneuvers had
determined that a surprise attack on Pearl Harbor was feasible, but it was
judged to be so unlikely that not much attention was paid to it. But these
maneuvers took place after the joint maneuvers in the Atlantic.

On 28 January 1939, the *Warrington,* in company with the USS *Houston,*
left Guantánamo, bound for Norfolk, Virginia.[23] Two days later, they
encountered a severe storm but arrived in Norfolk unharmed. Here, expecting President Roosevelt to come aboard, the *Warrington* had special
ramps installed by the navy yard, in place of some ladders. On 10 February,
the two ships sailed to Key West, Florida, where they "manned the rails" in
honor of the president's arrival. He disappointed the *Warrington* men,
however, by boarding the *Houston* instead.

Ten days later, they were back in Guantánamo, where the president
went fishing for two days. Then, with brief stops at San Juan, Puerto Rico;
St. Thomas, Virgin Islands; and Avis Island, the president continued his
fishing tour. All this fishing may well have been a cover for a much more
serious purpose. He may well have been surveying the possibilities for a
new naval base; it seems unlikely that any president, even Franklin Roosevelt, would have the arrogance to commandeer a cruiser and a destroyer
just to go on a fishing trip—and a naval base was established at Roosevelt
Roads, Puerto Rico, just a few years later. Returning to Culebra via San
Juan, the ships then rejoined the fleet. On the twenty-eighth, the *Warrington* escorted the *Houston* back to Charleston, where they again manned
the rails as Roosevelt debarked.[24]

The *Warrington* and the *Houston* parted company at this point, with the *Warrington* sailing back to Norfolk, where the recent modifications were "unmodified." She next sailed to New York for an extended overhaul.

In early June, with the overhaul completed, she sailed to Fort Hancock, New Jersey, where she began preparations for receiving His Majesty, King George VI, and Her Majesty, Queen Elizabeth.[25] The testimony of those present indicates that the ship became the scene of utter pandemonium. Although she had just completed a thorough overhaul, she received the scrubbing, painting, and polishing of a lifetime. One special operation, related by Maxwell Curry, carpenters mate 1st class, involved the replacement of the toilet seat in the squadron commander's cabin, which was to be occupied by their majesties.[26] Unfortunately, the new seat had no lid, which rendered Captain Wood most unhappy. Max bore this disgrace manfully; it was somewhat eased by his being able to sell the old seat to a "collector" for $100. The American entrepreneurial spirit was alive and well.

This frantic period lasted about a week, during which the *Warrington* lay at anchor off Fort Hancock, in full view of the bright and beckoning lights of New York City, with no liberty allowed. Thus it was with a somewhat frustrated crew that the *Warrington* finally moved alongside a pier at Red Bank on 9 June. The royal party was due to arrive the following morning, so Captain Wood, out of the goodness of his heart, granted liberty that evening, but only within the boundaries of the fort. This was well meant, of course, but proved to be a minor error.

The liberty party promptly repaired to the local Enlisted Men's Club, where all went well for a while, as they sat quietly drinking their beer. In due time, however, Seaman Willie G. "Bull" Johnson (who, some years later, as a chief boatswains mate was to lead a group of men in jettisoning an anchor) felt called upon to declaim his favorite poem, "The Wreck of the Hesperus." Mounting a chair, Bull held forth in full voice, to the frantic applause of the deck force sailors. The engineers, on the other hand, being sailors only by courtesy, were sadly lacking in the finer things of life, including an appreciation of classic poetry. To the dismay of the deck force, the engineers broke out into raucous song. Polite protests got nowhere, and soon fists began to fly. The club quickly became a shambles, and before long the battered but uplifted warriors found themselves marching back to their ship under the not-too-friendly auspices of the local military police.[27]

When the king and queen arrived the next morning, they were greeted by a very formal captain and crew manning the rails in spotless dress white uniforms (a uniform no longer in existence), embellished with split lips and

U. S. S. Warrington
Commemorates the Passage of
His Royal Majesty George VI
King of England, Emperor of India
Defender of the Faith On This Vessel

June 10, 1939

Commemorative envelope

black eyes. King George appeared not to notice, but little escaped the eyes of the queen, who seemed a bit amused by the spectacle. As she turned to climb a ladder to an upper deck, where chairs had been placed for the guests, she happened to glance into a small porthole nearby, which had steel bars across the opening. Inside, she saw Fireman Dave Miller, who was scheduled to go on watch, and was wearing dungarees, with orders to stay out of sight. The porthole opened into the officers' pantry, but, apparently misled by the bars, Queen Elizabeth mistook it for the brig, and gave Dave a sympathetic, motherly smile.[28]

As she climbed the ladder, the sailors standing at attention nearby got a brief glimpse of the royal garters. Machinists Mate Mike Ward still claims his right to the title of "Knight of the Garter." Mike, an unreconstructed Irishman, did not think much of the English king, but was most favorably impressed by the Scottish queen.[29] Those crewmen who had an opportunity to observe Queen Elizabeth fairly closely are unanimous in their belief that she was indeed a lovely lady. Most of the men had no particular feelings concerning King George, but the majority held a fairly poor opinion of his entourage.

Getting under way, the ship sailed to the New York Battery with the crew still manning the rails and returning salutes from other ships all the way. The *Warrington* was flying the royal standard at the fore truck (the top of the mast)—the first United States man-of-war ever to have done so.

The royal party disembarked at the Battery and proceeded to visit the World's Fair, then in progress. Seaman Charles W. Pickering, who had been one of the sideboys who greeted the party on arrival and who saw them off, says that shortly after they left, he saw Officers Steward "Pete" Satana walking around the deck, waving a roll of toilet paper, and offering to sell it for ten cents a sheet. It had come, of course, from the squadron commander's cabin.

The visit to the World's Fair was not the real reason for the king's visit to the United States. The clouds of war were becoming darker by the day; Hitler would invade Poland in less than three months, triggering World War II, and the king had come to see what help he might expect from Franklin Roosevelt when the blow fell.

After this episode, things returned more or less to normal. The ship sailed to Rockland, Maine, to conduct her usual training exercises. This did not last long; on 1 July, she was at Colón, Canal Zone, and on the next day she transited the canal and set a course for San Diego, California. Arriving on the thirteenth, she promptly became a member of the Battle Force.[30] Enroute, she passed through an area literally covered with black and yellow striped sea snakes, and later through a school of hammerhead sharks. Swarms of sea snakes are not very uncommon in Central American waters, but they were sufficiently uncommon to the *Warrington* personnel to tempt a few courageous but a bit foolish young men to try to capture one. Luckily for them, the attempt was a failure; these snakes are not aggressive, but if provoked, their bite is said to be more venomous than a cobra's.

Two days after reaching San Diego, the ship sailed to San Francisco, where the crew had the unique experience of visiting their second World's Fair. After several days, she returned to San Diego, where she took part in routine training exercises with other destroyers and cruisers, as well as participating in the annual fleet exercises. This continued for the remainder of 1939 and into the spring of 1940.[31]

In early January 1940, the *Warrington* went into the Mare Island Navy Yard for a brief overhaul, primarily for the purpose of acquiring a new coat of experimental bottom paint. She then resumed her normal activities until April.

By this time, World War II was under way, and the so-called phony war was about to end, as the Germans unleashed their blitzkrieg through Belgium and Holland, into France. Most Navy people assumed that we would be in the war sooner or later; rumors abounded. One such rumor had it that the ship's new coat of bottom paint had been invented by the Germans and the formula for it had been stolen by American frogmen from a German ship visiting New York.

Things were about to change.

chapter thirteen

PACIFIC PARADISE, 1940–1941

On April Fool's Day 1940, the fleet departed from its West Coast ports for Fleet Exercise 21, which was to be conducted around the Hawaiian Islands, and was scheduled to last about six weeks. The navy had been closely observing the wartime experiences of the Royal Navy for several months and had quickly learned that ships should remove as many inflammable materials as possible before engaging in combat. The U.S. Fleet instituted a new program, known as "Strip Ship," which called for the removal of any wooden furniture and all old, oil-based paint from the hull, and so on.[1] The *Warrington* was one of the first to strip ship, and although she did not have the thick, heavy coats of paint the older ships had, she still had problems enough to make the crew unhappy and uncomfortable. Drill ammunition was replaced by service ammunition, but worse, the glass in the portholes was removed and replaced by welded steel plates, making it impossible to open a port to catch a passing breeze. Air-conditioning was unknown in those days, and the blower systems were inadequate in that semitropical, humid atmosphere; crews' living spaces were often intolerable.

When the fleet problem ended, with all hands expecting to return to families and friends on the West Coast, there came an unpleasant surprise: part of the fleet was to remain in Hawaiian waters indefinitely. This group of ships, consisting mainly of cruisers and destroyers, became known as the Hawaiian Detachment (HawDet for short). Rumor had it that this arrangement was the result of a compromise between President Roosevelt, who wanted the whole fleet to stay, and Adm. J. O. Richardson, the commander in chief, U.S. Fleet, who wanted none of the fleet to stay. Since that day, some writers claim that Roosevelt thought that leaving the fleet at Pearl Harbor would serve as a warning to Japan to behave herself, but Richardson thought it would only present Japan with a temptation. History tells us who was right.

HawDet duty was anything but pleasant, in spite of Hawaii's reputation as the paradise of the Pacific. The ships' operating schedules were far from inspiring; the destroyers patrolled the waters around the island of Oahu at eight knots, listening for submarines, for two weeks at a stretch, and then were allowed to return to Pearl Harbor for "rest and recreation" for two days. Rest and recreation consisted of refueling and taking on provisions, cleaning the ship, and standing captain's inspections. It might remind one of the so-called creed of the sea, as quoted by Richard W. Dana in "Two Years before the Mast": "For six days shalt thou labor, and do all that thou art able, and on the seventh, holystone the decks and scrape the cable."

Liberty hours were short; the Hawaiian Islands were not prepared for an influx of sailors for more than short periods of time, nor were the inhabitants notably hospitable toward the men. Until the rest of the fleet returned, early in 1941, there was only one fleet landing, which was perpetually crowded, to the annoyance of some senior officers, as liberty parties came and went.[2]

When the fleet returned, for the next fleet problem, a second fleet landing, of sorts, was established at a nondescript place further up the harbor, known as Aiea (I-AY-ah). There was nothing at Aiea except a large field of sugarcane and a small, Toonerville-type railroad, used for hauling the cane, plus a somewhat rickety pier. There were no facilities for the comfort of the men. Returning liberty parties had nowhere to go and nothing to do but sit on the grass and wait for their ship's boats to arrive. Liberty expired at about 5:00 or 6:00 P.M.—it still being daylight—and men began arriving at Aiea in large groups; at times, there would be as many as five hundred men sitting and lying around.

Because liberty hours were so short, and because means of amusing themselves were so limited in Honolulu, many of these men had headed for the nearest bar as soon as they got into town, and stayed there until time to return, with expectable results. They were already frustrated and angry; liquor did nothing to improve their mood, so it was not unusual for free-for-all fights to erupt without warning.

A branch of the Shore Patrol known as the Beach Guard is assigned the duty of maintaining order at fleet landings. I fell heir to this duty several times in those days (I was serving aboard another ship at the time), and I found it to be a wise precaution to take several Shore Patrol armbands with me when I took over this duty. The normal Beach Guard consisted of only

David H. Miller after cleaning a boiler, Pearl Harbor, 1940. Note wooden bench on turret, which was removed to "strip ship." (Courtesy of D. H. Miller)

two men and one officer—not enough manpower to handle five hundred angry men.

I watched as trains came in, and tried to "capture" a few men who appeared to be in reasonably good shape, to reenforce the guard. The men thus captured resented their status, for which I could not blame them, but there was no other way to exercise control. When their own boats came in, I released them.

The morale of the fleet suffered badly during this period. Matters were not improved when Adm. H. E. Kimmel (who had relieved Admiral Richardson as CinCUS) issued orders that no officers were to leave their ships without wearing a jacket, tie, and hat. Up till then, they had been allowed to leave the ship in "aloha" shirts—no hats, coats, or ties were to be seen. The order had one effect the good admiral probably did not anticipate; most of the officers did not own a hat, and few wished to buy one, but the admiral's order was obeyed: they borrowed their wives' hats, and if there were not enough to go around, each officer would solemnly salute the colors, step down onto the gangway, and hand his hat back to the next in line. It was the general consensus that Admiral Kimmel did not have enough work to keep himself busy.[3]

According to Fireman David Miller, another phenomenon appeared during this time, which he calls "declaring oneself." This consisted of an otherwise good shipmate brooding until he developed a hatred for all mankind. He would then stand on the fantail with fists clenched and invite all and sundry to come and get him. This would go on until he himself was beaten.[4]

For the *Warrington,* this debilitating routine continued for fifteen months, with only one real break in the monotony. This break, in the form of a kind of déjà vu somewhat reminiscent of the first *Warrington* (DD 30), when she was rammed by the schooner, came one dark night in the fall of 1940, when a number of ships were carrying out night maneuvers at high speed. Her sister ship, the *Somers,* rammed the *Warrington* from astern.

Night maneuvers are always hazardous, and were especially so in the days before the advent of radar. When ships were operating at high speeds and in close quarters, an exceptional degree of alertness was called for, and the ability to make instantaneous course and/or speed changes was a most valuable talent. Luck and good seamanship were also most handy to have available.

In the case of the *Warrington,* luck was conspicuously absent. Captain Wood had been detached, and his relief, Cdr. Frank G. Fahrion, had not yet reported for duty. The executive officer, Lieutenant Commander Thieme, was in the hospital, so the command devolved temporarily upon the chief engineer, Lt. C. M. Dalton. This was not to be "Captain" Dalton's finest hour, although there were many extenuating circumstances.[5]

When the fleet got under way that morning, it had been divided into two "enemy" fleets, the Red and the Blue, and as they cleared the harbor, they separated, disappearing from each other over the horizon. After dark, they returned, looking for each other. Under the operational rules, they were not allowed to fire real ammunition at each other, of course; firing was simulated by the use of flares of various colors to indicate the type of firing going on (guns, torpedoes, etc.).

The *Warrington* was in the unusual (for her) position of leading a column of destroyers at twenty-five knots, with the *Somers* as the next ship astern. Suddenly, out of the darkness, a large ship loomed up—an enemy—almost dead ahead. In accordance with fleet doctrine, Dalton seized the opportunity; he ordered a hard turn and "commenced firing" torpedoes, thereby "sinking" the enemy ship. Here luck failed him; almost immediately, another large ship appeared ahead, and the *Warrington* had no more maneuvering room. Dalton rang up "emergency astern" and avoided ramming the enemy ship, but the *Somers,* unaware of the emergency ahead, plowed into the *Warrington*'s stern, squarely between the depth charge racks.

There is no mention of Dalton having turned on his red truck light, indicating his engines were stopped or backing, which would at least have given the *Somers* a few seconds' warning that something was amiss. The ships were darkened, since they were simulating combat, but this did not mean that they could abandon normal safety precautions.

Machinists Mate Mike Ward says that the electrician's mate standing his watch on the fantail forgot he was wearing a telephone headset, and nearly hanged himself, trying to run away from the bow of the *Somers.*[6] Dave Miller and three other men, at their battle station in the magazine for the number 4 gun mount, took off like birds at the terrible crash, like a mammoth automobile wreck, which occurred within fifty feet of them. On reaching the fantail, Miller and W. J. Czinky, another fireman, found two depth charges that had broken loose and were rolling back and forth. One was damaged, with its yellow explosive contents visible. The undamaged charge rumbled across the deck and through the snaking (netting) under the lifeline into the sea. Miller and Czinky tried to corral the damaged charge, but its three hundred-pound weight was more than they could handle, and it, too, went overboard. Both charges failed to explode.[7]

Temporary repairs were made to both ships at Pearl Harbor, then they sailed for the West Coast. At Mare Island, the bow of the *Warrington* was used as a pattern for the *Somers*'s damaged bow, and the stern of the *Somers* served as the pattern for the *Warrington*'s stern. Somehow, in the shuffle, the *Warrington* ended up some six feet longer than she had been before; she proudly advertised herself as the longest destroyer in the fleet for some time thereafter.

Repairs completed, the two ships returned to HawDet. Some time later, Secretary of the Navy Charles Edison visited the fleet, where, among other operations, he witnessed a fueling at sea—a fairly new operation at that time. The CinCUS, Admiral Kimmel, ordered the *Warrington* to come alongside the *Pennsylvania,* Kimmel's flagship, to conduct the exercise. At first, all went well; the fueling connection on the *Warrington* was located just abaft the break of the deck on the starboard side. The *Pennsylvania* started pumping oil—and a couple of minutes later one of the lines holding the ships together parted, allowing the ships to yaw apart. What followed happened in only a few seconds.

The *Pennsylvania*'s fuel pump was shut down within ten or twelve seconds; the hose connection aboard the *Warrington* was spun off; the lines securing the hose aboard the *Warrington* were cast off; the hose flew into the sea as the *Warrington* men jumped clear; the *Pennsylvania* began retrieving her hose; and the stern line was cast off from the *Warrington* as she pulled away from the *Pennsylvania* as smoothly as if it had all been rehearsed.[8]

This performance so impressed Secretary Edison that he sent the *Warrington* a "Well done!" and then had himself transferred to the *Warrington* so that he could congratulate the men personally, and also see how the operation was carried out aboard the destroyer. He made a tour of the ship, including the firerooms, where Dave Miller had the honor of explaining the workings of a boiler.[9]

When the fleet returned, in the spring of 1941, HawDet was absorbed. In July, the *Warrington* and *Somers* left Pearl Harbor on what seemed to be a routine training operation; but when at sea, they were handed sealed orders, which, when opened, directed both ships to escort an aircraft carrier on a south-southeast course. Their HawDet days over, they headed for a new phase in the *Warrington*'s career.

chapter fourteen

THE NEUTRALITY PATROL, 1941

It did not take long for all
hands to figure out that the group of ships was headed for Panama, but no
one knew what that portended.

The year 1941 was a bad one for the Allies; Adolf Hitler had made his
supreme blunder when he attacked Russia while leaving an undefeated
Britain in his rear, but at this time, it did not seem to be a blunder. The
German armies appeared to be invincible. Greece was lost; the Battle of
Crete was a British naval disaster; the cruiser HMS *Orion,* a survivor of that
battle, limped into Mare Island Navy Yard, having passed through the Suez
Canal, through the Indian Ocean, around Australia, and across the Pacific
with her dead entombed in her forward parts, to find that the navy yard
workmen would not help the British sailors remove the bodies of their
shipmates for burial.[1] The Battle of the Atlantic had not yet reached its
peak but was well underway, as Britain reeled under the terrible losses to
Axis submarines.

In America, President Roosevelt persuaded Congress to pass the Neutrality Act, designed to preserve America's status as a neutral while protecting her waters from the depredations of submarines. In reality, the act
worked strongly to the advantage of the Allies, as American warships,
patrolling two hundred miles offshore, were actively searching for and
tracking Axis submarines, while informing the whole world of their whereabouts. This permitted the Royal Navy to locate the subs and either attack
them or route convoys around them, or both. And this was obviously most
provocative toward the Germans; it could not go on indefinitely without
some reaction.

The carrier (which may have been the *Wasp*) and her escorts were headed for this tense situation.[2] The *Warrington* and the *Somers* had been out of the United States for about fifteen months, except for a brief overhaul period. They did not know that their exile was to last several more months; most people assumed they were headed for home.

While enroute to Panama, the group of ships stopped one day, and lay to, while men went over the stern of the carrier in bos'n's chairs and painted out her name, substituting another. While this went on, the destroyers enjoyed swimming call in midocean, with riflemen standing guard against possible sharks. It was fairly common knowledge at that time that Japanese spies infested the Panamanian jungle along the Canal route; this was the reason for the name change, and, when the ships passed through the canal, the destroyers hung canvas curtains over their hull numbers. Boatswains Mate Lew Parrillo remembers that while he was swimming in midocean "some idiot" grabbed him around the neck, thinking he was drowning, but no one suffered any harm.[3]

At Balboa the destroyers refueled, and on the next day they proceeded through the canal with the newly rechristened carrier. On reaching the Atlantic side, the carrier went her own way, while the destroyers sailed through familiar waters to Guantánamo Bay. They lay at anchor there for a few days, while the crew applied a new coat of paint, which would become the *Warrington*'s "uniform" until the middle of 1944. The familiar light blue-gray "war color" was replaced with a coat of dark grayish blue, and the large hull numbers on the forecastle were replaced by small numbers. A shipfitter rigged a special screen around the after anchor light on the mainmast. This was to be the only light permitted at night; it shone upward on the ensign and created the effect of a disembodied ensign floating around all by itself.

No liberty was granted during this stay in Guantánamo, much to the disgust of the liberty-starved sailors, even though the only liberty port available was the dilapidated little village of Caimanera.[4] Caimanera left a lot to be desired as a liberty port but beggars cannot be choosers. The village consisted of a dirt street running up from the boat landing, with no buildings on it, intersecting at right angles with another dirt street. If one turned to the right on the second street, one would find saloons and red-light houses. A turn to the left produced only red-light houses. I cannot recall ever having seen any other buildings in Caimanera. Those described were shabby shacks.[5]

Clearly, liberty parties had only limited fields of entertainment ashore; in addition to Caimanera, they could go ashore at the Naval Station to play baseball, tennis, or to swim, but that about ended the possibilities. And to men who wanted—and needed—to get away from the close living quarters inherent in shipboard life, Caimanera seemed like heaven. They should not be judged too harshly.

As usual, a few rebels found a way. One was Dave Miller, who seems to have been mixed up in everything that went on. Although sentries had been posted to keep men from slipping ashore via one of the many bumboats that hung around the ship selling fruits and vegetables, Dave and some accomplices managed to talk the executive officer into organizing a fishing party. Using this as a cover, he and a few conspirators visited Caimanera one night. Returning to the ship in a bumboat, they were almost caught by a pistol-toting officer clad only in his cap and drawers. This keeper of the peace did catch some of the evildoers, but Dave was not among them. He hung onto one of the propeller guards until the officer's attention was diverted, then he quickly climbed aboard and disappeared down below.[6]

When the ship was commissioned, in 1938, many of her crew were boots, fresh out of training stations; now, three years later, enlistments were beginning to expire, and men were eagerly looking forward to bidding farewell to the navy.[7] They were due for a rude disappointment. When the ship left Guantánamo, instead of heading for home, she headed for Trinidad. Here she joined the Neutrality Patrol, which, in this part of the Atlantic, consisted of two old "Model T" light cruisers, the USS *Memphis* and the USS *Cincinnati,* plus the destroyer USS *Davis,* an 1,850-tonner, but not a *Warrington* sister-ship.[8]

This group operated in pairs, with a cruiser and a destroyer patrolling together across the narrow waist of the Atlantic between Africa and South America. The 1,850-ton destroyers were ideal for this kind of work, since they carried enough fuel to enable them to make the round trip without difficulty; moreover, since these ships were woefully weak in antiaircraft defense, and in this part of the world, attack by aircraft was unlikely, they were able to concentrate their attention on their antisubmarine function. The accompanying cruiser would theoretically take care of any enemy raiders that might appear. The mission of these patrols was to intercept any Axis submarine attempting to pass up or down the Atlantic between the continents and to report all such contacts; later, some intermittent escort operations were added.[9]

Naturally, this made the "short-timers" exceedingly unhappy, but others enjoyed the much-improved liberty in Brazil. Lew Parrillo, for one, felt that this was really good duty, especially for young, healthy males with voracious appetites. Says Lew, "It was the cheapest liberty I ever had in the Navy. Our dollar exchange was real good. We could get a steak and eggs for

Shore Patrol, São Paulo, Brazil, 1941. From left: W. I. Alley, TC1c; R. J. Moore, TC1c; P. K. Reeder, WT2c. (Courtesy of Charles W. Pickering)

Liberty in São Paulo, Brazil, 1941. From left: C. F. Webb, S1c; J. H. Purdy, S2c; R. B. Mount, S1c; W. D. Hunter, S2c. (Courtesy of Charles W. Pickering)

15 cents, and that was really living."[10] On the other hand, the residents of Recife, Brazil, did not appear to be equally enthralled by their Yankee guests. Dave Miller, by now a watertender 2d class, and another man were threatened by a mob of Brazilians while on shore patrol, and were only rescued by the timely appearance of the shore patrol officer bringing reenforcements.[11]

The cheap liberties carried with them another blessing; when the *Warrington* left HawDet under a cloud of secrecy, her pay accounts had been left behind; no one could draw pay until the accounts caught up with the ship. In those days, and for some time thereafter, the mails were very slow and unreliable.

Two days after joining the Neutrality Patrol, the *Warrington* departed from Trinidad on her first patrol in company with one of the old cruisers. The men began standing wartime Condition watches, arranged to cover varying situations of possible danger. Condition I was General Quarters— all hands at their battle stations. Condition II had half the crew at battle stations at all times; this meant that the crew was standing "watch-and-watch"—that is, four hours on, four hours off—around the clock. No better way has been found to wear out a crew quickly. Theoretically, this Condition was to be used when combat was likely but was not imminent. Condition III had one-third of the crew on watch at all times, a four-hours-on, eight-hours-off routine, which could be tiring, but was far preferable to Condition II. One British naval officer once remarked to me that, if he were fighting the U.S. Navy, he would just sit back and let us wear ourselves out. There were some Yanks who agreed with this view.

In the case of the *Warrington,* the Condition watches lasted for two weeks, and then were followed by normal watches in port for two days, similar to the old HawDet routine. But in addition to the Condition II or III watches, Condition I was set every morning an hour before dawn, and lasted until an hour after dawn. Consequently, sleep became a thing ardently sought after whenever the opportunity arose.

Crew morale began to drop again, after its momentary lift on passing through the Panama Canal. In addition to the long-standing problems resulting from many months away from home, they now found the mails, as I have noted, to be slow and irregular. Strange behavior again became more or less common, but oddly enough, very few men mention it.[12]

Between August and November 1941, the *Warrington* made seven patrols. On 11 September, President Roosevelt issued his famous "shoot on sight" order, directing all naval vessels to attack any German or Italian "pirates" found in the territorial waters of the United States. Six weeks later came the long-delayed German response; a German U-boat torpedoed and sank the USS *Reuben James,* an old four-stack destroyer. This event was followed by congressional authorization to arm merchant vessels.

On 26 October, just a few days before the loss of the *Reuben James,* the *Warrington,* in the course of one of her patrols, came across the after section of a merchant ship, drifting and apparently abandoned. After checking carefully to see if any living people were aboard, the *Warrington* sank the derelict by gunfire, as a hazard to navigation. The next morning, she acquired a sonar contact and attacked it with depth charges. The accompanying cruiser launched an airplane, which made a bombing run on the point of contact. The pilot then delivered a message to the *Warrington* in the form of a note that was handed to the captain unopened. He never divulged its contents, but the crew was convinced for years afterward that the *Warrington* had sunk a U-boat but could not claim a "kill" because the United States was not then at war.[13] I have been unable, however, to find anything in German, British, or American records indicating that a submarine was lost in or near that location at about that time. After refueling at Recife, she was ordered to sail to Charleston, South Carolina, for overhaul, to the unbounded delight of all hands. The long drought appeared to be over. She was due to receive an extended overhaul, and her "over-timers" were due to get their discharges at last. However, for reasons that have never been explained, these men did not receive their discharges immediately, but had to wait until a fateful date—6 December 1941.[14] Naturally, they lost no time in heading for home, only to find themselves back in uniform a few days later.

By 7 December, the ship was about one-third the way through her overhaul, but there was still much to be done. Most of the normal liberty party had left the ship about noon on Saturday, the sixth, and when they returned on Monday morning, they found she was completely ready for sea, except for some minor details. She went to sea that day, carrying some navy yard workmen completing their jobs.[15] She then carried out coastal patrols until late in December.

During this patrol period, she was called upon to escort the new British battleship, HMS *Duke of York,* to Norfolk, and encountered a severe storm enroute. Mike Ward says, "Here we received a citation from Winston Churchill, congratulating us on being a super ship, and the captain of the *Duke of York* came over and inspected us for any damages on our ship from the terrible storm we had been in."[16] Shortly thereafter, the *Warrington* again sailed for the Panama Canal.

Dave Miller tells an anecdote regarding one of his shipmates, Officers Steward "Pete" Satana, which took place shortly before the last patrol:

Pete came to me with a puzzle concerning his father, back home in the Philippines. In a letter, his father wrote that some "strange bandits" were stealing his chickens and produce, and he asked Pete to send him a rifle and some ammunition so he could protect his farm, which was on the Island of Luzon, many miles north of Manila. Because Pete knew that I had done some hunting, he asked me what kind of rifle he should send.

I tried to learn more about the situation, but Pete himself was puzzled, and between Pete's limited English and his father's somewhat limited writing ability, all I knew for sure was that these "bandits" were something that had never been seen there before and they were stealing his father's crops and chickens . . . these were Japanese soldiers who had been secretly landed in large numbers, where they lay in wait for the surprise attack on December 7th.

Not realizing this, and fearful of getting Pete's father into serious trouble, I compromised, and instead of recommending a rifle, I told Peter to send his father a double-barrelled 12-gauge shotgun. . . . I never found out if they got there in time.[17]

In the days following the Pearl Harbor attack, many rapid changes occurred. The chief of naval operations, Adm. Harold R. Stark, was relieved by Adm. Ernest J. King, who, when assuming the additional title of commander-in-chief, U.S. Fleet, was said to comment, "When they get in trouble, they send for the sons of bitches." He knew whereof he spoke. He changed the abbreviated title of CinCUS to ComInCh, and then proceeded to reorganize the U.S. Fleet. Gone were the Battle Force and the Scouting Force, and in their places were the Pacific and Atlantic Fleets, each of which was subdivided into numbered fleets, with the odd numbers in the Pacific and the even in the Atlantic. The numbered fleets were further subdivided into forces, more or less on a geographical basis. Thus, Admiral Nimitz relieved Admiral Kimmel and became CinC, Pacific Fleet, or CinCPac, with Admiral Halsey in command of the South Pacific Force. This later became known as the Third Fleet.

In May 1941, Admiral Kimmel had sent Cruiser Division 3 (USS *Concord, Raleigh,* and *Cincinnati*) to Panama, under the command of Rear Adm. John F. Shafroth. The *Cincinnati* went through the canal, to become part of the Neutrality Patrol, but the other two ships remained in the Pacific, where they became the nucleus of the Southeast Pacific Force (SEPacFor), guarding the Pacific approaches to the canal.[18] Their mission was later expanded to include patrolling the west coast of South America, on the lookout for Axis raiders, and then the protection of convoys destined for Guadalcanal.

Shortly after we entered the war, the United States began establishing advanced bases at strategic points across the Pacific. One of these, code-named "Bobcat," was at Bora Bora, in the French Society Islands, on the route from Panama to both Australia and Guadalcanal.[19]

When the *Warrington* transited the canal in early January 1942, she joined the SEPacFor, along with the USS *Sampson,* a sister-ship. Her duties included escorting convoys to Bora Bora, where she would be relieved by other escorts for onward routing; she would then take over the escorting of convoys headed back to Panama.

In between these operations she and the other ships of SEPacFor visited various South American ports, such as Callao and Lima, Peru, or Guaya-quil, Ecuador. She even got as far south as Chile and Easter Island. On one occasion, she escorted the new battleship, USS *Washington,* to Brisbane, Australia, and, in late November, escorted the damaged USS *South Dakota* from Bora Bora to Panama. The *Washington* was on her way to one of the war's decisive battles: the Naval Battle of Guadalcanal. The *South Dakota* was returning from the same battle.

The Southeast Pacific Force became the "home away from home" of both the *Warrington* and the *Sampson* for the next sixteen months. In addition to the operations mentioned, they served as target and training ships for submarines and army bombers enroute to the war zones.[20]

In October 1942, the *Warrington* received what was to become her last major overhaul, and even this one was curtailed, lasting about six weeks. The principal purpose of this overhaul was to modernize, to some extent, the ship's weak antiaircraft capabilities. Repair work was done, of course, but was of secondary importance.

The infamous 1.1 inch pom-pom was replaced by a quadruple 40 mm Bofors short-range mount forward of the bridge, and another was mounted aft, in place of the number 3 five-inch mount. She now had a total of six five-inch guns remaining. One torpedo mount was removed and replaced by a 20 mm Oerlikon AA gun atop the midship deckhouse, just abaft the bridge structure. The after searchlight tower and the crow's nest were removed; surface and air-search radars were installed, and four K-guns were installed on the main deck.[21]

In the course of making these alterations to the ship, the navy yard workmen at Balboa removed the cover to the exhaust ventilation system for the forward emergency diesel generator room and failed to replace it, possibly through an oversight.[22] This omission, as we have seen, had serious consequences later.

This overhaul period might have been a good time to correct one of the *Warrington*'s original design flaws—the lack of a public address system—

but apparently no one considered this more than a minor inconvenience at that time.

In view of the tragedy two years later, these abbreviated overhauls deserve a good deal of emphasis. A normal peacetime destroyer overhaul lasted about ninety days. The ship's previous overhaul, in November 1941, had been interrupted by the outbreak of war at about thirty days; now the Balboa overhaul lasted only about forty-two days. The *Warrington* had not had a full overhaul since 1939—and she would never get one.

Her last voyage as a member of SEPacFor began in May 1943. Upon her arrival at Bora Bora on 4 June, she received orders to report for duty to CinCPac. Previously, her captains had been changed three times, as Commander Fahrion was relieved by Commander Fitz, who was relieved, in turn, by Commander Demarest.

CinCPac ordered the ship to further report to the commander, South Pacific Force (Admiral Halsey), whose headquarters were located in Noumea, on the French Island of New Caledonia. After reaching Noumea, she sailed to Guadalcanal, where I boarded her, as related in chapter 1.

EPILOGUE

It only remains to tell what
little is known of the three main figures in this tragedy.

Commander Quarles did the best he could to save his ship, and should
not be judged too harshly for his mistakes. Anyone can be a "Monday-
morning quarterback," but the man on the spot has no time to conduct
deep studies of various possible courses of action. After the courts-martial,
he served as executive officer of the cruiser USS *Canberra,* then served tours
in the Bureau of Ordnance, in Paris, France, and finally as commanding
officer, Naval Ammunition Depot, Fallbrook, California. He retired in
1952 and worked for an insurance company for the next twenty-two years.
He died in 1989.[1]

Lt. Wesley U. Williams was promoted to lieutenant commander, but
returned to civilian life after the war to work as a hospital administrator in
Olympia, Washington, until his death in 1991. He rejected my attempts to
get him to "integrate" into the regular navy, on the grounds that he felt that
the court-martial on his record would ruin his career, even though he had
been acquitted. At the time, he was not aware that the court-martial had
had no effect on Commander Wheyland's career.

I have little information on Commander Wheyland. He did make
captain and apparently left the service some time after the war. He died in
1988.

There have been a few inquiries as to the possible location of the final
resting place of the *Warrington.* The last reported position, calculated
roughly by Ens. John R. Dicken, was latitude 28°-26′N., longitude
73°-53′W. This was figured without the use of instruments, at about 1:50

A.M., after the ship had lost all power and was drifting in a westerly direction. Quarles later estimated the rate of drift at about two to two and a half knots,[2] which would indicate that she drifted some twenty to twenty-five miles from the estimated position. However, the storm was recurring during the twelve hours the ship was drifting, pushing her more and more to the north as time passed. The men in the water would not have been aware of this change in the direction of drift. The best estimate available, therefore, is that the ship lies somewhere within a twenty-five-mile radius of the reported position, and may now be lying on the slope of an area known as Blake Basin, some four hundred miles east of Vero Beach, Florida, at a depth of about fourteen thousand feet—two thousand feet deeper than the *Titanic*.[3]

The Dragon had done its worst. If the men it killed have left us worthwhile lessons, perhaps their deaths were not in vain.

a p p e n d i x   a

METEOROLOGICAL NOTES ON THE GREAT ATLANTIC HURRICANE OF SEPTEMBER 1944

Prepared by Richard J. Reynolds

The 247 officers and men of the USS *Warrington* who died at sea during the September 1944 hurricane comprised the majority of a total of 390 military and civilian lives lost on land and sea. In addition to the *Warrington*, four other vessels were sunk and ninety-six other navy and coast guard personnel were listed as dead or missing according to the report from the Fifth Naval District. The Coast Guard cutters *Jackson* and *Bedloe* capsized and sank while protecting a liberty ship that had been torpedoed off the North Carolina coast; the minesweeper *YMS-409* was lost at sea; and the lightship *Vineyard Sound* dragged her anchors and sank about a mile northeast of her station. These stories are told in chapter 5.

In terms of lives lost and property damage to the East Coast, the Great Atlantic Hurricane of 1944 was second only to the hurricane of 1938, which the *Warrington* also encountered (see chapter 12). The latter killed 494 people in New York and New England and caused an estimated $350 million in damages. While equal to or greater in strength than the 1938 hurricane at sea, the September 1944 hurricane took only 46 lives on land (344 at sea) and caused an estimated $100 million in property damage.

SIZE

In meteorological aspects, the September 1944 storm (or Great Atlantic Hurricane, as it was termed by the U.S. Weather Bureau) was one of the largest and most powerful storms to traverse the East Coast. It was also one of the first hurricanes to be flown into and tracked by the then newly formed Army Air Corps Hurricane Weather Reconnaissance Squadron. In terms of size, it was perhaps one of the largest Atlantic hurricanes ever recorded. The average-sized Atlantic hurricane generates hurricane-force winds over a diameter of about 100 miles, with gales extending across a diameter of 350 to 400 miles. The Great Atlantic Hurricane, at its peak on or about 12 September, "possessed hurricane winds over an estimated width of 200 miles, with gales covering a diameter of 600 miles."[1] In terms of size, central pressure, and wind speeds, the September 1944 hurricane, at its peak on 12–13 September, would almost certainly fall into Category 4 on the Saffir-Simpson Scale, which means it would have had sustained winds in excess of 131 miles per hour.

BAROMETRIC PRESSURE

Minimum central pressure is one of the key parameters used to gauge a hurricane's strength, and changes in central pressure indicate the storm's rate of intensification or decay. Most of the barometric data for the September 1944 hurricane were estimated or measured at shore points, as the hurricane recurved and sped northward along the East Coast from the fourteenth through the fifteenth. When the hurricane reached Cape Hatteras on the fourteenth, its central pressure, estimated from the pressure profile as it sped by the coast, was 27.88" (944.1 millibars); its radius of maximum winds (which is slightly larger than the eye) was nineteen miles; and its forward speed was twenty-four miles per hour. [The reader will recall that Captain Quarles was trying to keep ahead of it the night before with a speed of fifteen knots (thirteen miles per hour).] A day later, when the storm was becoming extratropical and was decaying, it struck Point Judith, Rhode Island, with a forward speed of thirty-four miles per hour, and still had a relatively low central pressure (measured by land barometer) of 28.31" (958.7 mb). At this time its radius of maximum winds had grown to thirty-six miles, indicating further decay. The lowest measured pressure for this storm (not a central pressure) was 27.97" (947.18 mb), measured at Cape Hatteras as the storm skirted the coast on the fourteenth. A synoptic surface map of the storm when it was off Cape Henry, Virginia, estimated the central pressure at that time to be 27.75" (940 mb).[2] These low pressures have only been matched or exceeded by a small number of Atlantic hurricanes: the 1938 New England hurricane (central pressure 27.75" at Hartford, Connecticut); Hurricane Hazel in October 1954 (27.66" at Tilgham Point, North Carolina); Hurricane Donna on 10 September 1960 (27.55" at Conch Key, Florida); Hurricane Hugo, 15 September 1989, (27.10", measured by aircraft at sea); and most recently, in August 1992, by Hurricane Andrew (minimum pressure 27.34" at landfall, Turkey Point, Florida).

When comparing the minimum pressures of these storms, it must be remembered that, in most cases, these pressures are measured at shore points, usually when the hurricanes had recurved and begun their northward march up the East Coast into colder Atlantic waters. When the *Warrington* and *Hyades* encountered the Great Atlantic Hurricane, they were well into tropical waters, some four hundred miles east of Vero Beach, Florida. Between 12 and 13 September, the hurricane was almost certainly intensifying or had reached its peak strength. Estimates of the storm's central pressure as it recurved north of the Bahama Islands, from 12 midnight to 12 noon on the thirteenth, were less than 27.00″ and "very probably 26.85 in."[3] Thus, the *Warrington*'s fate appears to have been sealed by its encounter with this hurricane of extraordinary strength, at or very near its peak intensity, and, as the course plot shows (see page 37) in the most powerful part of the storm—its northeast quadrant.

WINDSPEED AND EYE DIAMETER

On the evening of 12 September 1944, an Army Air Corps reconnaissance aircraft located the hurricane near latitude 27° North and longitude 74° West, and penetrated the storm. The weather officer aboard the aircraft estimated the sustained wind at about 140 miles per hour, and reported such extreme turbulence that with both the pilot and copilot at the controls, the aircraft could barely be kept under control. On several occasions during the flight, the crew feared that the plane would be torn apart. Upon returning to base, it was discovered that 150 rivets had been sheared off one wing alone.[4] The crew did not report penetrating the eye; however, based on the estimated wind speed, they were probably very close to the eye wall, in the area of maximum winds. The radius of maximum winds for a hurricane is an indicator of both its relative strength and the radius of its eye. Atlantic hurricanes are generally strongest in the lower latitudes where they are over warmer tropical waters, and grow weaker as they recurve and move northward over colder northern waters. As this happens, the eye, and thus the radius of maximum winds, increases, with a concurrent rise in the central pressure and a decrease in maximum wind speed. Meteorological data for the Great Atlantic Hurricane of 12 and 13 September is sparse, but what data there are suggests that the hurricane was at or near its peak intensity at this time. The radius of maximum winds was observed to be nineteen miles on the fourteenth, when the storm passed Cape Hatteras. Since the radius of maximum winds is, on the average, six to seven miles beyond the eye wall,[5] we can estimate the radius of the eye as being thirteen to fourteen miles on the fourteenth, resulting in an eye diameter of no more than twenty-eight miles, and a diameter of maximum winds of about forty miles. Since the storm had somewhat weakened by the four-teenth (central pressure of 27.88" vs. an estimate of 26.85" on the twelfth), we can estimate from statistical relationships between central pressure and radius of maximum winds[6] that the radius of maximum winds was probably on the order of fourteen miles on the twelfth. This would make the estimate of the eye diameter at no smaller than sixteen miles. This very small eye diameter is indicative of a well-developed and very powerful hurricane.

When the eye passed to the south and west of the *Warrington*'s reported position at about 0100 on 13 September, its center was only about forty-six miles southwest of the *Warrington* (see plot of hurricane's path, page 52). Since the eye radius was only about eight miles at this time, this means that the ship was only about thirty-eight miles from the eye wall, and only thirty-one miles from the radius of maximum winds, which were estimated at 140 miles per hour. Bear in mind, however, that at this time the Great Atlantic Hurricane had hurricane-force winds (over 74 mph) extending outward one hundred miles from the eye, with gales extending outward to almost two hundred miles from the eye. Since the eye passed so close to the *Warrington* in the early hours of the thirteenth, the ship and crew were probably experiencing sustained winds in excess of 100 miles per hour, and probably closer to 120 miles per hour. Moreover, the *Warrington*'s unfortunate location in the storm's northeast quadrant put her in the most powerful sector of the hurricane, due to its forward motion (13 miles per hour, added to wind speed, at this time), and mountainous seas and swells.

After its encounter with the *Warrington,* the hurricane continued to recurve to the north and began to accelerate. The hurricane moved almost due north at 25–30 miles per hour and passed over Cape Hatteras at about 8:20 A.M. (EST) on the fourteenth, with winds clocked at 90 miles per hour and a central pressure of 27.97".[7] It then turned slightly northeast-ward, moving up the eastern seaboard, with its forward speed accelerating to 40 miles per hour. At Cape Henry, winds were clocked at 85 miles per hour, with gusts to 134 miles per hour. The storm crossed Long Island, New York, at about 9 P.M. on the fourteenth, then moved ashore at Point Judith, Rhode Island, crossing Rhode Island and Massachusetts before emerging into Massachusetts Bay near midnight on the fourteenth. At this point, the storm had lost enough energy to be downgraded to a tropical storm [although witnesses say one would never have known it had been downgraded—RAD]. Once it passed the Maine coast and reached New Brunswick, it had become an extratropical low.

SEAS

It is extremely difficult to estimate sea heights from the deck of a ship in a full-blown hurricane. Rain and wave spray are driven horizontally; sea and sky are often indistinguishable, and under extreme wind conditions, the sea is actually flattened. Suffice it to say that, given the maximum velocity of the winds as 140 miles per hour, the size of the hurricane-strength wind field (about one hundred miles from the eye) and the radius of the gale-force winds (about two hundred miles), that the swells produced by this storm were undoubtedly monstrous. A published account of the observations of three weather bureau meteorologists who flew into the hurricane as it passed Cape Henry[8] can shed some light on sea state. As they penetrated the hurricane in their aircraft at an altitude of three thousand feet, they were below the cloud deck and could clearly see Chesapeake Bay. Colonel Wood writes:

> The waves in Chesapeake Bay were enormous. A freighter plowing through the Bay was being swept from bow to stern by huge waves which at times appeared to engulf the whole vessel at once. Spray was being thrown into the air at heights which appeared to reach 200 feet above the surface of the sea. From the appearance of the water, both within Chesapeake Bay and east of Cape Henry, it is not surprising that a Navy destroyer of the 1,850-ton class was sunk by the storm.[9]

Some of the largest ocean waves are generated by hurricanes. In a typical Atlantic hurricane (Category 2 or 3), open ocean waves of thirty-five to forty feet are common, and in extreme hurricanes (Category 4 or 5), wave heights may exceed forty-five feet (table 1). Moreover, since waves are additive when in phase, the crossing of two waves can produce peaks of fifty to fifty-five feet.[10] In a hurricane, the highest waves are produced just to the right of the eye wall, when viewed in the direction of travel. This is the result of two factors: (1) the strongest hurricane winds occur in this region, and (2) the winds act on the sea surface for the greatest length of time when they are moving in the same direction as the storm's track.[11] Therefore, the highest waves would be located in the northeastern quadrant of an Atlantic hurricane moving in a northerly direction. In addition, the speed of ocean waves set up by the one hundred-plus mph winds may range from thirty to fifty miles per hour, which means that these waves soon outrun the relatively slow-moving hurricane that generated them (the average forward speed of a hurricane is twelve to thirteen miles per hour). These hurricane swells produced by the right side

Table 1.
STATE OF THE SEA

Code number	Description	Height (feet)
0	Calm (glassy)	0
1	Calm (small ripples)	0–4 inches
2	Smooth (wavelets; no whitecaps)	4–18 inches
3	Slight wavelets (few whitecaps)	1.5–3.25
4	Moderate	3.25–7.5
5	Rough	7.5–12
6	Very Rough	12–18
7	High	18–27
8	Very High	27–42
9	Phenomenal	Over 42

of a hurricane may travel several hundred, and possibly one to two thousand miles ahead of the slow-moving hurricane.[12]

Thus, it is apparent that the *Warrington* and the *Hyades* may have encountered hurricane swells from the southeast as early as the morning of 11 September, when the hurricane was located some eight hundred miles to the southeast. Because the course of the hurricane was becoming more northerly as it approached the U.S. mainland, the *Warrington*'s position relative to the eye, along with her southerly course, resulted in the ship's

Table 2.
WIND FORCE

Force	Description	Range (knots)	Sea state
0	Calm	Less than 1	0
1	Light airs	1–3	0
2	Light breeze	4–6	1
3	Gentle breeze	7–10	2–3
4	Moderate breeze	11–16	3–4
5	Fresh breeze	17–21	4–5
6	Strong breeze	22–27	5–6
7	Moderate gale	28–33	6–7
8	Fresh gale	34–40	7–8
9	Strong gale	41–47	8
10	Whole gale	48–55	9
11	Storm	56–63	9
12	Hurricane	Over 65	9

being exposed to continually increasing winds and waves from the morning of the eleventh through the morning of the thirteenth, at which point the eye passed to the west of the *Warrington*'s last estimated position (see chart 1, page 37) (see also table 2). Neglecting other factors that can influence wave heights, a rough estimate of hurricane wave heights can be obtained from average wind speed. Dunn and Miller (1964) give a formula (developed by Cline, 1926) that estimates maximum wave height by dividing average wind speed (in mph) by 2.05. If we assume that the September 1944 hurricane attained Category 4 status during the early morning hours of the twelfth, with a maximum average wind speed of 140 mph, then it is conceivable that for their last twenty-four hours afloat, the *Warrington* and her crew experienced waves approaching seventy feet in height.

SINKING OF THE USS
WARRINGTON (DD 383)

A Review of the Testimony by David H. Miller, Watertender First Class

PREFACE

Those who survived that terrible night of 12 and 13 September 1944, and the horrible days and nights that followed in the sea have the memories of their own experiences seared in their minds. But for many of them their actual knowledge is limited by their positions on the ship. For example, the gunner's mate who rode high and dry the entire night in number three gun turret, looking out through the gun sighting ports from time to time to watch the green seas pounding across the fantail deck. Others in the after deckhouse watched green seas go over the torpedo tubes by at least six feet. The torpedo tubes were themselves twelve feet above the deck.

Those on the bridge next morning looked aft and saw what Captain Quarles described as men clinging and crawling around the superstructure like squirrels crawling on tree limbs as the ship heeled over farther and farther and settled deeper and deeper into the water below them. The rest of the events were related to them by their shipmates. It is like the parable of the three blind men who examined the elephant with their hands. One felt the tail, one felt the trunk, and the third felt the side of the beast. Their descriptions of the animal matched what they felt.

By carefully digesting and comparing over 1,000 pages of testimony covering thirty-eight days of the Inquiry, one cannot only get a clear overall picture of the tragedy, but also one can feel confident about understanding what happened—and what should *not* have happened. My perspective is enhanced by the three years and ten months that I spent aboard the *Warrington,* from the date of her commissioning on 9 February 1938, to 6

December 1941, when Vice Admiral Chuichi Nagumo's 33-ship task force was 19 hours from Pearl Harbor.

During that time I stood my watches in the after fireroom, my general quarters station for the most part was in number four magazine, and on one bored afternoon in port, I climbed the stack and looked down to see the four partitioned sections in the bottom where the fateful boiler uptakes vented their combustion gasses and smoke. I also crawled through her bilges and into her boiler steam drums, mud drums, and fire boxes, but not by choice.

While writing this review, from time to time I've looked out of my fifth-floor office window to the street below and recalled the 100-foot plus waves of the *Warrington*'s 1938 hurricane, that would have covered my office window, and I feel an empathy for all who were aboard her that terrible night.

Citations from the transcript of the proceedings before the Court of Inquiry in October and November 1944 are provided herein for significant points under discussion. For other factual statements, citations can be given from the record, if necessary. Citations from the oral testimony presented before the Court are identified as follows: C.I. Testimony 100 = Notes of testimony, page 100; C.I. Findings No. 23; 1300 = Finding of Fact number 23, page 1300; Action Report 30 = Captain's Action Report to the Secretary of the Navy, page 30.

Relative comments concerning events outside the testimony before the Court or the Action Report are in paragraphs or sentences enclosed in parentheses.

As in many disasters, several unexpected or unusual factors or events came together in an almost unbelievable coincidence of time to produce the tragic end of the American destroyer *Warrington* (DD 383), and two hundred forty-seven of the three hundred fifteen officers and men aboard her. Remove almost any one of these factors, and the tragedy would not have occurred.

Moreover, a review of the testimony of the witnesses who testified before the Court of Inquiry discloses that in this instance there were actually two tragedies. One, of course, was the sinking of the *Warrington*. The other was the heavy loss of life. Neither should have happened.

There was a failure of communication between the captains of the two ships in the Unit, Commander Morgan C. Wheyland, USNR, of the USS *Hyades,* and Commander Samuel F. Quarles, USN, of the USS *Warrington.* At 10:42 A.M. on 13 September, when the wrecked *Warrington* was dead in the water and within three hours of sinking, Captain Wheyland was specifically ordered by ComServLant: "REPORT IMMEDIATELY PRESENT CONDITION OF YOUR UNIT AND WEATHER." Wheyland replied by radio: "CONDITION OF UNIT GOOD WEATHER HEAVY BUT ABATING PROCEEDING AT REDUCED SPEED," even though he had not seen or heard from the *Warrington* since 6:10 P.M. the evening of the 12th, when the *Warrington* notified him by visual signals that she was compelled to heave to and change course because of the heavy seas and high winds.[1] The *Hyades* had also lost radar contact with the *Warrington* at 9:00 P.M. the evening of the 12th.[2]

Then, when he had not heard from the *Warrington* for a period of 26 hours, Commander Wheyland did not attempt to communicate with her to determine her condition or whereabouts until ordered to do so by another radio dispatch from CinCLant.[3] When he was finally ordered by CinCLant to proceed immediately to the *Warrington*'s assistance, he did not come about and begin the search for an additional 3 hours and 34 minutes.[4] When asked directly by CinCLant whether he was in company with the *Warrington,* Wheyland delayed another 4 hours and 15 minutes before replying that he was not, and this was the first time that he notified any authority that the ships were separated.[5]

When he discovered that she had sunk, by the *Hyades*'s collision with a *Warrington* life raft with survivors aboard at 4:50 A.M. on 15 September, Wheyland did not notify anyone else of the fact nor of the plight of her survivors for another 2 hours and 17 minutes. The Court found that these factors increased the loss of life.[6] [But in this connection, see chapter 8— RAD]

For Captain Quarles's part, he delayed before asking the *Hyades* for help. Although the *Warrington* had lost power on both engines at 11:00 P.M. on the 12th, and was dead in the water for about one-half hour, taking green seas over both sides, Quarles did not give orders to radio the *Hyades* to ask her to return to him and to tell her that the *Warrington* was "in trouble" until midnight.[7] Then, after giving the order to contact the *Hyades,* he did not make it a point to verify that this critical communication had been made. In fact, he only learned by accident two-and-a-half hours later that there had been no verification that contact had been made with the *Hyades.*[8] "To my horror, at this time (2:33 A.M. on the 13th) it was reported to me that either no message had been gotten off to the *Hyades,* or, if it had, she had not receipted for it."[9] By this time, the *Warrington* was permanently dead in the water, beginning to flood, and her situation was desperate.

And after the two ships parted company by mutual consent, at 6:10 P.M. on the 12th, neither captain thereafter communicated his course and speed changes to the other.[10]

Why the failure of this basic element of cooperation between these two ship captains? The record does not disclose how or why Commander Wheyland was designated to be in charge of the Unit (the voyage of two ships in company), but an examination of the background facts may shed some light on the question.

Both captains were graduates of the Naval Academy, but while Commander Quarles remained on active duty in the Navy since the day he graduated, on 2 June 1932, Commander Wheyland served only seven years on active duty—four years in the Regular Navy, and three in the Naval Reserve, hence his rank was USNR. That distinction was a subtle but significant factor throughout World War II. To some in the Regular Navy, Reservists were "feather merchants."

Aside from his shakedown cruise on the *Hyades,* this was Wheyland's maiden voyage as captain of a ship. He was more than ten years older than Quarles, and his ship was much larger than Quarles's ship. The *Warrington,* although a man-of-war, was "only an escort" in this Unit.

Thus there were several factors that could have made the relationship between the two ship captains awkward. Whatever the actual psychological situation may have been, it appears obvious that neither captain was anxious to communicate with the other. Actually, Quarles testified that he would have attempted to run before the storm earlier if he had not been in company with the *Hyades.*[11]

And so, on Sunday afternoon, 10 September 1944, ComServLant sent this Unit, consisting of a brand-new supply ship and a six-year-old destroyer badly in need of a general Navy Yard overhaul, carrying a staff of officers with newly assigned duties, and a substantial draft of new recruits, practically none of whom had ever been to sea, out of Hampton Roads, Virginia, on a non-urgent voyage toward the path of a known hurricane. And both ships were under the command of new skippers.

The proximate cause of the first tragedy, the sinking of the *Warrington,* was the 180-degree turn to the leeward, putting her stern into the teeth of the hurricane, and placing her vulnerable, low, midships engineering spaces at the mercy of the huge seas. This decision was made, of course, by Captain Quarles. There were several other contributing factors to this first tragedy, however, and they must be given proper weight.

DESIGN FLAWS IN THE HULL

1. LOW FREEBOARD AMIDSHIPS.

Perhaps it could be said that the seeds of this disaster were sown in the Great Depression. During those bleak times, Congressional pork-barrelling undoubtedly contributed to the sporadic distribution of orders for naval shipbuilding for economic reasons rather than for the common-sense efficiency of selecting the best design before embarking upon construction. As a result, during the Thirties at least a half-dozen different designs were used to build destroyers, all but thirteen of which were 1,500-tonners. All, however, were "broken-deckers." [The discussions held by the General Board, partly described in chapter 10, tend to refute the idea that design differences were the result of congressional pork-barrelling. These designs seem to have been carefully thought out by senior naval officers, on the basis of what might be called the advanced thinking of the times. —RAD]

There were five broken-deck, 1,850-ton, squadron leader destroyers of the *Somers* class, of which the *Warrington* was one, built in the 1930s. The major flaw in their hull design was the very low freeboard of the main deck amidships, where the engineering access hatches and blower intakes were located. (The main deck is the uppermost continuous deck, from bow to stern.) In fact, when the *Warrington* was tied up in a nest alongside a 1,200-ton, four-stacked, destroyer of the World War I type, with her flush deck, it was startling to see that her deck amidships was lower than that of the little four-stackers.

When the *Warrington* was under way, the secondary bow wave came back and hit the ship's side amidships, just forward of the after fireroom hatch, and even in moderate seas this secondary bow wave would splash aboard on the windward side. Accordingly, until the bulwarks were added on the deck amidships after the New England hurricane of 1938, deck traffic was limited to the leeward side whenever seas of any consequence were encountered. It is easy to understand why the after fireroom was the first major compartment or space to flood. The after fireroom was the crack in the dike that ultimately sent the *Warrington* to the bottom.

2. BLOWER INTAKE AND HATCHES.

The low freeboard amidships made the intakes for the engineering blowers in this area vulnerable to sea water in heavy seas (the intake openings were only four feet above the deck), and it severely limited the use of the windward hatch to the fireroom. Although it had about an 18-inch coaming (raised rim), the access hatch was located right on the surface of the deck. Accordingly, it became standard operating procedure to close the fireroom blower intakes on the windward side topside, open the blower room door down in the fireroom, and use the open leeward fireroom access hatch topside to draw intake air down and through the fireroom for the forced-draft blowers for the boilers.

This arrangement for air for the boilers was made possible because of the then-new air casings around the boilers, and it resulted in greatly cooling the fireroom itself. Prior to these air casings, ships had "closed" firerooms, which meant that the entire fireroom was under air pressure, requiring the access hatches to be kept closed at all times, and also requiring all entrance and exit to and from the fireroom to be through "air locks."

The access hatches for the forward fireroom were located just aft of the break of the forecastle deck and were, accordingly, somewhat protected from the seas. During the hurricane, until conditions became critically severe, the forward starboard hatch was left open and air for the blowers was drawn through it. Both starboard and port access hatches for the after fireroom were kept closed, of course, as soon as the weather began to worsen, and air was drawn down through the intake vent of Number 7 blower on the starboard (leeward) side.

The Court of Inquiry concentrated intently upon the question of whether or not the boiler uptakes were bashed in or torn away from the deck, allowing the sea to enter the firerooms. To assist the reader in understanding this point, as well as the discussion of other events that occurred in and about the firerooms, it would be well to describe the construction and location of the uptakes, the blower rooms, and the boilers themselves.

The uptakes are rectangular ducts or "chimneys" made out of somewhat lighter gauge steel than the ship herself. A separate uptake curves upward from the top of each of the four boilers, and they all discharge their combustion gasses or smoke into the bottom of the single smokestack. Where they come through the relatively heavy steel of the deck in the center of the ship, the sides of the uptakes are welded to the deck, in a bead, or seam. The uptakes require a substantial opening in the heavy steel of the deck; this opening is filled by the uptakes themselves.

Aboard a Navy ship, there is a standard pattern for numbering multiple items, beginning forward with the starboard (right) side and working aft; odd numbers come down the starboard side, while even numbers are on the port side. With regard to the uptakes, Uptake Number 1 (for Boiler No. 1) is the farthest forward uptake, and it comes aft to the bottom of the smokestack on the starboard side of the centerline of the ship. Uptake No. 2 is next in line; it runs adjacent to Number 1 part way, then goes back to the stack on the port side of the centerline.

Uptake No. 3 is just abaft the stack, and it comes to the stack on the starboard side of the centerline. It will be shown later that this uptake played a pivotal role in the loss of the *Warrington*. Uptake No. 4 came to the stack from Boiler 4, on the way passing outboard of No. 3, on the port side. When she entered the storm, the *Warrington* was steaming on boilers No. 1 and 4.

The bottom of each uptake connects to the top of its boiler fire box. The fire box is lined with fire-brick on the bottom and on its front and back. The fire box is also divided into two compartments by a fire-brick wall. The right side of the fire box generates the steam to nearly 600 pounds per square inch pressure, and the left side of the fire box superheats the steam to 800°F. At the top of the boiler, in the center, is the thick steel drum from which steam goes to the engines through heavy steel pipes; and on the bottom of the fire box, on each side, is a heavy steel "mud" drum. This catches the by-products of converting fresh water to steam, such as salt and other impurities.

These were "water tube" boilers, with banks of tubes running down each side on an angle from the steam drums to the mud drums. The intense heat from the oil burners passed up around the tubes and then on up into the uptakes as combustion gasses or smoke. The entire fire box area of the boiler is encased in a metal "box" into which the forced-draft blowers discharge air under pressure to feed the fires and to prevent flarebacks from the fire box into the fireroom itself.

On the *Warrington* there was a history of the uptakes separating from the deck along the seam where they were welded, causing a leakage of seawater into the firerooms. An unsuccessful attempt had been made to caulk this open seam in Espíritu Santo or Purvis Bay.[12] Also, the *Warrington*'s engineering department had tried unsuccessfully to have these uptake seams repaired in Brooklyn Navy Yard. Chief Watertender Teague testified, "We had job orders to have them fixed at the Yard, but it was not done. . . . We had a job order in for it, when we went to the Yard. They gave us a fifteen-day emergency overhaul. They did not do anything to them."[13]

Before the "Big Shot" of water which came aboard at the broaching, there was water coming into the after fireroom down the *outside* of No. 3 uptake, but not in sufficient quantity to cause a flooding.[14] Nevertheless, this demonstrates that the uptake had separated from the deck before broaching. All that remained now was for the heavy pounding of the seas to cave in the relatively light metal of the uptake.

Chief Watertender Teague testified that he examined No. 3 uptake both before and after the *Warrington* took the "Big Shot" of water. He said, "There was a film of water running down all the time" on the side of the uptake before broaching. And further, "It was a fair amount of water coming down the uptake then." But after the broaching, "Every time one would hit those uptakes after the Big Shot, it would just pour down on the starboard side."[15] He also testified that the water was entering the fireroom and into No. 3 boiler itself through the caved-in uptake.[16]

Accordingly, upon the broaching it would appear that the bulk of the water which rapidly flooded the after fireroom in one massive surge entered through the gap in the deck which was created when No. 3 uptake was smashed in by the sea in one tremendous blow. Fireman second class Clarence Strunk was on burner duty on the floor plates in the after fireroom when the *Warrington* broached, rolled hard over to starboard, and took the Big Shot of water, filling the fireroom nearly to the gratings in one big surge. He testified that "all the water that amounted to anything was coming through Numbers 7 and 8 blowers *until the uptakes caved in*" (Emphasis added).[17] This topic will be discussed more fully hereafter.

3. HIGH ISOLATED BOW.

Although the bow of the *Warrington* was no higher than those of the later 2,100-ton flush-deckers of the *Fletcher* Class, the contrast between the high bow and the low main deck caused the bow to act like a sail in a strong crosswind, or perhaps more like the tail of a weathervane. This was no problem ordinarily, but according to the testimony before the Court of Inquiry, in the hurricane it was very difficult to keep the *Warrington*'s bow headed into the storm. As the bow would rise completely out of the water at the crest of a huge wave, the fierce wind, just a few degrees to port, would slam against the bow and drive it sideways off course.

Captain Quarles likened the riding of the *Warrington* on these mountainous waves to a child's seesaw.[18] He said that when the ship crested a huge wave she would sit down momentarily with her midsection on top of the wave, and with her bow and stern out of the water at the same time.[19] When this happened, of course, the bow acted even more like the tail of a weather-vane.

The helmsman, in the early evening of the 12th stated that when they hove to and he was ordered to bring the ship around to a course of 90°, he had "a lot of difficulty getting around there. You could not exactly carry on the course two to five degrees on either side."[20]

TIRED SHIP AND TIRED CREW

The *Warrington* was long overdue for an extensive Navy Yard overhaul. The discrepancies which helped send her to the bottom did not occur overnight, and during her long years of tropical duty the ship had not been subjected to weather conditions which would expose the severity of those discrepancies.—e.g., seas heavy enough to send substantial slugs of water into the blower intakes and down into the blowers themselves.

The *Warrington* had been away from the States and out in the Pacific or South Atlantic for three and a half years preceding her rendezvous with her fatal Atlantic hurricane, and on that extended warm-weather duty she had not encountered life-threatening weather. Because she had not been in extended heavy combat operations, perhaps it was felt that she had not suffered much wear and tear. But the *Warrington* was neglectfully abused by the Navy for years before she succumbed.

For this hurricane weather, probably the most significant discrepancies in need of repair, aside from the ventilation blowers in the enginerooms, were the blower intake covers and the fireroom access hatches. There were two intake covers for each blower, making a total in all of sixteen covers for the eight blowers, and these covers were stowed in racks on the sides of the intake trunk. However, three of the covers were missing, and this left open intakes on blower Number 3 (starboard side of forward fireroom), Number 4 (port side of forward fireroom), and Number 7 (starboard side of after fireroom).[21]

When the ship took her first damaging roll to starboard, Number 7 blower was one of two places where the first serious water entered the after fireroom, the starboard access hatch being the other. Also, water entering the ventilation blower intakes in the enginerooms at 11:00 P.M. put those already faulty blowers completely out of commission, starting the intolerable build-up of heat in those compartments.[22] "For want of a nail, a shoe was lost; for want of a shoe, a horse was lost; and for want of a horse, a battle was lost." The "nail" in this instance was the entire group of faulty blowers in the enginerooms, which led to the difficulties in the operation of the enginerooms and helped Captain Quarles to make his decision.[23]

In addition to the missing covers for the fireroom blowers, the fittings, or fasteners, for these covers had thick coats of paint, making them difficult to operate, and when the heavy seas hit them they were carried away, exposing more faces of the intake vents. Also, some of the covers were bent, making it difficult to fit them into place.[24]

Some of the latch-catches on the quick-opening covers on the access hatches were damaged or worn, so that they did not hold when hit by heavy seas.[25] They kept springing open of their own accord, and eventually the fireroom crews had to wire them shut from the inside.[26] But when the firerooms were abandoned and the crews left them, there was no way to wire the hatches from the outside. Consequently, the seas continued to flood down into the firerooms. Several unsuccessful attempts were made during the night to tie down the covers to the fireroom hatches from the outside, at great risk to life.

The *Warrington*'s crew was weary and frustrated by the ship's long, boring tours of bleak routine duty on the "edge" of the war. Their work was important, and carried its own element of risk, but for the most part it lacked the invigorating thrill of combat. It was debilitating. The counsel for Captain Quarles, in his summation before the Court, quoted a *Warrington* officer as saying that he had not read a newspaper over his morning cup of coffee in two years, and the counsel said to the Court, "Gentlemen, that is a very significant statement."[27]

The morning newspaper was not the only thing that officer missed, and no one who has not been in his shoes can truly appreciate the significance of that statement and the depressing, life-sapping existence it portrays, as precious years of a man's life are passing away, whether he is in his late teens, early twenties, or thirties.

The *Warrington*'s skipper in the Pacific, Lieutenant Commander Robert A. Dawes, Jr., recognized the effects their extended tour of overseas duty had on his officers and men, and when he got his orders to proceed to the Brooklyn Navy Yard for maintenance overhaul, he promised that they would all receive a richly deserved leave. [Not quite true; the first news of going to the Yard also contained the news that it would be for only fifteen days. I knew only a fraction of the crew could get leave in that short time, so I only promised as much leave as the time limit would permit.—RAD]

As Captain Quarles testified, the scuttlebutt (rumor) that they were coming from the Southwest Pacific to the East Coast of the United States for an extended Navy Yard overhaul and 30 days' leave before assignment to better wartime duty, had all hands charged as high as a kite.[28] [I have no idea how or when such a rumor ever got started, if it ever did. I never heard it during my time aboard.—RAD] Then their morale plunged to the depths of martyrdom when the ship got only a brief "lick and a promise" in the Navy Yard, and there was very little leave. As one result, when the *Warrington* left New York after only 15 days in port, about a dozen crew members "missed the ship," which was a very serious matter, even in peacetime.[29]

Although Captain Quarles was aware of this morale problem, his chosen solution left much to be desired. He stated that several of the *Warrington*'s officers pointed out that many in the crew had been overseas for a long period of time without leave, and Quarles himself saw that "some had the characteristics of operational fatigue." So, "I decided that I had to conduct matters in two ways to correct or offset this matter, and decided that I had to demonstrate a great deal of interest and forcefulness (Quarles's favorite word), and urge the rest of the officers to do the same, and at the same time, forward a few requests to the Commander, Subordinate Command, for exchanges of personnel where warranted."[30]

Quarles also stated, "I do know from my observation that to some extent the *Warrington* was suffering from what you might call a martyr complex."[31] His solution brought a swift reaction. "The Engineer Officer burst into my cabin one time, very excited, and said that a terrific calamity had overtaken him, and I inquired what it was, and he was waving his hands and he said, 'Captain, I have thirteen requests for transfers!'" Quarles's response was that "that always happens when people are feeling sorry for themselves."[32]

On one occasion in Casco Bay, the *Warrington*'s crew suffered mass arrests by the Shore Patrol, resulting in one Captain's Mast with twenty or thirty offenders in one "shot." Upon checking, Quarles learned that most of the men had clean records, and after hearing from Lieutenant (jg) Moore that the men claimed that the Shore Patrol was "down on them, and that all the Shore Patrol has it in for the *Warrington*," he allowed the Executive Officer to conduct the Mast and give the men just one day's restriction, so that their records would remain clear.[33] Nevertheless, there is nothing in the record to contradict the proposition that, almost without exception, every man and officer aboard fought to the end to save his life and his ship.

CHANGE OF COMMAND

Despite the extended, morale-lowering duty the *Warrington* had endured, Captain Dawes had maintained a loyal crew and staff of officers, and the *Warrington* had efficiently carried out every assignment she had received. Discussions with the officers and men who served with him leave no doubt that Captain Dawes commanded by respect.

From Commander Quarles's testimony, it appears that the personnel aboard the *Warrington* had good reason to believe that their new skipper had every intention of making the *Warrington* a "hot ship." He stated that his transfer to take command of the *Warrington* was "abrupt," with the inference that there was a situation aboard which needed his special abilities to square away. As an example, he stated that, on a lower-deck inspection, he was "determined to find as many things wrong as possible, to shock them out of their, what I presumed, was a state of complacency. So, in common vernacular, I 'raised hell' from one part of the ship to another."[34] On another occasion, he called the officers together and gave them a "very forceful lecture." His favorite adjective when describing his orders or activities throughout his tenure was "forceful."

In relating a problem with sentry duty in Casco Bay, a day or so after assuming command, Quarles stated, "I suspected the cause of this sentry information, that there was some laxity in obeying orders at that time, and generally the performance of duties in a fully military fashion. During some of my conferences with the officers, I indicated that I thought that was the case, and regardless of how much the men had been through, regardless of how much leave they thought they were due, regardless of anything else, that they were to take charge forcefully, and that I would back them up at Mast if they should ever find occasion to bring in people to Mast for failure to carry out orders."[35]

When the *Warrington* encountered this hurricane it was only her second trip to sea under the command of her new captain, the first being the run from Norfolk to Casco Bay. He had not yet become acquainted with her or her officers or crew, and they were in the process of dealing with their first impression of him.

This strained atmosphere probably made it difficult for the other officers of the *Warrington* to use initiative in a timely fashion when the emergency conditions began developing. The Court of Inquiry condemned Lieutenant Wesley U. Williams, the Executive Officer, for not being with the captain and offering assistance during the storm, but when Quarles bypassed Williams by summoning Lieutenant Patrick B. Davis to the bridge to assist him, Williams quite logically traveled about the ship on his own, seeking places to help and providing that help.

When presented repeatedly with reports of the difficulty being encountered in the engineering spaces, Captain Quarles scolded the Engineering Officer, Lieutenant (jg) William V. Keppel, over the telephone and ordered him to do the job. Lieutenant Keppel and those under him in the engineroom were literally being stewed alive in the 196° steam vapor.

The unfortunate man refused to don a life jacket and went down with the ship, along with the injured Chief Radioman Arthur B. Tolman and Lieutenant (jg) Robert M. Kennedy, the ship's doctor, who was attending Chief Tolman. After shaking hands with the captain, Keppel said "good-bye" and "confided that he could not swim and wanted this to be the end."[36]

Quarles testified, "I was fully aware of the vulnerability of the after part of the *Warrington* class ship to storm damage."[37] "About 10 P.M. on the evening of the 12th I stated to the Navigator [Lieutenant Davis] that it was then too dangerous to attempt it [a 180° turn] as the stern of the ship would be swept by waves before the maneuver could be completed."[38]

His officers had told him of the terrible conditions in the enginerooms, but he went down there after making the turn. "It was indicated to me by the various people on the bridge at the time that I shouldn't send anyone up from the engineering spaces to get Keppel [who was up on deck, recovering from having fainted from the heat below], that he was in too bad a condition to go down below to answer the phone. So I wouldn't be outdone in the matter of talking to him and decided to go down on deck."[39]

When Commander Quarles left the bridge he had just swung the *Warrington*'s stern into the face of the hurricane. He testified that when he told the Chief Engineer over the telephone, a little earlier, he wanted him to make 15 knots (to turn and run before the storm), the Chief "reported that he didn't know whether he could make that speed or not. He seemed to despair of making that speed. Just why he couldn't make it, I didn't take time to ask him or inquire. I merely told him that he had to do it, in a very forceful fashion."[40]

Quarles testified that the ship came around to a westerly heading without any immediate problem, *other than a temporary derangement with the steering mechanism,* and after they rode on a heading of 280° for awhile, he decided to go down on deck to visit the Engineer Officer by the engine-room hatch. He also said, that the ship "seemed to be doing well, except, periodically, large amounts of rudder had to be used to keep her on her course. She would fall off first to one side and then to the other. A little bit."[41]

Radarman third class Arel B. Smith testified that, before making the 180° turn, the ship was making 5 knots into the seas, and after making the turn, the pitometer log showed that she was making 17 knots until she broached. He also testified that she had been steaming on the new course for 15 to 20 minutes before the broaching occurred.[42]

Captain Quarles went on to say that "with the great length of the ship, it naturally would be hard steering with the seas. It would require the frequent and most rapid use of the rudder, which was apparent."[43] Old pilots often tell their young students, "The wind is your friend, but if you turn your back on him, he'll kill you." Captain Quarles's final remark was, "There was no particular danger at this time of running one way or the other, because it was six of one and half a dozen of the other."[44]

(Atlantic hurricanes generally are spawned in the semitropical latitudes above the Equator and move westward toward Florida as they grow. Their doughnut-shaped winds blow counter clockwise in a circle that can measure hundreds of miles across. The entire mass continues westward and then, as they approach the U.S. coast, they often turn northwesterly and eventually northward [see appendix A] as they reach the temperate latitudes and begin to fade. This northward turn is called "recurving."

The 1938 hurricane at times moved across the sea at a speed of 65 knots, with winds as high as 138 knots. As explained earlier, the position of the *Warrington,* in the top of the "doughnut," made it impossible for her to have turned to the west and outrun the storm.—DHM)

The success of Quarles's drastic maneuver depended on three things: (1) Perfect steering; (2) No engineering problems; and (3) No "rogue" waves. Quarles testified that he was being plagued by the first two.[45] In a hurricane (or any other large storm) the waves do not come rolling along in neat rows as they do when breaking on a seashore. There is always a lot of giant "chop," and at any moment a giant wave can come out of nowhere at a freak angle and smash down on a ship. If the "turn and run" had turned into a disaster, there could be no turning back.

Earlier, Quarles had testified that when the *Warrington* regained main engine power about 11:30 P.M. on the 12th, after the first outage of about a half hour, the ship was on hand steering. He sent an order to bring the ship around to the left to a course of 110°, but to the consternation of everyone on the bridge the indicator showed the rudder moving to the right. Realizing that this would swing the ship's stern into the wind and into a disastrous position, everyone on the bridge began yelling over the phone to get the helmsman to reverse the rudder.[46]

Eventually they succeeded, and the ship began to swing back to the left. In the meantime, however, she was hit by a giant wave on the starboard quarter. Quarles says it "was a jar similar to one boxer hitting another one on the chin, but I heard no structural failure. I noted no water up around the bridge, and got no particularly alarming reports as far as structural damage was concerned as a result."[47]

(In the 1938 hurricane, the *Warrington* was also hit by such a wave, which appeared to come from the port quarter, even though her bow was headed into the seas at the time. I was lying on my bunk in the engineers' compartment when suddenly there was a tremendous "bang" overhead, and the ship shuddered as though a mountain-sized boulder had crashed down on top of the after deckhouse, which was above the engineers' compartment. The sound was much greater than the sound of the collision when the *Somers* rammed us off Pearl Harbor in 1940. A giant rogue wave had crashed down on top of the deckhouse, and seawater came pouring in through the ventilators. At the same time, both compartment hatchways were filled with solid green water, and this solid water continued to flood in for what seemed like the better part of a minute. How long the stern was under this wave I don't actually know, but when it stopped coming in the water was about a foot deep in the compartment.—DHM)

Before the Court, Quarles stated that he decided to leave the bridge shortly after reversing course because he wanted to discuss with the Chief

Engineer whether potential engineering repairs could be made aboard ship or would necessitate a visit to Charleston Navy Yard. He testified that others on the bridge tried to persuade him not to go down to the engineroom at that time, but "I would not be put off . . . I would go below into the engineroom and walk in and tell them, 'This is not bad. I have seen it a lot worse a thousand times.' "[48] What he saw in the engineroom, however, shocked him into reality. It was a scene from Hell.

The high temperature, combined with the seawater sloshing around the floorplates, created a steam vapor that made it difficult to see. Quarles testified, "I noticed that the heat was very excessive, worse than I had ever seen it before in any engineroom—but not so much the heat but steam and vapor was apparent. I could hardly see the lights that were on in the engineroom and could hardly distinguish faces."[49] If he had been close enough to see their faces, he would have seen that the men's sweat-soaked hair was plastered to their flushed foreheads above their red-rimmed, bloodshot eyes, and that every inch of their dungarees was drenched with sweat and clung to their bodies. Even their shoes were sodden with sweat.

The crowning ironic tragedy is the fact that it was at this exact moment of revelation of the truth to him that the *Warrington* took what was to be her fatal roll, cascading green seas down into the engineroom on top of the captain, stopping her engines for the last time, and making a return to a proper course impossible.[50]

REASSIGNMENT OF OFFICERS

[It is the prerogative of a commanding officer to reassign all but a few key officers as he sees fit, when he takes command of a ship. The captain stands or falls by the results; in this case, the timing was bad, but Quarles would have had no way of knowing that.—RAD]

Before getting under way on his second and final voyage, the new captain reassigned several officers to new duties as part of a reorganization of the ship's operating structure. Among other things, he removed the duties of Navigator from the Executive Officer and assigned them to a junior officer. He also assigned a new officer to the duties of First Lieutenant and Damage Control Officer, thereby relieving the former First Lieutenant (Lt. Patrick Davis) of one job and Lt. Keppel of another. The new First Lieutenant, Lt. (jg) Pennington, thus had two jobs to learn. It is interesting to note in passing that there had been considerable division of opinion in the Navy for some years as to who could best handle the duties of Damage Control Officer; but it always seemed to end up being a sort of secondary duty to either the Chief Engineer or First Lieutenant. In this present case, the Court saw fit to charge both officers with dereliction of duty, for reasons known only to themselves.

Obviously, this reassignment to new duties worked against smooth operation under the stressful conditions which were immediately encountered. This awkward situation was compounded during the storm when Captain Quarles by-passed this Executive Officer and worked directly through a junior officer whom he summoned personally to the bridge from the wardroom. It was a bitter ironic injustice that the Court of Inquiry cited the Executive Officer's "failure" to "work with the captain" during this emergency as their basis for recommending that the Executive Officer's commission be revoked.

CAPTAIN'S EXPERIENCE

Captain Quarles had five years' experience in destroyers. He was deeply impressed by the *Warrington*'s length; she was 371 feet at the waterline, which was 37 feet longer than 1,500-ton destroyers, but she was only 18 inches wider—36 feet, 2 inches, compared to 34 feet, 8 inches of beam for the smaller destroyers. Quarles's service had been on two 1,200-ton four-stackers with flush decks and adequate freeboard amidships, and much of that service had been on the relatively long, smooth swells of the Pacific. He had seen plenty of *nasty* weather in two winters in the north Atlantic, but as nasty as these storms were, they were not Caribbean hurricanes.

USS Noa (DD 343), a typical four-stack destroyer. Note the flush deck and relatively high freeboard amidships, with enclosed deckhouse. Engineering spaces are well protected. (Courtesy of the Yangtze Patroller)

He testified that, during his two winters on North Atlantic duty, he experienced severe weather. "There were numerous occasions where we had winds of between 70 and 100 knots, sometimes possibly greater."[51] [See the table of wind force in appendix A.] According to the U.S. Weather Bureau reports, there were 14 hurricanes during the years 1941 to 1943, six of which reached the latitudes where Captain Quarles might have encountered them, but by the time they got that far, into cold northern waters, they had been down-graded into extratropical storms.

He testified further that his four-stacker experience convinced him that the *Warrington*, being "twice their size," should be able to ride out the hurricane. He may not have believed what he said he had heard about the midships vulnerability of broken-deck destroyers. He said, that after he saw the results of his 180° turn, he wanted to turn the *Warrington*'s bow back into the storm, but it was too late. Her engines were stopped forever.[52]

SEQUENCE OF DERANGEMENTS AND CASUALTIES

There was nearly simultaneous entry of water in many areas of the ship, some of which disabled some machinery (the Diesel emergency electric generators, electric ventilation blowers in the enginerooms), but the major flooding which eventually caused her to sink occurred first in the engineering spaces. The first to flood was the after fireroom, followed shortly thereafter by the forward engineroom. Then, quite some time later, came the after engineroom; and last, almost simultaneously, the forward fireroom and the engineers' living compartment. The latter was probably still filling when she rolled over and went down, stern first.

The first serious trouble took the form of waves coming aboard amidships and knocking out the remaining electrical ventilation blowers in the enginerooms. Other ventilation blowers in the enginerooms had already been put out of operation by failure of their bearings. The waves had also, simultaneously, brought water into the after fireroom through the forced-draft, steam-driven blowers, but this water was being kept readily under control by the fire and bilge pump.

At about 11:00 P.M. or midnight (take your pick from the testimony) the ship took a hard roll to starboard and shipped heavy water down the blowers into the forward engineroom. This first heavy roll was apparently caused by the bow falling off to starboard, perhaps from the exposed bow being driven to starboard by a particularly fierce burst of the hurricane's winds.

Considering the attitude of the helmsman in his testimony,[53] it was entirely possible that, despite his utmost efforts, he was not able to keep the ship's head into the wind at that point, thus falling into the yaw that

David H. Miller repairs a forced-draft blower in Number 2 Fireroom. (Courtesy of D. H. Miller)

brought in the first serious water and triggering the whole chain of events that ended with the sinking. This first slug of heavy water shorted out the steam-driven generator and darkened the whole ship momentarily, before the diesel generators kicked in. The diesels kept running for about half an hour before they were both disabled by seawater. In the meantime, the steam-driven generator was re-started. However, the main engines also stopped at this time and remained stopped for nearly a half hour.

The ship continued to struggle against the storm, and water continued to enter all four engineering spaces, primarily through the blower intakes, but not in sufficient quantities to create a danger of flooding the spaces. However, the steamy heat in the enginerooms created nearly unbearable conditions, and men had to stand watches in shifts of only ten minutes each. An atmosphere of desperation began to develop. Captain Quarles testified that they were having difficulty keeping the ship headed into the storm, with the bow frequently falling off to starboard into the trough.

The broaching, which occurred about 1:30 A.M. on the 13th, in one giant surge flooded the after fireroom nearly to the upper gratings (about eight or nine feet above the floor plates, which would be the same distance above the floor of the boiler fire boxes), and required the immediate emergency shut-down of Number 4 boiler and all machinery in that fireroom.

Although the fireroom itself was rather spacious, it should be remembered that most of that space was taken up by the two boilers themselves. Both are encased in the forced-draft air casing, forming a huge, nearly airtight, box. Hence, although seawater eventually entered and filled the internal boiler spaces, initially it would not require a solid "half of a fireroom" of seawater to flood the room nearly to the gratings. Moreover, the amount of water that did surge in on that roll (or dual roll) was far more than could have come in on one surge through the blower vents and the access hatch.

HOW AND WHERE THE WATER ENTERED

Captain Quarles's decision was: (1) to turn tail to the seas and winds of a hurricane, and (2) to try to run through those seas at 15 knots. The ship's speed under these conditions was a major factor in causing the damage which doomed her.

The *Warrington* was actually plowing through those huge seas at 17 knots, being driven by her screws and a 100-knot tail wind.[54] When she skidded into that port sheer, she rolled over to starboard and slammed into a mountain of water almost broadside, still at 17 knots or more. It amounted to a virtual collision with a solid wall of water, and hitting solid water at substantial speed is like hitting concrete. Her Number 3 boiler uptake (on the starboard side) was obviously carried away by the blow, instantly creating a cavernous opening in the main deck through which the seas dumped in one great surge, into the fireroom.

Fireman first class Fred J. Kieser was on watch in the after fireroom, checking water levels on the upper gratings when the *Warrington* broached. He testified that the water "came in all at once in one big shot" from the overhead.[55] Kieser added, "We rolled over, picked up this water, and it [the fireroom] was full."[56]

A. B. Smith, who was on watch as a radarman in the CIC, testified that the ship took a big roll to starboard, took a long time coming only part way upright, then rolled back on her starboard side again. He said that she never straightened up again after that, but remained in a starboard list which gradually grew more severe until she sank.[57]

Fireman second class Clarence Strunk was on watch on the oil burners in the after fireroom at this time, below Kieser, and he was positive in his testimony that the big surge of water came in on the starboard side. However, he also testified that he couldn't tell if the water came in by the uptakes because the lights were out and he was holding a hand lantern and looking at the steam gauges.[58] When questioned further as to where the water entered on the starboard side, he answered, "It entered through the Number 7 blower, most of it. Part of it, anyway. I don't know where else it entered unless the side of the ship came loose."[59] He and others also testified that it was not possible for that amount of water to enter "in one big shot" through the blowers.

Strunk was questioned repeatedly about the point of entry of the "big shot" of water, and he stuck to his guns. He insisted that only a relatively small amount of water came in from the port side, and that it entered through Number 8 blower. When asked, "Did this big shot of water appear to come from the vicinity of the starboard hatch?" he replied, "I don't know where it came from, except from Number 7 blower, if the side of the ship didn't come out."[60]

Witnesses said that the *Warrington* stayed over at this time in a "dual roll," with her starboard side buried in the sea. She laid way over for awhile, came back only part way, and then laid over again, all the while with water cascading into the fireroom. Strunk estimated the time she was laid over in this dual roll as "three to five minutes."[61] That is probably not realistic, but whatever the period of time it was on the clock, when the *Warrington* finally came more or less back to upright, her after fireroom had been instantly flooded with about eight or nine feet of water. That amount of water could not have entered through the blowers or even the access hatches in that brief a period.

Strunk was asked, "Did the water hit you suddenly or were you in a position to see it coming before it entered the fireroom or while it was still coming into the fireroom?" He replied, "It hit me before I knew anything about it."[62] Within a minute or so, he was standing in front of a steaming, high-pressure boiler, up to his armpits in relatively cold seawater. Instantly, everyone in the fireroom began to yell, "Secure the boiler!" "We wouldn't keep it lit off with water coming over the burners," said Strunk. He couldn't duck down under water to shut off the oil burners, so, instead, he reached up under the gratings and shut the globe valves through which oil flowed down to the burners.[63]

If she had been steaming on Number 3 boiler instead of Number 4, she *would* have experienced that calamitous boiler explosion, the absence of which puzzled the Court, because much of this water would have dumped in on a hot boiler through the *inside* of the torn uptake itself. As it was, the hot boiler, Number 4, was protected from this water by the air casing which surrounded it. The air casing, being nearly airtight, was also water-tight, except for the relatively tiny apertures required for the oil burners' air register handles. Water could only sprinkle through these air register handles in tiny streams, and it would have taken a long time to reach the dangerous parts of the boiler.

But the sailors in that fireroom did not have the time nor the conditions in which to make such a fine analysis of the situation, and their actions in remaining at their stations, in the dark, for the ten or fifteen minutes it took to secure the boiler, the machinery, and the fireroom itself, was an outstanding example of disciplined bravery which should have been recognized officially, but never was. Instead, one of them, Fireman Strunk, was so infuriated by the skeptical cross-examination to which he was subjected at the courts-martial that he leaped to his feet, knocked over his chair, and proclaimed, "I am not a liar!"

Captain Quarles testified (as did Clarence Strunk)[64] that by daylight the starboard main deck was awash, and with the seas sweeping across the deck it was not possible for anyone to inspect the uptakes *on the starboard side* (Emphasized phrase added). But Fireman Strunk had the courage and intellectual curiosity to investigate for himself. He testified that after daybreak he examined the uptakes *on the port side* and observed that an uptake was "bashed in." This testimony is so important that it should be set forth in detail:[65]

Q. Did you notice it [the uptake] when you went up on deck after you secured the fireroom?

A. Yes sir. I didn't notice it at the time I went up after we secured the fireroom. I didn't notice it until that morning after daybreak.

Q. Now, can you describe what this bashing in looked like when you saw it in the morning? How big was the hole, and so forth?

A. Well, it looked to me like she was bent in about seven or eight feet.

Q. Was there a hole?

A. No, sir. I didn't see a hole there. It was swept off from the deck, part of it, by the stack.

Q. Just what was ripped loose?

A. Where it was welded to the deck, it was loose from the deck, by the stack there.

Q. Was this bashing in near the forward fireroom hatch?

A. Yes, sir, on the port side.

Q. On the port side?

A. Yes, sir.

Quite probably, most of the uptake damage on the port side occurred after the ship lost her engines permanently and then wallowed in the trough, allowing the seas to pound aboard on both sides. Hence, the flooding of the after fireroom is still ultimately traceable to its location in the low freeboard amidships where the starboard uptake took the full impact of the broaching at 17 knots.

The damage to the starboard uptake is further documented by the witnesses who, at daybreak, saw the "dirty water" coming out of the starboard access hatch above the after fireroom. This dirty water could only have come from *inside* Number 3 boiler's fire box, and it could only have entered and left that fire box through the large opening where the uptake was ripped apart and loose from the fire box.

Chief Watertender Teague testified that just before the forward fireroom was abandoned, on the morning of the 13th, he received orders to light off Number 2 boiler, but that he was unable to do so because he found that the fire box was "full of water."[66] This water could only have entered the fire box through Number 2 uptake, which by that time was also battered in and separated at the seam.

20-20 HINDSIGHT

Considering the known vulnerability of the after fireroom, one can't help but wish that appropriate action had been taken to guard against that vulnerability when the decision was taken to "prepare for hurricane weather," or during the 12 or so hours between that pronouncement and midnight, when the *Warrington* took the hard roll to starboard which shipped in the first serious water.[67] It would have been relatively simple to do so.

The after fireroom could have been secured and battened down completely. The forward fireroom was operating and could have provided all the steam necessary to ride out the entire storm at reduced speed. Furthermore, the second boiler in the forward fireroom could have been lit off if additional steam had been needed.

The blower covers missing from the after fireroom could have been replaced with covers from the forward fireroom blowers, because the forward blowers were partially sheltered by their location, just behind the break of the deck, and were not particularly vulnerable to the incoming seas as long as the ship continued to head into the wind.

The forward engineroom did not fill as rapidly as the after fireroom, but it followed soon after, because the water in the fireroom, now under the hydrostatic pressure of its own depth, streamed forcefully into the engineroom through the various openings in the bulkhead between the two rooms, around the cables and manholes, as had been observed earlier in the evening. These openings were caused by the installation, over the years, of various additional cables without the necessary watertight flanges that should have been installed, but weren't. Again, this laxness was apparently the result of the "new" air casings around the boilers, which made it unnecessary to maintain an airtight (and therefore, watertight) fireroom.

Although the massive flooding of water at the time of the broaching cut off the ship's electric power again and brought both engines to a stop, it did not mean that the ship had to remain dead in the water. The forward fireroom and the after engineroom were still unflooded. Furthermore, the forward fireroom was normally the one to supply steam to the after engineroom, except when the main steam line was cross-connected. The forward fireroom still had a full head of steam on its Number 1 boiler, and Number 2 boiler could still have been lit off at that time, if it had been deemed necessary. However, main feed water pressure had been lost to the forward fireroom, requiring the men to switch to their emergency feed pump and its own emergency feed water tank, which they did.

All that is required to run a boiler is fuel oil, air pressure, and feed water. The forward fireroom had oil, air, and emergency feed water, but the supply of emergency feed water was limited, and Chief Watertender Teague testified that the lack of feed water was all that caused him to secure the fireroom when he did so at 5:20 A.M. on the 13th. ("W J" Sapp claims to have given the order to abandon the fireroom himself.) This was the final decision which sealed the *Warrington*'s fate.

Paradoxically, it was also testified that the crew in the after engineroom was also ready eventually to light off (restart) the port engine, but they could not do so without adequate steam pressure to operate their auxiliary machinery. They had no adequate steam because the supply of emergency feed water to the forward fireroom had been exhausted, and the manifold valves to switch to a full water tank were in the bottom of the after fireroom, buried under tons of sea water.

Telephone communications between the fireroom and the engineroom were out. So, at 5:30 A.M. on the 13th, after securing Number 1 boiler, Watertender first class "W J" Sapp left the forward fireroom to seek a supply of feed water. He went first to the after fireroom, and after finding it completely flooded, putting the supply valves at the bottom of the fireroom out of reach, he went further aft to the forward engineroom. There he encountered Lt. (jg) Robert B. Moore, the Assistant Engineer Officer, who told him, "No, all the pumps are out in the forward engineroom." "So," says Sapp, "I said I'd go back to the forward fireroom. As I started to go up the ladder the wind seemed to increase its speed, so he told me to wait until daylight. I was in the air lock."[68]

This leaves a tantalizing thought: if Sapp could have made it to the *after* engineroom, could the after engineroom have supplied feed water to the forward fireroom, enabling the forward fireroom to supply steam to the after engineroom, thereby getting the *Warrington* underway again, and keeping her bow headed into the seas?

One must constantly remember the conditions that existed. The fiercely screaming wind, the biting sea driving into these men in the darkness, the violently heaving ship, and the constant danger everywhere of injury and death. Nevertheless, one can't help but wish that there had been some communication between the forward fireroom and the after engineroom, resulting in a supply of feed water to Number 1 boiler. They already had the oil and the air.

SUMMARY

It appears that the destructive chain of events was set in motion at about 11:00 or 12:00 on the evening of the 12th, when the bow fell off to starboard and the first serious water entered the forward engineroom, knocking out the ship's electric power.

Power was restored, and the ship maintained headway until about 1:00 A.M. on the 13th, when she made her fatal 180° turn to starboard, then sheered to port and broached at 17 knots, taking in the heavy slug of water that flooded the after fireroom, knocked out the electric power, and stopped her engines permanently, leaving her dead in the water at the peak of the hurricane.

The broaching was caused by her inability to run at 17 knots before the hurricane and the mountainous following seas that then came crashing down upon her vulnerable midsection.

Therefore, the ultimate proximate cause of the sinking of the *Warrington* was the decision to make the 180° turn and attempt to run at 15 knots at that stage of the hurricane. Captain Quarles testified that he wanted to return to an easterly course immediately after the broaching, but he had no engines left with which to make the turn.[69]

appendix c

ACTION REPORT
SECRET

U.S.S. WARRINGTON
    SERIAL: NONE   25 SEPTEMBER 1944
    SUBJECT: LOSS OF U.S.S. WARRINGTON, 13 SEPTEMBER 1944.
          REPORT OF ESCORT OF U.S.S. HYADES 10–12 SEP-
          TEMBER; OF EFFORTS TO WEATHER HURRICANE
          OFF EAST COAST OF UNITED STATES 12–13 SEP-
          TEMBER; AND RESCUE BY HUNTER/KILLER GROUP
          OF U.S.S. CROATAN 15–16 SEPTEMBER[1]

UNITED STATES ATLANTIC FLEET
DD383/L11-1   SERVICE FORCE
Serial   25 September 1944
                          Care of Fleet Post Office
                 Naval Operating Base, Norfolk, Va.

DECLASSIFIED
From: The Commanding Officer, U.S.S. WARRINGTON (DD383).
To   : The Secretary of the Navy.
Via : (1) The Commander, Task Force Twenty-Nine.
       (2) The Commander Destroyers, U.S. Atlantic Fleet.
       (3) The Commander-in-Chief, U.S. Atlantic Fleet.
       (4) The Commander-in-Chief, U.S. Fleet.
Subject: U.S.S. WARRINGTON—Report of Loss of.
References: (a) Art. 841, U.S. Navy Regulations.

1. In compliance with reference (a), a report is herewith submitted containing all of the pertinent facts within my knowledge relating to the loss by sinking of the U.S.S. WARRINGTON (DD383) during a hurricane on 13 September 1944.

2. The U.S.S. WARRINGTON departed from the Naval Operating Base, Norfolk, Virginia, at 1715 (Z plus 4) 10 September, 1944, having been ordered by the Commander Task Force 29 to escort the U.S.S. HYADES (AF28) to the Panama Sea Frontier, then to proceed independently to Trinidad, reporting there to the Commanding Officer, U.S.S. ALASKA for duty prior to 0900 (Z plus 4) 17 September, 1944. Prior to departure, several conferences were conducted by the operations officer of the Commander Task Force 29, relating to the operational assignments of the U.S.S. WARRINGTON and U.S.S. HYADES. The Commanding Officers and Communications Officers of both ships attended these conferences. At the first conference, it was ascertained by the Operations Officer that the Commanding Officer, U.S.S. HYADES was the senior of the two Commanding Officers. It was mutually agreed upon by all parties that he would act as officer in tactical command of the unit. The Commanding Officer, U.S.S. HYADES issued a communication plan and voice code table for TBS-TBY use. Both were drawn up with both ships working in close collaboration, and as far as I know were satisfactory to both vessels. Escort station for the WARRINGTON and other matters were discussed and agreed upon by both Commanding Officers. It was decided that the WARRINGTON should take station 2500 yards ahead of the HYADES and patrol station so as to be ahead of her by the time she completed her turn to each new zigzag course. A set of mimeographed zigzag plans were given to each ship by the Operations Officer of Commander Task Force 29 for potential use. Both ships were issued routing instructions and given all necessary or available hydrographic and weather information by the sailing authority. At some time during the afternoon of 10 September, 1944, either immediately before or after sailing, the first of a series of hurricane notices was noted by me and plotted on the WARRINGTON's Atlantic Chart by someone in the Navigation department. Before sailing a final muster was taken, during which it was ascertained that approximately two men were absent without leave and that the Chief Commissary Steward was absent, probably because of his having been given misguided instructions regarding liberty by some undetermined officer. The report of changes required to be submitted before sailing was sent ashore, to the best of my knowledge, by the pilot, for mailing, the pilot being a commissioned officer. This report of changes did not reach the HYADES because she had gotten underway from alongside the Naval Operating Base piers about an hour and a half earlier

with the intention of anchoring out in the stream near Old Point Comfort for compass checks, assisted by a tug.

3. Upon sailing, no deficiencies affecting the ship's ability to perform any assignment reasonably well, were known to the Commanding Officer and I am confident that none existed except those of a controversial nature to be discussed in later paragraphs. Morale was very satisfactory. The ship had been fully fuelled and provisioned. Water tanks were full. Replacement ammunition had been obtained for that expended during a previous training period.

4. The WARRINGTON joined the HYADES off Old Point Comfort as she was completing her compass checks and proceeded ahead of her along the prescribed route. After clearing the swept channel, the HYADES gave the order to commence zigzagging, prescribing plan and course. The WARRINGTON patrolled station as planned. WARRINGTON's speed was about 15 knots. At the instigation of the HYADES, many TBS-TBY tests were made, during most of which communication was poor, but from my observations, almost normal for TBY performance. The WARRINGTON remained on station ahead of the HYADES until heaving to during the late afternoon of 12 September 1944. In paragraphs immediately following, events will be arranged by dates in log form, to the best of my memory. No ship's logs or records were saved.

5. *Sunday, 10 September 1944.*

Departed Norfolk, Va., with U.S.S. HYADES, uneventfully, leaving the vicinity of Old Point Comfort about 1800 (Z plus 4). At Buoy "18" HYADES set South Southeast course at about 14 knots. Conducted TBS-TBY test which proved unsatisfactory. Asked HYADES if she expected to zigzag during the night. HYADES replied by signalling zigzag plan number and execution. Commenced patrolling as planned. Plotted first hurricane warning received. It appeared would pass clear of our route to Eastward. Sea was smooth. Wind was light. Received impression that HYADES was making every effort to improve TBY performance by tuning and other means.

6. *Monday, 11 September, 1944.*

Weather was generally good throughout the day. Wind was light from S.E. Sky was partially overcast. Received and plotted additional hurricane warnings which indicated storm would cross our track, either ahead or behind us, and that we could expect to run into some part of it. Barometer remained steady. Exchanged noon positions with HYADES. Determined that we had made only 12.5 knots good. Suggested to HYADES that we zigzag only during daylight in order to make better speed. Exercised at General Quarters, steering shifting, engineering casualty, damage control, and other drills. The WARRINGTON's Engineering Office reported to the Commanding Officer, in the presence of the Executive Officer, that one ventilation blower in each engineroom had failed since sailing and asked if I would sign a letter, to be originated by him, to the Bureau of Ships, requesting new design blowers be installed in the enginerooms. He stated that the WARRINGTON's engineroom blowers were not good and were different from those on other ships of the WARRINGTON class. One of his complaints concerning the blowers was that gyroscopic action caused damage to bearings while the ship was rolling. I do not remember whether he added anything as to vulnerability to damage from water. He was assured that the Commanding Officer would gladly sign and forward such a letter via the usual chain of command. He assured me at the time that the blower failures meant some discomfort to personnel, but would not affect the ship's ability to carry on unless other blowers should become inoperative before those were repaired. There were four ventilation blowers in each engineroom in all. Ceased zigzagging at dark. WARRINGTON continued to patrol station. Tested TBS-TBY during the day. Noted some improvement.

7. *Tuesday, 12 September 1944.*

Sea was moderately rough during morning, becoming progressively more so during the day. Swells were noted as being much larger than to be expected with a wind of the force then blowing. Wind force was 18–25 knots until late afternoon, blowing from East Northeast. Swells appeared to come from a direction more southerly than the wind. Additional hurricane warnings were received indicating that the hurricane was closing us although its exact location and path was a matter of doubt because the various warnings which had been received varied considerably as to location and direction of movement. By applying the rules which I had learned from Knight's Seamanship and Bowditch, it appeared that the low pressure area was to SSE of us at an unknown distance. We were on a southerly course (about 183° True). One rule I remembered was that the rate of barometer drop was an indication of the distance from the center of the storm, with due consideration being given to ship's movement. The barometer did not behave as though the center of the low pressure area was close to us. As I recall, the barometer remained relatively high and steady during most of the day until evening when it commenced dropping rapidly. The steadiness of the barometer at a time when it should have been falling led me to believe that we were going to miss the most violent portion of the storm. Wind direction was watched all during the day for a shift, but none was apparent. I suggested to HYADES during the morning that we cease zigzagging in order to increase our speed and pass ahead (to westward) of the storm center. HYADES replied that information received indicated storm was stationary. Apparently HYADES was not alarmed by the data at hand. Nevertheless, HYADES soon ceased zigzagging and apparently put on best speed. WARRINGTON ceased patrolling about noon to avoid weather damage.

The Engineering Officer reported evaporator trouble early in the day and cut off fresh water to washrooms while the evaporators were being checked. The trouble with the evaporators was never reported to me in detail other than that the salinity of the water being made was too high for use as feed water. The last report received by me from the Engineering Officer concerning the evaporators was that he thought the trouble had been eliminated. The amount of feed water on hand was adequate to have more than carried us through the emergency and therefore the question of whether the evaporators were in working order or not has little if any bearing on the disaster to the ship.

At approximately 1430 (Z plus 4), at the direction of the Commanding Officer, an order was passed throughout the ship, by boatswain's mates, as follows: "Make ready for hurricane weather. Batten down and secure all loose gear." The order was properly passed as far as I could observe and considerable activity resulted about the topside. The ship did not have a general announcing system and suffered considerably in its ability to circulate information and orders quickly and effectively. In a storm, when access is difficult and limited, the need of a general announcing system is most keenly felt. The fact that a storm was due and likely was, as I believed, common knowledge throughout the ship without the necessity of any word being passed.

Material Condition BAKER was maintained until the ship was completely closed up during and after the engineering casualty which will be described later.

During the day, the ship rolled moderately with wind and sea on the port beam. I estimate that the greatest roll was between 20 and 30 degrees. The ship's stability impressed me as being very good and had been so reported to me by the former Commanding Officer and all officers who had been on the ship sufficiently long to be qualified to express an opinion. Most officers had previously complained that the ship was under armed and that her stability could stand a lot more added anti-aircraft guns.

During the afternoon, the Gunnery Officer reported that shells in the turret handling rooms were breaking loose from their battens and that he was generally alarmed over the situation. I was equally concerned and ordered him to put every man in the ship, not otherwise occupied, down in the handling room, if necessary, to prevent shells from rolling around. He got the situation under control by the use of additional battens and shores, and no serious troubled developed so far as I know. This situation, however, influenced me to heave to very early to lessen the ship's roll.[2]

During late afternoon, approximately 1700 (Z plus 4), I noted that the port bulwark had been bent inboard in two places. I sent a TBS-TBY message to the HYADES suggesting that it seemed advisable for me to heave to. No immediate answer came back, leading me to suspect that the HYADES had not received it or could not get an answer back on that circuit. With this in mind, I abruptly slowed to 5 knots and swung my bow left into the wind, at the same time sending a visual message to HYADES as follows: "It is necessary for me to heave to." HYADES immediately replied visually: "Heave to at discretion, do you wish us to stand by you." I replied, "Negative, will overtake you after the storm," and then summoned my Communication Officer. I asked the Communication Officer what radio circuit would be best for communicating with HYADES, other than TBS-TBY, which was unreliable, even at short distances. He replied that we were not on an operating circuit together, but that 2885 was available to both ships for use. I then originated and sent a message to HYADES about as follows: "If we separate, I will communicate with you over 2885 kcs." My decision to decline HYADES's offer to stand by WARRINGTON was based on the following:

(1) Barometer had not dropped excessively, leading me to believe the most violent part of the storm might miss us.

(2) We were already behind schedule and WARRINGTON would be pushed to make Trinidad on time.

(3) HYADES would be in less danger from submarine attack if she continued on at her best speed.

(4) The WARRINGTON had suffered no storm damage or other casualty to the engineering plant, other than what has been previously noted in this report.

(5) I considered that I was "babying" the WARRINGTON to heave to so early in a storm and did not want the HYADES to suffer from what I considered my almost over-concern about minor structural storm damage.

(6) I had personally encountered many violent storms in a smaller, older, destroyer and thought that a destroyer of twice the size and relatively new should have no trouble if the seas were kept away from the low after part of the ship. I was, however, fully aware of the vulnerability of the after part of the WARRINGTON class ship to storm damage.

Upon heaving to, course was set at about 100°T so as to keep wind and sea about one point on the port bow. Engine speed was varied between 5 and 7 knots, attempting to keep steerage way only. The pitometer log showed a speed through the water of about 4 knots. The ship rode fairly well until later in the night.

Soon after heaving to, the Engineering Officer called me by phone and requested that I make 12 knots to stop the main injection flapper valve from pounding. I refused this request, explaining that the ship would break its back if it headed into the seas at such a speed. He then replied that he probably could lash the valves so as to stop the banging.

About an hour after heaving to (approximately 1800 Z plus 4), the Engineering Officer requested permission to stop the port engine in order to find out where some salt was coming from. Permission was granted as the ship's bow could be held up-wind easily with one engine. The port engine remained stopped for about an hour as well as I can recall, and was then reported ready to go ahead. Went ahead one-third on both engines again.

As the night wore on, wind and sea increased in velocity and size. Even with the ship practically stopped, the ship pounded very hard. Sometimes I wondered why the keel did not break. The ship's great length (381 feet) worked to her disadvantage in riding the waves. At times it seemed that both bow and stern would be out of the water at once, causing the midships section to "mush" down, allowing the crests of the waves to rise very high along the section of the ship enclosing the engineering spaces. I am confident that this phenomena [sic] caused the first serious water damage to the engineering plant. From time to time, before 2300, the Engineering Officer called me by phone to complain of various minor ailments in the engineering plant. One of the ailments was excessive heat in the engine-rooms. I offered him sympathy, terminating each conversation with the order to keep the engines going at all costs as the life of the ship and his life depended upon it. I do not know whether or not he fully appreciated my statement then, but the truth of it was carried home in the worst possible way later. At any rate, he seemed to do his best. Shortly before 2300 (Z plus 4), he called me to the phone to report that his engineroom blowers were out and that water was coming down the vents. He also said he needed more men to work relays in the heat. I sent the first available officer, the Navigator, down to lend him a hand and sent others around to stir up various other officers and various men from the engineering compartments. Soon afterwards (about 2300 Z plus 4) the ship lost electric power for a short interval. This loss of power caused the main engines to lose vacuum, the steering engine and steering mechanism to go out of commission, and the engine order telegraph to go out of operation. All of the above-mentioned casualties were to be expected upon a loss of electric power except the loss of vacuum. The loss of vacuum was caused by the stopping of electric condensate pumps then in use in each engineroom. A main steam condensate pump was already warmed up and was immediately put on. Enough vacuum was recovered to run the engines after an appreciable and costly delay. Electric power was temporarily restored by means of No. 2 auxiliary diesel generator. A shift to hand steering was made until electric power was restored. The ship's bow fell off to southward, allowing the ship to wallow in the trough of the seas during the period of lost main engine power. The ship was headed upwind as soon as headway was regained. Other than the water which had knocked out ship's power and had grounded or drowned out all engineroom ventilators, no serious amount of water had been taken in the engineering spaces before midnight. To the best of my knowledge, all engineroom ventilation blowers were out of commission by 2300. Omitted in the narrative so far is the fact that the port bulwark plating peeled off about an hour after heaving to. The starboard bulwark plating peeled off about three hours after heaving to. The starboard side of the ship was always, to the best of my knowledge, kept to leeward during the whole episode. Except for the extraordinary violence of the storm and the poor riding qualities of the WARRINGTON, I know of no reason for the starboard bulwark to have been knocked off so readily. The structural members supporting the bulwarks were, in my opinion, much too weak for the job they had to perform. I recall having made a mental note of this before the storm.

Also omitted so far from this narrative, is a conversation I had with the Navigator about 2200 (Z plus 4) about the storm and my action in heaving to. It is of interest inasmuch as the Navigator is a survivor and might remember it. I recall having said to the Navigator that I was disappointed over the way the ship rode the seas when hove to and that it would have been better for me to have put the stern into the sea and run for it. At the same time, I stated that it was then too dangerous to attempt it as the stern of the ship would be swept by waves before the maneuver could be completed.

The HYADES was being tracked by the radar in CIC until the first power failure. As well as I can recall, she was at about 55,000 yards at about 2300 (Z plus 4), in a southerly direction. Such long surface ranges were not unusual with this radar. Destroyers had been tracked out to ranges greater than 60,000 yards.

6. *Wednesday, 13 September 1944.*

At some time, to the best of my memory, between midnight and 0100 (Z plus 4), I gave the Communications Officer orders to send the HYADES a message in plain language, asking her to rejoin the WARRINGTON as quickly as possible. I told him to try and get it out by any means at his disposal. It was felt all along that in case of disaster to us, the HYADES was our natural and logical rescue ship. This is mentioned to point out that our first efforts to call for help would naturally be, and were made, in her direction. My estimates of time are not very accurate because my wrist watch was lost at some unknown time. The bridge clock was mounted in a rather obscure spot on the after bulkhead so that in order to see it, one had to face completely away from ahead and from the helmsman and compass. At any rate, the Communications Officer left the bridge on his assignment and was not seen by me for an undetermined length of time.

During the period from midnight to about 0230 (Z plus 4), there were several lapses of emergency power and main engine power. The ship's bow fell off occasionally to Southward in spite of every effort being made to keep it headed up. Some very bad waves were taken over. I held frequent conversations with the Engineering Officer by sound powered telephone. My principal reaction to these calls was that the Engineering Officer's voice sounded weak from exhaustion and that conditions down below were deplorable in every way. I repeatedly told him that the engines would have to be kept running or the ship would be lost. This was done to make certain that he should develop a feeling of disregard for the engines for the sake of the ship as a whole and also because, to the best of my knowledge, he had had little previous experience to entitle him to know how a ship had to be handled in a bad storm. At some time around 0230 (Z plus 4), I called him by phone and talked over the situation. He indicated that the water was getting out of control. He stated that the water was coming in from ventilators, blowers, and various other places. In answer to my question as to why he did not put covers on the engineroom ventilators, he replied that the covers were gone.

I explained to him that in my opinion we had one last chance which was to put the stern into the sea and run at 15 knots. He seemed to despair of making the speed but indicated he would try. The ship gathered speed and swung its stern into the sea without, as I can recall, shipping any excessive amount of water. Course was set at 280°T, with wind and sea dead astern or slightly on the port quarter. The ship rode easily on this course and as long as speed was maintained, did not ship water. I recall having had the feeling that the ship was saved.

Shortly before this burst of speed, someone in the main radio room called me on the 21MC inter-communication circuit and stated that he had radio New York on the line ready for a message. The radioman asked me if I desired to send any message. I was about to decline to send a message, thinking that the HYADES had been called back to rejoin us. To my horror at this time, it was reported to me that either no message had been gotten off to the HYADES, or, if it had, she had not receipted for it. In short, they had not raised the HYADES by radio. I then hurriedly dictated a distress message to the radioman over the 21MC circuit. While I was dictating the message, the OOD or his assistant was getting the ship's position off the chart. This position was tacked on to the end of the message. Everyone knew that seconds counted because power might go off at any moment. My instructions were to send the message in plain language, avoiding any mention of ships by name for purposes of security, leaving the identity of the ship to be revealed by its call. This precaution prevented me from doing as I now know should have been done. The words, "Relay to HYADES" should have been included in the body of the message. The distress message actually dictated to radio and broadcast was as follows: "In distress X Need assistance X Engineering spaces flooded X Have lost power X Wind of hurricane force X 27–57N X 73–44W." I purposely exaggerated the conditions prevailing because I wanted to be sure we received a lot of attention and also because it was generally apparent that a distress message had to be gotten off while the main radio was functioning. The emergency radio had been reported as having too little or no power to reach anyone.

The delivery of the message to Radio New York was reported to me. I asked the Communications Officer what circuit the message was transmitted on. He replied hurriedly, "All circuits." I was anxious for it to reach the HYADES. As I recall, he stated that she should have gotten it, but if she did, she did not receipt for it.[3]

Shortly after the message was delivered, the ship's doctor came on the bridge and reported to me that he had been administering to the engineers who were suffering from heat exhaustion. He recommended to me that I have the word passed throughout the ship that whatever should happen, personnel should stay with the ship, as that was their best chance of survival. I immediately ordered this word be passed. At about the same time, I sent various people around to make certain that all officers were aroused and knew that the ship was in trouble. While the doctor was on the bridge, I attempted to call the Engineering Officer by sound powered phone. He could not be reached in the engineroom. The doctor explained that he and others were out on deck recovering from the effects of heat. At this time, we were apparently safely headed westward at about 15 knots. I wanted a summary of damage suffered in order to make plans regarding where to take the ship. My thought at the moment was to try to make for Navy Yard, Charleston. Realizing that the only way that I could get a qualified report was to see the Engineering Officer in person, I decided to go down on deck to talk to him. The doctor argued that it was too dangerous. Nevertheless, after telling the OOD to keep the ship on 280°T and explaining to him that his life depended on not letting it get off this course, I went down on deck to see the Engineering Officer, being guided to where he was by the Navigator, as well as I can recall. The engineer was on deck outside the forward engineroom. He made his report and advised me to look down below to see for myself how bad it was. I stepped inside the engineroom just as a great wave of water came through the overhead. This shot of water put all electric power off again. I quickly went back to the bridge and found that steering power had stopped. The OOD reported that he held the ship on its course until electric power failed. A hand steering detail was on hand, but regardless of how quickly a shift was made, the ship could be steered with stern to the sea only by electric power as it required maximum and most rapid use of rudder. Steering by hand steering was much too slow. The bow fell off to SSW allowing wind and sea to come over the port beam. The engines were never turned over again. Electric power, either from main or emergency generators, was never restored again. No radio power was ever available again. I immediately ordered all hands out of all compartments and ordered the ship to be completely closed up fore and aft. This order was expeditiously carried out and many reports were soon received that everything was closed up. Various reports were received by messengers from the engineering spaces, but none by telephone. The lack of telephone communication indicated that engineering personnel could not get to their telephones. As soon as the engineering situation appeared hopeless with reports being received that most of the engineering spaces were flooded, I ordered the execution of the Jettison Ship Bill. This order was given, as well as I can recall, about 0330–0400 (Z plus 4). My first concern was to get the torpedoes off. All eight torpedoes, set on safe, were fired over the starboard side about 0400. The motor boat swinging at its davits on the starboard side was partially filled with water and swinging wildly, having broken most of its securing rigging. It was cut adrift with an axe by a deck petty officer. All topside ready ammunition was jettisoned immediately. As dawn broke, additional items were thought of and jettisoned.

The foremast came in for a long discussion. It offered a great capsizing moment because of its great height and sail area, having mounted on top a SC radar array. There was some question as to whether it would break or merely bend, adding to our peril if its guys were cast loose. It was made of hollow steel tubing with an average diameter of about 10–12 inches. At about 0800 I gave the order to cast loose the foremast guys. This was promptly done and the mast almost as promptly broke at about the height of the top of the main battery director. Wind was 70–100 knots from the port beam. The upper part of the mast fell, but remained suspended from the standing part by unbroken ligaments for nearly an hour. It finally fell into the water over the starboard side and disappeared. Starboard 20mm and 40mm guns were jettisoned about 1000 (Z plus 4). The starboard pelorus and various miscellaneous gear were jettisoned throughout the forenoon. A long discussion took place between the Commanding Officer, the Torpedo Officer, and various torpedomen, regarding the advisability of releasing the depth charges. All assured me that all depth charges were set on safe, but all advised that there would be some danger involved in releasing the charges by the bridge release, as the charges would have their forks wiped off and might go off. I decided not to attempt to release the charges. It was reported to me that seas prevented the racks from being safely reached by personnel. I was unwilling to order personnel back there under such conditions.

During the time that the upper part of the mast was dangling over the side, two men were swept overboard to starboard, both wearing life jackets. Ring life buoys were thrown out to them. One was rescued and brought back on board. The other caught a line near the bow and held on for an appreciable time. I called for volunteers to go on the bow and give him a hand. One or two people responded, going on the bow near the starboard hawsepipe to attempt to haul him on board. The man in the water became exhausted before he could be rescued and released his hold on the line he had caught. He drifted around the bow and disappeared upwind as the ship was rapidly blown to leeward.

Reports reached me throughout the morning that the ship was not taking water anywhere except the engineering spaces which were believed to be entirely flooded except for the after engineroom. A bucket brigade had been functioning back there and as far as I could determine kept the water fairly well under control. Access and communication fore and aft was very difficult and dangerous. Seas were sweeping across the after part of the ship consistently.

About 1130 (Z plus 4), I decided there was no longer anything to be gained by staying on the bridge. There were a large number of personnel taking shelter in the bridge and chart house. So much weight so high hurt our stability. I directed all hands there to follow me. I took everyone down to the squadron commander's cabin, which was on the port side of the ship and was located in the superstructure with a quick-opening door to either side of the ship. From this location I could observe the starboard rail and the progress of the ship's settling. It seemed to me that nothing else could be done, but watch and wait. All drainage pumps and handy-billies of every type had been verified as inoperative. The emergency radio apparatus had been repeatedly reported as unserviceable. At about 1230 (Z plus 4), the ship became noticeably more sluggish in righting itself. I walked around the superstructure and estimated that the ship soon would capsize. The order was given for all hands to line up on the port rail and prepare to abandon ship but not to abandon until I gave the order. The port side was chosen because after personnel were in the water, the ship would drift away from the men. I reasoned that if men were in the water to starboard they would be pressed against the side of the ship by the ship's leeway as had been noted earlier with the two men who fell overboard.[4] This would be extremely dangerous as it would cause them to be hit by the superstructure as the ship capsized and make them subject to being sucked under as the ship went down as well. The order was effectively passed throughout the forward part of the ship and readily obeyed by most all persons.[5] I could see some progress in the execution of the order amidships and aft, but due to poor access aft, it was reasonable to expect some delay. Personnel were kept lined up in a state of readiness to abandon ship for 5–10 minutes. Ship's stability continued to deteriorate. Detailed instructions for abandoning ship were impossible because they could not be heard. The wind was blowing at about 70–100 knots, carrying sheets of water with it. It was an instance where individual initiative figured more heavily than anything else. As far as I knew, practically all life rafts on the starboard side were already adrift.[6] However, I actually knew of only one. I knew that such rafts as were on the starboard side that could be reached would undoubtedly be released and be filled to capacity.

At about 1250 (Z plus 4) the order was passed to abandon ship.[7] Personnel immediately started abandoning ship forward. I shouted and gestured to personnel amidships and aft, climbing higher on the bridge structure in order for my signals to be seen. While climbing to the bridge, I noted that securing cords were being cut away from floater nets aft in order that they might float clear. The ship very gradually listed to starboard. By the time I reached the bridge, the ship was listed about thirty or forty degrees to starboard, not tending to right itself. Several officers and men were on the bridge, or came on at their own choice, having received the order to abandon ship. Among them were the Executive Officer and Engineering Officer. After securing a pillow from my emergency bunk, I climbed out the port side of the bridge and stood on the port bulkhead which by then had become nearly horizontal. The Engineering Officer came up and shook hands with the Executive Officer and me. Noting that he was without a life jacket, I urged him to get one and make for a raft. He rejected all advice and refused to accept the pillow which I offered him. He confided that he could not swim and wanted this to be the end. Most all personnel seemed to have life jackets, either kapok or air inflated rubber belts. I recall having offered my life jacket to a seaman who did not have a jacket just before abandoning ship. He would not accept it. Other men standing in the vicinity told him that there were lots of them round about. My conscience was clear in the matter as I had started a drive on the wearing of life jackets soon after taking command of the WARRINGTON on 30 August 1944.

The WARRINGTON very slowly continued heeling to starboard until it lay completely on its starboard side. I experienced no difficulty in walking on the port side. The ship paused in this position for an appreciable time. One man who accompanied me seemed to think she would stay afloat for a considerable time in that position. I was soon lifted up, after having sat down, by a wave and deposited somewhere near the keel where undertow carried me under. When I regained the surface, the bow had raised up as if the ship was sinking stern first. The Executive Officer swam up to me about this time, stopped, showed me where he had received a blow on the chin and lost some teeth. He pointed out a life raft to me and then swam for it himself. As soon as I could get clear of the ship's bow which was threatening to come down on my head, I swam for the raft myself and made it. Men on the raft hauled me on board. The ship disappeared before I reached the raft. While still submerged in water up to my waist, three depth charges exploded. I felt no shock and thought the charges had exploded too deep to hurt anyone. The raft which I caught was apparently one which the seas had knocked off the starboard side before the ship was abandoned. It had about four persons on it then, later collecting three more, which were all we could find alive. One dead man in a kapok life jacket floated past us about an hour after the ship went down. He was not identified. The raft had been badly banged around. The bottom had been knocked out and water breakers dashed off. Men on the raft fished a can of food out of the water and secured it to the raft. It was a can of food apparently which had been originally secured to this raft but knocked off.

As well as I can recall, the wind subsided within a few hours after we were on the raft, but the seas did not.[8] The raft was capsized many times during the remainder of the afternoon and night. It kept us busy extricating ourselves from underneath and climbing back on top again. Everyone swallowed lots of salt water on these occasions. The lucky ones vomited profusely. Two less fortunate ones did not and died in agony before rescue reached us.

9. *Thursday, 14 September 1944.*

When day broke, the wind had reduced to a moderate breeze, the sky was mostly overcast and remained so throughout the day.[9] The sea was choppy, making the sighting of a raft extremely difficult by a surface vessel and hard by an aircraft. A PBY patrol plane flew within three thousand yards of us about 1000 (Z plus 4) and within eight thousand yards during mid-afternoon. Each time, one man on the raft stood up and waved a white cloth. We knew that white was not such a good color because of the possibility of its being mistaken for a white-cap. It was the next day before we thought of using my khaki shirt. The first patrol plane might have sighted us if he had been looking for life rafts instead of the WAR-RINGTON itself. A merchant type vessel and a small escort passed us about noon within four thousand yards, but seas were too choppy for either to have sighted us. The raft which I was on had no water, but ample tinned food. We subsisted mainly on malted milk tablets which contained lots of vitamins and provided some moisture. All hands showed remarkable composure, cooperation, and self-discipline. Food was intelligently used and preserved. The first man who died, became crazy during the day, died in the afternoon, as well as I can recall, and was buried. He was identified as Engleman, a fireman first class.

10. *Friday, 15 September 1944.*

At daylight, low-lying clouds were observed making visibility limited during the morning until about 1000 (Z plus 4). The sea was relatively calm with a very light breeze blowing.[10] At about 0900 (Z plus 4) the HYADES was sighted. She was observed cruising back and forth. We attempted to paddle the raft with our hands to close her, but she did not sight us. Later it was learned that she was busy at the time picking up other survivors. About an hour or two after sighting the HYADES, carrier planes were seen flying around her.

Ensign Dicken, USNR, was observed to be suffering from mental and physical disorder during the early morning. His condition became rapidly worse and he died about this time and was buried. His defection [*sic*] and death was similar in all respects to the death of Engleman, both apparently being due in a large measure to salt water poisoning.

Some planes flew near us but did not sight us immediately. We were still waving white objects. During the afternoon (my estimate of time may be off) I took my khaki shirt off and it was thereafter used for waving. After it was used, the first plane which came within sighting distance of us sighted us, dropped smoke bombs, and circled around us until the U.S.S.

HUSE (DE-145) came over and rescued us. We were picked up by boat without mishap and with utmost care and concern for our welfare and exhausted condition. We spent the night on the HUSE, being very kindly treated and properly administered medically. The Commanding Officer of the HUSE had me placed in his stateroom bunk. As soon as we were on board the HUSE, the Commander Task Group 22.5 (Commanding Officer of the U.S.S. CROATAN) inquired by TBS as to the total number of rafts and floater nets to be expected. I gave him an exaggerated estimate to be on the safe side.[11]

11. *Saturday, 16 September 1944.*

Survivors on the HUSE were transferred by breeches buoy to the U.S.S. CROATAN without discomfort or mishap. Soon after arrival on the CROATAN, I, who was apparently in the best physical condition of most all the survivors, attempted to be of assistance to the Commanding Officer, Captain J.P.W. Vest, USN, in advising search areas at his suggestion. I soon ascertained that the most likely areas had been and were being very thoroughly searched. I received the general impression that searching operations were very well coordinated between planes and ships. The searching group consisted of the U.S.S. CROATAN (CTG 22.5), U.S.S. FROST, U.S.S. HUSE, U.S.S. INCH, U.S.S. SNOWDEN, U.S.S. SWASEY, U.S.S. HYADES, U.S.S. WOODSON, U.S.S. JOHNNIE HUTCHINS, ATR-62, and the ATR-9. It may be safely stated, I think, that after the arrival of the U.S.S. CROATAN's searching group all living survivors were rescued. All rafts and floater nets which the WARRINGTON survivors knew to have been launched were accounted for. The Commanding Officer of the CROATAN was most helpful in constructing survivor lists, the record of those known to have died, and assisting in the safekeeping of the few personal effects found on deceased persons.

The WARRINGTON sank, having on board twenty (20) officers and about three hundred and one (301) men. Of these, five officers and sixty-eight men were rescued.[12] Three men who were rescued died on board the CROATAN resulting from exposure and exhaustion. Forty-five bodies were recovered and buried by the searching vessels. A separate report will be made to the Bureau of Naval Personnel concerning survivors and those known to have died after all available information is sifted.

Survivors, except six who were retained in the CROATAN and one in the HYADES, were landed at Norfolk by the WOODSON and JOHNNIE HUTCHINS and immediately transferred to the U.S. Naval Hospital, Naval Operating Base, Norfolk, Va. Those men retained by the CROATAN and HYADES were retained for medical treatment, it being considered unwise to risk transfer from one ship to another due to their poor physical condition. Enroute to Norfolk, all survivors were cautioned not to discuss any matters concerning the WARRINGTON disaster with anyone except proper Naval authorities.

12. In this narrative so far, an attempt has been made to write down events, decisions, and other matters as they were apparent to the Commanding Officer at the time of occurrence. Some omissions have occurred. In succeeding paragraphs, an attempt will be made to summarize, draw conclusions, and to fill in data omitted so far in the narrative. Paragraphs will be given a heading.

13. *Confidential Publications.*

Prior to abandoning the WARRINGTON, the Communications Officer was directed by me to lock up the confidential publications and leave them to sink with the ship. To the best of my knowledge, this was done.

14. *Stability, Flooding, and Counter-Measures.*

At the time of the disaster, the WARRINGTON had on board about 150,000 gallons of oil which was close to 85% of normal loading capacity of 176,000 gallons. Fuel had been used about equally from forward and after tanks.

The water account is not well known, but I estimate that the ship had on board about two-thirds of its water capacity of around 30,000 gallons.

The ship's draft on departure from Norfolk was approximately 13½ feet forward and 14 feet aft.

The WARRINGTON's athwartships metacentric height had been reported to me as between two and three feet. The ship's stability was very good when normally loaded with no spaces flooded.[13]

The ship had the following devices for potential use in clearing water from flooded compartments: One fire and bilge pump in each fireroom and in the forward engineroom, a main circulating pump in each engineroom, one semi-permanently installed 4-cylinder, Model 500 handy-billy on the main deck near the boundary between the forward and after enginerooms, four portable gasoline handy-billies, and four portable submersible electric pumps.

All fire and bilge pumps, both main circulators, and one portable electric submersible pump were used to clear water from the engineering spaces. No gasoline handy-billies were made to operate. All or nearly all gasoline handy-billies were run during general quarters on Monday, 11 September 1944.

All bulkheads were reasonably watertight except the bulkhead between the after fireroom and the forward engineroom. This bulkhead had a large leak around electric cables.

Until immediately before capsizing, no compartments were known to have shipped any appreciable amount of water except the I.C. Room, engineroom, and firerooms. The approximate estimated times that spaces were flooded are as follows:

Forward fireroom—0400 (Z plus 4) 13 September 1944.

After fireroom—0230 (Z plus 4) 13 September 1944.

Forward engineroom—0300 (Z plus 4) 13 September 1944.

After engineroom—0600 (Z plus 4) 13 September 1944.

Firemen's compartment (possibly flooded)—Possible immediate cause of capsizing.

By flooding is meant the shipping of enough water to render machinery inoperative and to provide a dangerous free surface.[14]

Water entered compartments in the manner enumerated below:

I.C. Room.

Through open exhaust ventilation trunk, kept open to operate emergency diesel generator.

No. 1 Fireroom.

Fireroom hatches (were not watertight and in addition were probably dashed open). Flaps on exhaust blower would not close.

No. 2 Fireroom.

All fireroom hatches, flaps on No. 3 and No. 4 blowers, cable holes, blower trunks, and between decks and uptakes.

No. 1 Engineroom.

Ventilation system and through bulkhead from No. 2 fireroom. Some ventilators were closed. Other ventilator closures were carried away.

No. 2 Engineroom.

Ventilation system.

Firemen's Compartment.

Not definitely verified as flooded, source unknown but probably some access was opened.

A casualty was suffered by the main circulator in No. 2 Engineroom at about 0200. Fire and bilge pumps seemed to be inadequate. The four-cylinder, semi-permanent, gasoline handy-billy was rendered inoperative by the seas. Its location prohibited its use anyway in heavy seas.

15. *Communications Summary.*

The WARRINGTON was equipped with a TBK main radio transmitter and a TCS emergency transmitter. The TCS transmitter was not successfully used at any time, due either to low power or its antenna being down. This transmitter was used in an attempt to call the HYADES on both 2716 kcs. and 2885 kcs. between the hours 0100–0130 (Z plus 4) 13 September 1944. It was used at this time because ship's electric power was off, prohibiting the use of the TBK. At about 0230 (Z plus 4), 13 September 1944, when the ship's emergency power was on, the HYADES was called on the main TBK transmitter on both 2716 kcs. and 2885 kcs. No reply was received. The WARRINGTON's distress message was then delivered to Radio New York as previously narrated. As well as can be recalled, the communication plan issued by the HYADES gave the HYADES the guard on 2716 kcs., the WARRINGTON the guard on 500 kcs., and both vessels guarding the "Fox" Schedules. The WARRINGTON used a frequency meter. Its TBK transmitter had been calibrated on 2885 kcs.

16. *Supplementary Engineering Data.*

Boilers 1 and 4 were in use in split plant operation with feed water and fuel suction split forward and aft. No attempt was ever made to use boilers 2 and 3. Electric condensate pumps were in use in each engineroom before casualty occurred. A main steam condensate pump was warmed up and ready in the after engineroom, capable of cross-connection to the forward engineroom. This pump was cut in when power failed about 2300 (Z plus 4). The ship had two emergency diesel generators, one in the I.C. Room and one in the after engineroom. Both were used to generate emergency power at various times between 2300 (Z plus 4), 12 September 1944, and 0300, 13 September 1944, until each was rendered inoperative due to water. Engineroom ventilator failures at about 2300 (Z plus 4), 12 September, caused the enginerooms to become too hot for efficient operation by personnel. In some parts of the forward engineroom, temperature reached 194°F., and above 148°F. in the after engineroom. Personnel worked in short, 5-minute shifts in the forward engineroom. Several instances of heat prostration occurred.

17. *Comment on Life Saving Equipment.*

Life rafts and floater nets had been properly equipped before the disaster. Many articles were destroyed, cast adrift, or lost by the storm before being used. No instance is known wherein emergency signal equipment was used, although it was on some rafts after abandoning ship. My experience indicated that emergency signalling equipment such as smoke bombs would have been more desirable than water. The packing of rations in small tin cans is very satisfactory. A similar system must be developed for carrying water. The use of large kegs for water is highly unsatisfactory because one inadvertent error or keg failure will destroy a complete raft water supply. All rafts should be equipped with a red cloth to attract attention. The rated capacity of life rafts is too high. During the second day, the raft I was on would not support half the weight of six people. Floater nets leave a lot to be desired in a heavy sea. Casualties on those were very heavy. Kapok life jackets were considered far superior to the air inflated type.[15]

18. *General Summary and Conclusions.*

It is felt that the vulnerability of the engineroom ventilation system to damage by water, together with its attendant hazard to main ship's electric power, was the primary and most important cause of the disaster to the WARRINGTON. The loss of engineroom ventilation caused sub-normal casualty performance by personnel. The loss of ship's electric power, leading to a loss of vacuum and temporary losses of steering control, hampered ship control at a vital time and undoubtedly contributed towards flooding in general.

The engineroom main circulators could probably have controlled flooding in both enginerooms and both firerooms if they had been effectively operated under more favorable conditions. The WARRINGTON's engineering spaces contained many serious deficiencies in topside watertightness which were not previously realized by the ship's personnel, both officers and men. The ship, as far as I could determine, had not had sufficient rough weather experience to learn how to get ready for it and to know the ship's deficiencies. Many personnel were not storm toughened themselves. The heavy loss of life is chargeable to the violence of the storm, inadequate life saving equipment, and delayed rescue. The order to abandon ship was given at a most opportune moment. Some few personnel were apparently hurt by depth charge explosions and some were lost as a result.[16] Many meritorious deeds were performed by personnel. Recommendations for awards will be submitted by separate correspondence.

19. No records, public money, nor public property, were saved. The Ship's Service Officer saved twenty-three dollars ($23) of Ship's Service money.

S. F. QUARLES

Copy to:
    ComInch (Direct)
    C.O., U.S.S. CROATAN

MOTHER CAREY'S CHICKENS

Kenneth S. Davis, Lieutenant, Sonar Officer (Temporary)
John Denny, Jr., Lieutenant (jg), Asst. Communications Officer
John R. Dicken, Ensign, Assistant First Lieutenant
John P. Hart, Lieutenant (jg), Communications Officer
Glenn W. Johnson, Lieutenant (jg), Torpedo Officer
Robert M. Kennedy, Lieutenant (jg), Medical Corps, Medical Officer
William V. Keppel, Lieutenant (jg), Engineer Officer
Louis R. Kroll, Lieutenant (jg), Assistant Gunnery Officer
Thomas S. Luerssen, Ensign, Assistant Engineer Officer
Robert B. Moore, Lieutenant (jg), Assistant Engineer Officer
Coleman S. Pack, Lieutenant (jg), Gunnery Officer
J. Marvin Pennington, Lieutenant (jg), First Lieutenant & Damage Control
    Officer
William L. Rogers, Ensign, on temporary duty
John R. Sullivan, Ensign, in training
Sidney M. Vickers, Lieutenant (jg), Supply Corps, Supply Officer

■ ■ ■

Julian W. Ahlers, Sonarman 2d Class
Robert C. Aldinger, Fireman 2d Class
Lloyd F. Allen, Fireman 2d Class
Emil E. Anderson, Seaman 1st Class
Norman I. Andress, Boilerman 1st Class
Gerard H. Andrews, Chief Machinists Mate
Melvin E. Andrus, Fireman 2d Class
Eugene F. Arbogast, Seaman 2d Class

Donald R. Bagley, Machinists Mate 2d Class
Robert L. Bailey, Seaman 1st Class
Marvin P. Bandkau, Fireman 2d Class
Herbert M. Banke, Fireman 2d Class
Stephen J. Barker, Seaman 1st Class
Bernie A. Basuini, Boilerman 2d Class
Bill H. Baugh, Seaman 2d Class
Chester A. Bennett, Fireman 2d Class
Roger Bennett, Seaman 2d Class
Andrew L. Berger, Fireman 2d Class
James F. Bienapfi, Seaman 2d Class
Fred W. Bond, Machinists Mate 2d Class
Harold Bonstrom, Fireman 2d Class
Perley J. Boyd, Stewards Mate 1st Class
Thomas R. Brady, Signalman 3d Class
James A. Brand, Seaman 1st Class
John D. Breeze, Fireman 2d Class
Robert M. Brown, Seaman 2d Class
William E. Brown, Fireman 2d Class
John W. Burton, Fireman 2d Class
Cimuel P. Campbell, Stewards Mate 2d Class
William S. Carlin, Radio Technician 3d Class
Billy R. Chapman, Sonarman 2d Class
Sidney W. Coleman, Stewards Mate 1st Class
Henry F. Collier, Seaman 1st Class
Joseph N. Cooper, Stewards Mate 2d Class
Chester M. Craig, Seaman 2d Class
Lige Crawford, Jr., Seaman 1st Class
Clyde B. Cross, Radioman 2d Class
Joseph S. Davidson, Machinists Mate 2d Class
Donald C. Davis, Fire Controlman 3d Class
William DeLee, Seaman 2d Class
Salvatore L. DeMarco, Radioman 3d Class
Clarence Dillon, Jr., Seaman 2d Class
Edward T. Dillon, Seaman 2d Class
Benjamin M. DiLorenzo, Seaman 1st Class
Joseph DiNardi, Machinists Mate 3d Class
Thomas E. Dotson, Seaman 1st Class
Robert A. Duncan, Seaman 2d Class
Louis Duvall, Jr., Seaman 1st Class
Elmore R. Easton, Watertender 3d Class

Dallas F. Edwards, Electricians Mate 2d Class
Samuel D. England, Sr., Seaman 2d Class
Jack Engleman, Fireman 2d Class
Jake M. Erickson, Seaman 2d Class
Donald T. Ermert, Seaman 2d Class
Ernest D. Estes, Fireman 2d Class
Lawrence M. Everette, Seaman 1st Class
Joseph Farkas, Fireman 2d Class
Horace G. Ferguson, Jr., Torpedoman 3d Class
Paul W. Forester, Seaman 1st Class
Wendell M. Gates, Yeoman 2d Class
Ernest Ginnett, Jr., Machinists Mate 2d Class
Frank P. Gschwend, Fireman 1st Class
Robert H. Hagan, Machinists Mate 3d Class
Harold J. Hamel, Watertender 2d Class
Edward J. Hammon, Jr., Seaman 1st Class
Robert D. Hammond, Storekeeper 3d Class
Glenn W. Hays, Machinists Mate 1st Class
Albert F. Head, Fireman 1st Class
William C. Heglin, Machinists Mate 1st Class
Carl E. Hendrick, Seaman 2d Class
Lynn A. Hill, Fireman 1st Class
Clayton Hines, Seaman 2d Class
John D. Hocken, Seaman 2d Class
Homer S. Hodges, Fireman 1st Class
John B. Hoffman, Seaman 2d Class
Kenneth E. Hoy, Seaman 1st Class
Robert B. Humphrey, Jr., Seaman 2d Class
Larry E. Hunter, Seaman 2d Class
Talmadge C. Jenkins, Seaman 2d Class
Charles S. Johnson, Seaman 2d Class
Harvey L. Johnston, Seaman 1st Class
Vaul W. Jones, Fireman 2d Class
William J. Jones, Seaman 2d Class
Charles R. Kantner, Seaman 2d Class
Morris Kantor, Seaman 1st Class
Roland Kaufman, Fireman 1st Class
Clifford L. Keith, Torpedoman 2d Class
Nick Kellemen, Radioman 3d Class
Harold L. Kelm, Seaman 2d Class
Arthur T. Kenary, Seaman 2d Class

Robert G. Kern, Fireman 1st Class
Reuben G. Kilmer, Seaman 2d Class
Leroy F. King, Seaman 2d Class
Thomas J. King, Seaman 2d Class
Kenneth Kirby, Signalman 1st Class
Elmer C. Koelling, Jr., Seaman 2d Class
James W. Kohr, Seaman 2d Class
John J. Kolfcycle, Seaman 2d Class
John E. Kuka, Seaman 2d Class
Frank A. Kulkkula, Seaman 2d Class
Lester J. Kreiser, Seaman 2d Class
Charles V. Kunath, Seaman 2d Class
Edward J. LaBuda, Chief Storekeeper
Doyle D. Laird, Sonarman 2d Class
Willard J. LaLonde, Seaman 2d Class
Clarence F. Lambert, Seaman 2d Class
Carl C. Lapp, Seaman 1st Class
Paul J. LaRussa, Seaman 2d Class
Ross G. Latimer, Fire Controlman 3d Class
George A. Lawing, Seaman 1st Class
Milton E. Lease, Radio Technician 3d Class
Leonard J. LeFebvre, Machinists Mate 1st Class
Donald L. Leggett, Yeoman 1st Class
Ernest J. Long, Watertender 1st Class
Ted Lynn, Seaman 2d Class
Junior L. Mainzer, Seaman 1st Class
Ralph P. Majewski, Seaman 2d Class
Thomas J. Mallon, Quartermaster 3d Class
Richard P. Marklund, Watertender 3d Class
John D. Martin, Quartermaster 1st Class
Ernest S. Matson, Seaman 2d Class
Charles F. Matthews, Seaman 2d Class
Stephen Maydan, Machinists Mate 1st Class
Lawrence T. McLean, Stewards Mate 3d Class
Damon L. Meeke, Seaman 2d Class
Fred K. Meinze, Gunners Mate 3d Class
Charles F. Meitzel, Jr., Storekeeper 2d Class
Glenn C. Melson, Ships Cook 3d Class
William R. Minnick, Fire Controlman 1st Class
Roy A. Miskimmon, Seaman 2d Class
Alfred B. Mitchell, Seaman 1st Class

Clarence C. Morgan, Electricians Mate 3d Class
John Munoz, Seaman 1st Class
Elvin K. Neaville, Chief Gunners Mate
Vernon A. Olson, Ships Cook 2d Class
Harry J. O'Malley, Boilerman 2d Class
James T. O'Neal, Stewards Mate 1st Class
William F. Owens, Machinists Mate 2d Class
William H. Pardee, Chief Yeoman
Raymond Parton, Fireman 1st Class
William E. Parsley, Seaman 1st Class
Bert O. Patterson, Fireman 1st Class
Garret H. Peratt, Ships Cook 3d Class
Victor H. Peristere, Pharmacists Mate 3d Class
Howard B. Perry, Machinists Mate 1st Class
Norman A. Perry, Gunners Mate 2d Class
Lawrence J. Pesek, Yeoman 2d Class
Linder G. Pirtle, Radioman 3d Class
Thomas O. Pool, Seaman 2d Class
Kenneth H. Pratt, Gunners Mate 3d Class
William J. Preuster, Electricians Mate 2d Class
John C. Proven, Seaman 2d Class
Harry Pszczola, Seaman 2d Class
Sylvester A. Rayburg, Jr., Gunners Mate 2d Class
Clair K. Raymer, Coxswain
Benjamin E. Redhead, Watertender 3d Class
Joseph F. Reiner, Electricians Mate 2d Class
William R. Reoch, Boatswains Mate 2d Class
Robert E. Reville, Radarman 2d Class
Howard T. Reynolds, Shipfitter 1st Class
Robert H. Rice, Watertender 2d Class
Don R. Richards, Seaman 1st Class
Walter W. Ricketts, Fire Controlman 2d Class
Colin N. Ridley, Turret Captain 1st Class
Victor A. Rippa, Machinists Mate 1st Class
Raymond C. Roberge, Seaman 1st Class
Charles E. Roberts, Watertender 3d Class
Joseph H. Rockford, Gunners Mate 3d Class
Stanley H. Roellich, Seaman 2d Class
Paul Romeo, Boatswains Mate 2d Class
Mark P. Ryder, Seaman 2d Class
Luigi G. Santini, Fireman 1st Class

Herbert P. Schoenfelder, Seaman 1st Class
Russell J. Schott, Torpedoman 3d Class
Eddie Scott, Stewards Mate 1st Class
William J. Seeback, Seaman 2d Class
Roy E. Seekford, Seaman 1st Class
Gordon K. Selking, Seaman 2d Class
Clifford S. Senior, Seaman 1st Class
George L. Shepherd, Machinists Mate 3d Class
Carl W. Sifford, Chief Pharmacists Mate
Joe L. Simon, Seaman 1st Class
Onofrio A. Simone, Seaman 2d Class
Melvin Smelesky, Seaman 1st Class
Clarence H. Smith, Seaman 2d Class
Clifford L. Smith, Torpedoman 2d Class
Nolan C. Smith, Seaman 1st Class
Theodore S. Smith, Seaman 2d Class
James L. Snoddy, Watertender 3d Class
William B. Snow, Quartermaster 3d Class
John E. Sosnak, Watertender 3d Class
Joseph C. Spencer, Jr., Radioman 3d Class
Walter Springel, Seaman 2d Class
William P. Staats, Watertender 1st Class
Crosley Steinbrecker, Seaman 1st Class
Roger Stewart, Seaman 2d Class
Joseph W. Stone, Chief Machinists Mate
Everett G. Stout, Seaman 1st Class
Ira Stout, Coxswain
Layton W. Strong, Seaman 1st Class
Lonnie P. Studdards, Seaman 2d Class
Paul E. Sublette, Seaman 2d Class
Samuel E. Sulanke, Gunners Mate 2d Class
David H. Swartz, Seaman 1st Class
Hubert H. Swift, Fireman 2d Class
Frank S. Szopa, Carpenters Mate 3d Class
Stephen Ternyak, Fireman 1st Class
Vernon E. Thomas, Seaman 1st Class
Clifford Thompson, Seaman 1st Class
John D. Tipton, Seaman 1st Class
Arthur B. Tolman, Chief Radioman
George H. Trousdell, Machinists Mate 2d Class
Gerard J. Tucholka, Seaman 2d Class

Earl M. Tucker, Stewards Mate 1st Class
Loren D. Turner, Watertender 2d Class
Jack S. Tuttle, Fire Controlman 3d Class
William L. Underwood, Seaman 2d Class
Harold Upton, Ships Cook 1st Class
Frank H. van Hoesen, Motor Machinists Mate 1st Class
Joseph H. Vipperman, Seaman 2d Class
Washington L. Voorhies, Fireman 1st Class
Jack W. Wagner, Seaman 1st Class
Vernon R. Waid, Seaman 1st Class
Leroy E. Walker, Chief Machinists Mate
Charles S. Welcker, Gunners Mate 1st Class
Theron Williams, Seaman 2d Class
Herbert E. Wilson, Seaman 1st Class
Gerald C. Wintjen, Seaman 2d Class
John Wolosin, Machinists Mate 3d Class
Andrew E. Wood, Carpenters Mate 2d Class
William J. Woolsey, Seaman 1st Class
Stanley Wright, Jr., Seaman 2d Class
Harry A. Yarmat, Seaman 2d Class
Antonio L. Zarelli, Radio Technician 2d Class

R.I.P.

SURVIVORS

Eugene E. Archer, Ensign, Ship's Secretary
Patrick B. Davis, Lieutenant (jg), Navigator
Samuel F. Quarles, Commander, Commanding Officer
Donald W. Schultz, Ensign, Assistant Gunnery Officer
Wesley U. Williams, Lieutenant, Executive Officer

■ ■ ■

Lawrence D. Allphin, Torpedoman 2d Class
O. E. Anderson, Seaman 1st Class
F. Bencie, Seaman 1st Class
Daniel D. Berman, Seaman 1st Class
Glenn W. Bivins, Gunners Mate 2d Class
J. N. Blanton, Seaman 1st Class
Thomas E. Braendle, Fireman 2d Class
A. D. Browning, Fireman 2d Class
Sterling R. Bussey, Fireman 2d Class
Elmer R. Canady, Chief Motor Machinists Mate
John M. Connolly, Torpedoman 3d Class
J. A. Davis, Seaman 1st Class
J. J. Devitt, Seaman 2d Class
John L. Eichman, Seaman 1st Class
Charles A. Everts, Chief Torpedoman
William J. Ferry, Seaman 1st Class
George H. Finch, Ships Cook 3d Class
N. Grabko, Seaman 1st Class

William C. Greene, Quartermaster 3d Class
Alfred (n) Hanson, Machinists Mate 1st Class
L. H. Hoffstetter, Seaman 2d Class
Charles L. Hutton, Seaman 1st Class
L. O. Jasmin, Sonarman 3d Class
Willie G. Johnson, Chief Boatswains Mate
Fred J. Kieser, Fireman 1st Class
Paul (n) Klingen, Radioman 2d Class
B. H. Knabb, Seaman 2d Class
B. B. Larson, Seaman 2d Class
John J. Latronica, Machinists Mate 2d Class
R. G. Lemon, Electricians Mate 1st Class
R. J. Lierse, Fire Controlman 3d Class
John M. Major, Seaman 2d Class
Anthony F. Martin, Seaman 2d Class
William A. McKinnon, Gunners Mate 2d Class
M. E. Minard, Seaman 1st Class
H. H. Norman, Seaman 1st Class
Raymond W. Padgett, Torpedoman 2d Class
Lewis (n) Parrillo, Boatswains Mate 2d Class
Robert B. Ralph, Radioman 3d Class
J. Reis, Gunners Mate 3d Class
John I. Richards, Boatswains Mate 2d Class
L. V. Riley, Machinists Mate 2d Class
Deryl (n) Rowell, Gunners Mate 2d Class
"W" "J" Sapp, Watertender 1st Class
D. Satana, Officers Steward 1st Class
W. Schroerlucke, Jr., Seaman 1st Class
H. Simons, Seaman 1st Class
William R. Singletary, Seaman 1st Class
J. J. Skelton, Sonarman 2d Class
Arel B. Smith, Radarman 3d Class
S. A. Smith, Seaman 2d Class
Garland S. Stewart, Seaman 1st Class
E. C. Stroud, Seaman 1st Class
Clarence (n) Strunk, Fireman 2d Class
E. M. Swanson, Seaman 1st Class
Walter C. Teague, Chief Watertender
A. K. Thurston, Seaman 1st Class
A. J. Vassallo, Fireman 1st Class

G. R. Voss, Seaman 1st Class
H. H. Wallin, Fireman 1st Class
J. Washkwich, Seaman 2d Class
Walter (n) Wright, Jr., Shipfitter 3d Class
William L. Zwick, Seaman 1st Class

NOTES

1. SOUTH PACIFIC DAYS

1. Greene, William C., Quartermaster 3c; Letter to Mrs. G. H. Traylor, undated.
2. Ibid.

3. THE FRANTIC ATLANTIC

1. In the light of what followed later, the absence of noise in the port reduction gear at full power is almost miraculous.

4. RENDEZVOUS WITH DISASTER

Unless otherwise indicated, all notes in this chapter are taken from the transcript of the record of the Court of Inquiry. These are shown as "Testimony," "Findings," "Opinions," or "Recommendations," as appropriate. Notes taken from Commander Quarles's Action Report are shown as "A.R."

1. Quarles, Samuel F., Commander, Testimony, pp. 1180–82, 1187–88.
2. Ralph, Robert B., Radioman 3c; interview, 13 September 1993.
3. Quarles, Testimony, p. 1254.
4. Wheyland, Morgan C., Commander, Finding No. 193, p. 1328. Also, Quarles, Testimony, p. 1175.
5. Doyle, Edwin G., Chief Radioman, Testimony, p. 1127.
6. Mayo, Charles N., Lieutenant Commander, Testimony, p. 1165. Also Quarles, A.R., p. 177.
7. Mayo, Testimony, p. 1165.
8. These men had at least a partial college education, but no seagoing experience.
9. Quarles, A.R., p. 177.
10. Quarles, Testimony, p. 1193; and A.R., p. 179.

11. Quarles, A.R., p. 178.
12. Quarles, Testimony, p. 1192; and A.R., p. 178.
13. Ibid.
14. Koelsch, Philip C., Rear Admiral, USNR, Letter to the author.
15. Finding No. 205, p. 1329.
16. Schultz, Donald W., Ensign, Letter to the author.
17. Quarles, Testimony, p. 1200.
18. Smith, Arel B., Radarman 3c, audio tape.
19. Doyle, Testimony, pp. 1116–17.
20. Quarles, Testimony, p. 1197; also A.R., p. 179–80.
21. Quarles, Testimony, p. 1196; also A.R., p. 180.
22. Quarles, Testimony, p. 1196.
23. Ibid., pp. 1199, 1200.
24. Ibid.
25. Ibid., p. 1200. Also, Finding No. 44, p. 1312.
26. Wright, Walter, Jr., Shipfitter 3c, Testimony, p. 824. Also, Finding No. 47, "Wind on the port bow" Force 9, at p. 1830; and Quarles, Testimony, p. 1209; also, A.R., p. 182.
27. Finding No. 45, p. 1312.
28. Finding No. 46, p. 1312.
29. Smith, Arel B., Testimony, p. 943.
30. Quarles, Testimony, p. 1209.
31. Quarles, Testimony, pp. 1216, 1262.
32. Notably, a liberty ship in Alaskan waters in 1943.
33. Quarles, Testimony, p. 1221.
34. Ibid., pp. 1201, 1215, 1261. Also Davis, Patrick B., Lieutenant (jg), Testimony, p. 1264.
35. Findings Nos. 48–50, p. 1313.
36. Davis, Testimony, p. 1272.
37. Quarles, Testimony, p. 1222.
38. Ibid., pp. 1222–23; also A.R., p. 185.
39. Quarles, Testimony, p. 1223.
40. Ibid., p. 1215.
41. Ibid., pp. 1216–17, 1220.
42. Ibid., p. 1221.
43. Ibid.
44. Ibid.
45. *Encyclopedia of Nautical Knowledge* (Centreville, Md.: Cornell Maritime Press), p. 59. By permission.

5. THE DRAGON BREATHES

1. Canady, Elmer R., Chief Motor Machinists Mate, Testimony, p. 1141–42.
2. Sapp, "W J", Watertender 1c, Letter to the author.
3. Strunk, Clarence, Fireman 2c, Testimony, pp. 544–45.

4. Latronica, John J., Machinists Mate 2c, Testimony, p. 1031. Also, Ralph, Robert B., Radioman 3c, Testimony, p. 699.
5. Parrillo, Lewis, Boatswain's Mate 2c, Letter to the author.
6. Latronica, Testimony, p. 1030.
7. Schultz, Donald W., Ensign, Testimony, pp. 623, 637–38.
8. Klingen, Paul, Radioman 2c, Letter to the author.
9. Allphin, Lawrence D., Torpedoman 2c, Telephone interview.
10. Schultz, Letter to the author. The timing of this event is somewhat doubtful, but Schultz's account is believed to be more accurate.
11. Finding No. 130, p. 1320.
12. Schultz, Letter to the author.
13. Holmes, Barton M., Captain, U.S. Merchant Marine (Ret), Letter to *Naval History* magazine, Summer, 1991: 2. Reprinted from *Proceedings* with permission; © 1991, US Naval Institute.
14. Ehrman, William E., Commander, U.S. Coast Guard (Ret), "Lost on a Voyage to Nowhere," Coast Guard Alumni *Bulletin,* July–August 1984: 28.
15. Ibid., p. 29
16. Ibid.
17. Flagg, Harold W., Senior Chief Boatswains Mate, U.S. Coast Guard, Letter to the author.

6. THE SHOUTS OF MEN

1. Klingen, Paul, Radioman 2c, Testimony, pp. 591–93.
2. Greene, William C., Quartermaster 3c, Letter to the author.
3. Finding No. 206(g), (h), and (i), p. 1330.
4. Williams, Wesley U., Lieutenant, Letter to the author.
5. Ralph, Robert B., Radioman 3c, Letter to the author.
6. Greene, Letter to the author.
7. Parrillo, Letter to the author.
8. Smith, Tape transcription.
9. Schultz, Letter to the author.
10. Greene, Letter to the author.
11. Teague, Walter C., Chief Watertender, Testimony, pp. 479–80.
12. Greene, William C., Quartermaster 3c, Letter to Mrs. G. H. Traylor.
13. International Oceanographic Foundation, "Sea Secrets," *Sea Frontiers,* Jan./Feb., 1993.
14. Allphin, Telephone interview.
15. *Sea Frontiers,* "Sea Secrets."
16. Davis, Patrick B., Lieutenant (jg), Telephone interview.
17. Latronica, Testimony, p. 1071.
18. Williams, Wesley U., Lieutenant, Personal interview.
19. Latronica, Testimony, p. 1074.
20. Klingen, Paul, Radioman 2c, Telephone interview.

7. IN THE CRADLE OF THE DEEP

1. Finding No. 184, p. 1327. The following named vessels participated in the search and rescue operation: USS *Croatan,* USS DE-146, USS DE-246, USS ATR-9, USS ATR-62, USS *Hyades,* USS DE-144, USS DE-359, USS DE-145, USS DE-360, USS DE-248, USS *Croatan* Air Group, USS *Cherokee,* and Shore-based Air Groups.

8. THE USS *HYADES*

1. Findings Nos. 20 and 21, p. 1309.
2. Finding No. 24, p. 1309.
3. Finding No. 25, pp. 1309–10.
4. Finding No. 29, p. 1310.
5. Finding No. 30, p. 1310.
6. Smith, Testimony, p. 943.
7. Finding No. 45, p. 1312.
8. Finding No. 44, p. 1312.
9. Finding No. 24, p. 1309.
10. Doyle, Testimony, p. 1121.
11. Ibid., p. 1113.
12. Ibid., p. 1114.
13. Ibid., pp. 1032, 1126–27.
14. Ibid., p. 1121.
15. Finding No. 44, p. 1312.
16. Doyle, Testimony, pp. 1129–30.
17. Mayo, Testimony, p. 1163.
18. Klingen, Letter to the author.
19. Mayo, Testimony, p. 1163.
20. Finding No. 110, p. 1318.
21. Doyle, Testimony, pp. 1117–18. Doyle's answers to the court's questions regarding the receipt and handling of this and subsequent messages are interesting. For example, Question 65 asks, in part, "this indicates that the message was rebroadcast and that you received it. Is that correct?" Answer: "The heading indicates that this is a double heading. Originally it was from ComGulfSeaFron—action to AT-170 and ATR-62 as this address indicates."
22. Finding No. 164, p. 1324.
23. Finding No. 165, p. 1325.
24. Finding No. 167, p. 1325.
25. Finding No. 168, p. 1325.
26. Finding No. 169, p. 1325.
27. Opinion No. 4(i), (j), (k), and (l), p. 1329.
28. Norfolk Weather Bureau Report, Appendix A, p. 218.
29. Doyle, Testimony, pp. 115–16, 1135.
30. Wheyland, Testimony, p. 1297.

31. Latronica, Testimony, p. 1071.
32. See Note 1, Chapter 7.
33. Finding No. 186, p. 1327.
34. Finding No. 190, p. 1327.
35. My wife and several survivors claim to have heard this broadcast. Others have reported the effect upon their families.
36. Vuono, Michael, Personal interview.
37. Finding No. 185, p. 1327.
38. Archer, Eugene E., Ensign, Letter to the author.
39. Opinion No. 4(h), p. 1339.

9. THE COURT OF INQUIRY

1. Wheyland, Testimony, p. 1297.
2. Roberts, Norman K., Commander, USNR, Testimony, p. 1173.
3. Quarles, Testimony, p. 1246.
4. Ibid., pp. 1252, 1257–58.
5. Notably, Chief Boatswains Mate Willie G. Johnson and Chief Watertender Walter C. Teague, both of whom were veterans of the great 1938 hurricane.
6. Quarles, Testimony, p. 1256. It is worthy of note that Williams never made any attempt to refute Quarles; even forty-five years later, he never uttered one word against him.
7. Quarles, Testimony, p. 1257.
8. Ibid., p. 1263.
9. Quarles, A.R., p. 283.
10. Quarles, Testimony, p. 1244.
11. Parrillo, Letter to the author.
12. Wright, Walter, Shipfitter 3c, Testimony, pp. 823–27.
13. The following names were submitted: Canady, Elmer R., Chief Motor Machinists Mate, 385-84-91; Thurston, A. K., Seaman 1c, 653-87-97; Kennedy, Robert M., Lieutenant (jg), 327934, MC-V(G), USNR; Hart, John P., Lieutenant (jg), 173967, D-V(G), USNR; Pack, Coleman S., Lieutenant (jg), 161411, D-V(G), USNR; Pennington, Jesse M., Lieutenant (jg), 184468, D-V(G), USNR; Davis, Patrick B., Lieutenant (jg), USNR; Martin, John D., Quartermaster 1c, 223-85-29; Tolman, Arthur B., Chief Radioman, 368-29-41; Wright, Walter (n), Shipfitter 3c, 224-50-73; Johnson, Willie G., Chief Boatswains Mate, 261-79-84; Reynolds, Howard T., Shipfitter 1c, 646-18-12; Stout, Ira (n), Coxswain, 279-70-19; Kroll, Louis R., Lieutenant (jg), D-V(G), USNR.

    Kroll was not included on Quarles's list. Also, in naming the men who accompanied Johnson to the forecastle to release the starboard anchor, Quarles inadvertently omitted the name of Minnick, William R., Fire Controlman 1c, 243-76-80.

14. Klingen, Letter to the author. The courageous and intelligent behavior of Radiomen Klingen and Pirtle has been called to the attention of the chief of naval personnel, with recommendations for appropriate recognition. The recommendations were disapproved.

10. THE WHOLE IS THE SUM OF ITS PARTS

1. Forwarding endorsement, attached to the record of the Court of Inquiry.
2. The first of these two meetings was held on 27 January 1933 and the second on 10 March 1933. There were undoubtedly other meetings, but these are of particular interest. Both meetings were attended by representatives of the Office of the Chief of Naval Operations—War Plans Division, Fleet Training Division, Ships' Movements Division, Material Division, Inspection and Survey Division, and Communications Division; Bureau of Navigation; Bureau of Ordnance; Bureau of Engineering; Bureau of Construction & Repair; and Bureau of Supplies & Accounts.
3. The war plans in effect before World War II included a concept (among others) under which the war foreseen to take place between the United States and Japan would end in a huge naval battle, in which ships of various types would more or less "pair off" against each other. Part of this involved a kind of "Charge of the Light Brigade," consisting of destroyers, led by these new "monsters," the 1,850-ton squadron leaders. As the world now knows, this idea went by the board on 7 December 1941.
4. Record of meeting, 27 January 1933, p. 17. This exchange follows a long discussion of the relative merits of guns versus torpedoes. It is mainly of interest because the majority of the people present agreed with both of these officers; the only strongly dissenting voice is that of Admiral Robinson, chief of the Bureau of Engineering, who first claimed that the question was beyond the purview of his bureau; when pressed, however, he pointed out that World War I destroyers used other weapons, such as guns and depth charges, ten times as often as they used torpedoes, and he felt that the next war would be the same, only more so. Admiral Robinson was obviously a very intelligent gentleman.
5. Record of meeting, 10 March 1933, p. 47. Admiral Hepburn's name is not included in the roster of officers attending the meeting.
6. Admiral Cole is the only member who even mentions seaworthiness, but he appeared to accept the low freeboard of the 1,850s with complacency; he even refers to their "high" freeboard.
7. Parrillo, Letter to the author.
8. Finding No. 27, p. 1310. Also, USS *Hyades* War Diary lists barometric readings as follows:

Time	Date	Barometer	Time	Date	Barometer
0100	9/11	30.12	1200	9/12	29.80
2400	9/11	30.00	1300	9/12	29.76
0800	9/12	29.80	1400	9/12	29.72

A graph of these figures is instructive; it will make it clear why Quarles was deceived by the apparent "steadiness" of the barometer in the early stages of the storm.

9. Quarles, Testimony, pp. 1195–96.
10. Normally, this was the first lieutenant. Rear Adm. Charles A. Curtze, in a letter to the author, mentions that at one time his job required him to visit various ships, delivering lectures on the subject of damage control, but few people seemed deeply interested.
11. Opinion No. 6(B)(7), p. 1340.

11. A LADY WITH A PAST

1. Office of Naval Records & History, Ships History Section, p. 115.
2. Ibid., pp. 115–17.

12. THE PEACETIME NAVY, 1920–1939

1. Beginning about 1937, two destroyer divisions—one in the Atlantic, the other off Hawaii, began testing the tactical applications of sonar. In the process, they also helped to develop procedures for the use of voice radio (TBS).
2. Miller, Edward S., War Plan Orange (Annapolis, Md.: Naval Institute Press, 1991), p. 79.
3. Office of Naval Records, p. 115.
4. Simmons, Alfred E., Fireman 2c, Response to questionnaire.
5. Register of Naval Academy Alumni, 1993, p. 181.
6. Miller, David H., Fireman 2c, Letter to the author.
7. Miller, David H., Letter to the author.
8. Office of Naval Records, 114.
9. Miller, David H., Letter to the author. Unless otherwise noted, all references to the 1938 hurricane are from this source.
10. Ibid.
11. Ibid.
12. McDermott, Frederick P., Yeoman, Telephone interview.
13. Miller, David H., Letter to the author.
14. Ibid.
15. Ibid.
16. Ibid.
17. Ibid.
18. Simmons, Response to questionnaire.
19. Ibid.
20. Ibid.
21. Short Range Battle Practice (SRBP) was the only practice for which personal awards were given.
22. Office of Naval Records, pp. 115–16.
23. Ibid.

24. Miller, David H., Letter to the author.
25. Miller, David H.; Ward, John M., Machinists Mate; and Curry, Maxwell, Carpenters Mate, Response to questionnaire.
26. Curry, Response to questionnaire.
27. Miller, David H., Letter to the author.
28. Ibid.
29. Ward, Response to questionnaire.
30. Office of Naval Records, p. 115.
31. Ibid.

13. PACIFIC PARADISE, 1940–1941

1. Miller, David H., Letter to the author.
2. Ibid.
3. Personal recollection.
4. Miller, David H., Letter to the author.
5. Ibid.
6. Ward, Response to questionnaire.
7. Miller, David H., Letter to the author.
8. Ibid.
9. Office of Naval Records, p. 114. There is some question as to the identity of this carrier; she has been named variously as the *Wasp, Ranger,* or *Enterprise.*

14. THE NEUTRALITY PATROL, 1941

1. Personal recollection. I was serving aboard a ship undergoing overhaul a few piers away from HMS *Orion.*
2. Miller, David H., Letter to the author.
3. Parrillo, Letter to the author.
4. Miller, David H., Letter to the author.
5. Personal recollection.
6. Miller, David H., Letter to the author.
7. Ibid.
8. Office of Naval Records, p. 115.
9. Miller, David H., Letter to the author.
10. Parillo, Letter to the author.
11. Miller, David H., Letter to the author.
12. Ibid.
13. Ibid.
14. Ibid.
15. Parrillo, Letter to the author.
16. Ward, Response to questionnaire.
17. Miller, David H., Letter to the author. I have been unable to locate any historical confirmation regarding the alleged early, covert landing of Japanese troops in the Philippines.

18. Personal recollections.
19. Ibid.
20. Office of Naval Records, p. 115.
21. Alexander, Harold H., Gunners Mate, and Koelsch, Letters to the author.
22. Latronica, Testimony, pp. 1030, 1065–66.

EPILOGUE

1. Naval Academy Alumni Association Magazine, "Shipmate."
2. Quarles, Testimony, p. 1244.
3. Those interested in further information are referred to the Bathymetric Projection prepared by the National Oceanic and Atmospheric Administration (National Ocean Service), Department of Commerce, 1986.

APPENDIX A

1. Dunn, G. E., and B. I. Miller, *Atlantic Hurricanes* (Baton Rouge: Louisiana State University Press, 1964), p. 375.
2. Wood, Col. F. B., *Bulletin of the American Meteorological Society* (May 1945): 153–56.
3. Norfolk Weather Service, 1944, from a report on the September 1944 Hurricane, unpublished, p. 2.
4. Summer, H. C., "The North Atlantic Hurricane of September 1944," *Monthly Weather Review* 72, no. 9 (1944): 187–89.
5. Ho, F. P., Schwerdt, R. W., and Goodyear, H. V., *Some Climatological Characteristics of Hurricanes and Tropical Storms, Gulf and East Coasts of the United States,* National Oceanic and Atmospheric Administration Technical Report NWS 15 (Washington, D.C.: NOAA, 1975), p. 85.
6. Ho et al., p. 69.
7. Summer, pp. 187–89.
8. Wood, pp. 153–56.
9. Ibid.
10. Dunn and Miller.
11. Ibid.
12. Ibid.

APPENDIX B

1. Finding No. 44, p. 1312. Findings Nos. 164, 165, pp. 1324–25.
2. Finding No. 157, p. 1323.
3. Findings No. 168, 169, p. 1325.
4. Findings No. 168, 174, pp. 1325–26.
5. Finding No. 170, p. 1325.
6. Findings No. 185, 186, p. 1327.
7. Quarles, Testimony, pp. 1211–12.
8. Ibid., p. 1223.
9. Quarles, A.R., p. 185; and Finding No. 104, p. 1318.

10. Finding No. 6, p. 1307.
11. Quarles, Testimony, p. 1200.
12. Teague, Testimony, p. 460.
13. Ibid., p. 477.
14. Ibid., p. 460.
15. Ibid.
16. Ibid., p. 462.
17. Kieser, Fred J., Fireman 1c, Testimony, pp. 525–27; and Strunk, Clarence, Fireman 2c, Testimony, p. 542.
18. Quarles, Testimony, p. 1202.
19. Quarles, A.R., p. 182.
20. Stewart, Garland S., Seaman 1c, Testimony, p. 871.
21. Teague, Testimony, p. 457.
22. Finding No. 66, p. 1314.
23. Quarles, A.R., p. 184.
24. Teague, Testimony, pp. 455–57.
25. Strunk, Testimony, p. 542; and Johnson, Willie G., Ch. Boatswains Mate, Testimony, p. 575.
26. Sapp, "W J", Watertender 1c, Testimony, p. 486.
27. Quarles (by Counsel), Argument, p. 1293.
28. Ibid., p. 1177.
29. Ibid., p. 1182.
30. Ibid.
31. Ibid., p. 1177.
32. Ibid., p. 1183.
33. Ibid., p. 1185.
34. Ibid., p. 1254.
35. Quarles, Testimony, p. 1185.
36. Quarles, A.R., p. 189.
37. Ibid., p. 181.
38. Ibid., p. 183.
39. Quarles, Testimony, p. 1216.
40. Ibid., p. 1215.
41. Ibid., p. 1217.
42. Smith, Arel B., Testimony, p. 951.
43. Quarles, Testimony, p. 1216.
44. Ibid., p. 1215.
45. Ibid., pp. 1191–92.
46. Ibid., p. 1208. This testimony indicates there may have been considerable confusion on the bridge.
47. Quarles, Testimony, p. 1208.
48. Ibid., p. 1221.
49. Ibid.
50. Ibid.

51. Ibid., p. 1176.
52. Ibid., p. 1222; also Finding No. 97, p. 1317.
53. Wright, Walter, Jr., SF3c, Testimony, pp. 823–57.
54. Smith, Arel B., Testimony, p. 951.
55. Kieser, Testimony, p. 533.
56. Ibid., p. 526.
57. Smith, Testimony, p. 950.
58. Kieser, Testimony, p. 551.
59. Ibid., p. 552.
60. Strunk, Testimony, p. 543.
61. Ibid., p. 539.
62. Ibid., p. 553.
63. Ibid., p. 540.
64. Ibid., p. 555.
65. Ibid., p. 544.
66. Teague, Testimony, p. 468.
67. Quarles, Testimony, p. 1196.
68. Sapp, Testimony, p. 493.
69. Quarles, Testimony, p. 1222.

APPENDIX C

1. This report was prepared from memory, without benefit of notes of any kind, although Commander Quarles doubtless conferred with several of the other survivors. Consequently, all times are estimates, and the reader will probably note a number of apparent contradictions between this report and the testimony of various survivors, as presented to the Court of Inquiry. The fallibility of human memory must be accepted, and discrepancies should not be given undue weight. With respect to times, as noted, it seems appropriate to explain here that the phrase, "Z plus 4" denotes times in Time Zone Plus 4 (where the *Warrington* was throughout this episode). In naval terms, this time zone is also designated as "Queen."

2. Quarles's memory may be at fault here; Ens. Donald W. Schultz, who took part in restowing the ammunition, says, in a letter to me, that this incident took place on the morning of the thirteenth, only a few hours before the ship went down; in fact, Schultz adds that he and his men would not have worked so hard had they had any idea that the ship was about to sink.

3. Radio New York receipted for this message at 0157. This time is exact, and might be used as a reference point in judging the accuracy of other times. The wording of the distress message as received by New York differs considerably from that quoted by Quarles, who later said, "I purposely exaggerated the conditions prevailing."

4. In view of the roaring wind and towering seas, it would be interesting to know how this word was passed. Other survivors make no mention of any preparatory orders at all, or only state that they heard none. Most agree that the

first definite indication that the ship was about to be abandoned came when Quarles climbed the bridge structure and signaled with his hands.

5. Note that this alleged order was passed "throughout the forward part of the ship" only. Men actually went overboard from both sides of the ship, without any concerted plan.

6. Wrong. All the starboard rafts and nets, with one exception, were lost when the ship went down.

7. See Note 5.

8. Others claim the cold wind blew all night. See Chapter 7.

9. Others complained of sunburn.

10. The volunteers who manned the *Hyades*'s whaleboat reported that the seas were still high enough to be dangerous.

11. In his testimony, Quarles says that he deliberately exaggerated the number of rafts in order to ensure that a very careful and thorough search would be made.

12. These figures are slightly in error. After the courts-martial were completed, Quarles and Williams were sent to the Bureau of Naval Personnel on temporary duty, to write letters of condolence to the families of the men who died. Naturally, this required extreme care and accuracy. Their final figures were:

    Total on board on departure from Norfolk: 315
    Total lost, 13–15 September: 247
    Total rescued, 15 September: 68
    See Appendixes D and E.

13. A ship's metacentric height (briefly) is the vertical distance between the center of gravity of the hull and the center of buoyancy. As long as the center of buoyancy is *above* the center of gravity, the ship is said to be stable; that is, if heeled to one side or the other, she will tend to right herself. The greater the distance between the two points, the greater the stability.

14. "Free surface" has been compared to the surface of water in a bucket when the bucket is tipped, causing the water to "slosh" back and forth.

15. Quarles later changed his mind on this point.

16. The Court of Inquiry found that no one was injured by the depth charge explosions. Only two survivors ever made contradictory claims, but neither gave definite evidence to substantiate their claims.

BIBLIOGRAPHY

BOOKS

Hammell, Eric. *Guadalcanal: The Decision at Sea.* New York: Crown Publishers, Inc., 1989.

McEwen, William A., and Alice H. Lewis. *Encyclopedia of Nautical Knowledge.* Centreville, Md.: Cornell Maritime Press, 1953.

Marchaj, C. A. *Seaworthiness: The Forgotten Factor.* Camden, Maine: International Maritime Publishers, 1986.

Miller, Edward S. *War Plan Orange.* Annapolis, Md.: Naval Institute Press, 1991.

PERIODICALS

Bulletin (U.S. Coast Guard Alumni), July–Aug., 1984: 27–30.

Bulletin of the American Meteorological Society (May 1945).

Naval History, Summer 1991: 2.

"Sea Secrets," *Sea Frontiers,* Jan.–Feb., 1993.

DOCUMENTS

Office of Naval Records & History, Ships History Section, Navy Dept.

Report of Meeting, Navy General Board, Washington, D.C., 27 January 1933; 10 March 1933.

Transcript of the Court of Inquiry, Norfolk, Va., Oct.–Nov. 1944, pp. 452–1328.

INDEX

ABOUT THE AUTHOR

A native of Annapolis, Maryland, and a 1933 graduate of the Naval Academy, Commander Dawes served at sea aboard one battleship, two cruisers, five destroyers (including one former German ship), and one fleet oiler, during his twenty-six-year naval career. He commanded three of these ships. His shore assignments included tours at the Naval Academy, Washington, D.C., Guam, Pearl Harbor, and Springfield, Massachusetts. Following retirement in 1960, he lived and worked in Massachusetts until 1974, when he fully retired and moved to Kilmarnock, Virginia, where he now resides with his wife Louise. He has one daughter and two grandsons.